Design and Analysis
of
Time-Series Experiments

Design and Analysis
of
Time-Series Experiments

Gene V Glass

Victor L. Willson

John M. Gottman

INFORMATION AGE PUBLISHING, INC.
Charlotte, NC • www.infoagepub.com

ISBN: 978-1-59311-980-5

Printed in the United States of America

To

Donald T. Campbell
and
Julian C. Stanley

Scholars, scientists, and inspiring colleagues

~July 1974

Both gone now,
But their mark is indelible and still bold.

~July 2008

TABLE OF CONTENTS

APPENDIXES

ABOUT THE AUTHORS

GENE V GLASS is Regents' Professor at the Arizona State University. He earned a PhD in educational psychology and statistics in 1965 from the University of Wisconsin. His early work in statistics led to the development of meta-analysis in the mid-1970s, now a widely used tool in medicine and social sciences. He was elected President of the American Educational Research Association (AERA) in 1975, and to membership in the National Academy of Education in 2000. Among his many writings are *The Benefits of Psychotherapy* (with M. L. Smith & T. I. Miller), *Meta-analysis of Social Research* (with B. McGaw & M. L. Smith), *School Class Size: Research & Policy*, and three recent books with Charalambos Vrasidas: *Distance Education and Distributed Learning*, *Online Professional Development for Teachers*, *Preparing Teachers to Teach with Technology*. He is the author of the recently published *Fertilizers, Pills and Magnetic Strips: The Fate of Public Education in America* (Information Age Publishing, 2008).

VICTOR L. WILLSON is Chairman of the Department of Educational Psychology at Texas A&M University. He has served as President of the Southwest Educational Research Association and as Chair of the Structural

Equation Modeling SIG of AERA. He is the author (with C. R. Reynolds and R. L. Livingston) of *Measurement and Assessment in Education* (2005) and (with C. R. Reynolds) of *Methodological and Statistical Advances in the Study of Individual Differences* (1985), and is a featured contributor to the *Encyclopedia of Special Education*.

JOHN M. GOTTMAN is Emeritus Professor of Psychology at the University of Washington, and world renowned for his work on marital stability and divorce prediction, involving the study of emotions, physiology, and communication. His breakthrough research on marriage and parenting has earned him numerous major awards including four National Institute of Mental Health Research Scientist Awards and the American Psychological Association Division of Family Psychology, Presidential Citation for Outstanding Lifetime Research Contribution. He is the author or co-author of more than 150 published academic articles and 37 books, including his most recent book, *The Relationship Cure, A 5-Step Guide for Building Better Connections with Family, Friends, and Lovers* and the *New York Times* bestseller, *The Seven Principles for Making Marriage Work*.

INTRODUCTION TO THE REPUBLICATION

Lee J. Cronbach once remarked that we, as social scientists, and our work sink without leaving a trace. And so it is all the more gratifying when a publisher decides, that after more than thirty years there is still merit in making readily available again someone's early effort to put one thing down right.

Design and Analysis of Time-Series Experiments was an attempt by myself and my colleagues Victor L. Willson and John M. Gottman to put down on paper some of the excitement that attached to the publication of Donald Campbell and Julian Stanley's famous *Experimental and Quasi-experimental Designs for Research* (1966), a republication of the "Campbell and Stanley chapter," as it was quickly to become known, from the 1963 N. L. Gage *Handbook of Research on Teaching*. I was in my first semester in graduate school in 1962 when Julian Stanley asked me to copyedit an ante-penultimate draft of the Campbell and Stanley chapter. It was immediately apparent to even a neophyte like myself that an extremely important step was being taken in the evolution of research methods in the social and behavioral sciences. I was particularly impressed with what seemed then the power and wide potential application of what Campbell and Stanley named the "interrupted time-series design" for discovering or testing causal claims. The basic logic of the design was convincing; the best way of handling the statistical analysis for separating signal from noise was unclear.

I had the good fortune at that time to be earning a PhD minor in the best mathematical statistics department in the world. G. E. P. Box and George C. Tiao, to name just two luminaries, were at that time exploring the power of the Auto-Regressive-Integrated-Moving-Averages (ARIMA) model to decompose time-series into predictable and random portions and, in a very early effort limited to one particular model—the first-order integrated moving averages model—to estimate and test the statistical significance of an intervention effect (Box & Tiao, 1965). At about that time I was finishing my own dissertation research in the area of factor analysis and had put aside my interest in the time-series experiment analysis problem, to be taken up at a later date.

"Later" proved to be much later; almost ten years in fact. While at the University of Colorado in Boulder in the early 1970s, I had the good fortune to come in contact with two remarkable young colleagues who shared my feeling that work on the interrupted time-series design and analysis was far from complete. It was John M. Gottman, then engaged in an internship in the Psychiatry Department at the University of Colorado Medical Campus, who came to me and said that more work needed to be done and that he was interested in our working together. His dissertation in clinical psychology at the University of Wisconsin was focused on time-series analysis (Time-series Analysis in the Behavioral Sciences and a Methodology for Action Research, 1971), and he had followed up that work with two *Psychological Bulletin* papers that were being widely cited. At the same time, my PhD student, Victor

L. Willson, was being drawn closer to the notion that concomitant variables would ultimately play a role in time-series experiments even as they had in conventional experimental design. We decided to collaborate, and *Design and Analysis of Time-Series Experiments* was the result in 1975.

In devoting an entire book to the topic, we were able to explicate many more possibilities for powerful time-series designs than was possible for Campbell and Stanley in their omnibus treatment of quasi-experimental designs. Moreover, no work had been published on the statistical analysis of time-series experiments since the Box & Tiao article in 1965 on the first-order integrated moving averages model. I was on sabbatical in the Spring of 1974 and used the opportunity to consult with both George Tiao, still at Wisconsin then, and Gwilym Jenkins at the University of Lancaster in the UK (Jenkins being Box's co-author on the landmark *Time-series Analysis: Forecasting and Control*, 1970) on the generalization of the ARIMA model to testing intervention effects. Throughout the rest of 1974, Willson, Gottman, and I worked feverishly to prepare the final draft of the book that was published in 1975 and is now republished here.

The initial reception of the book was more gratifying than we had any right to expect. James A. Walsh, reviewing the book in *Educational and Psychological Measurement*, remarked that "...this book will come to be viewed as a true landmark....[It] should stand the test of time exceedingly well." Perhaps this republication exonerates his enthusiastic prediction. And the source of wisdom on quasi-experimental design gave us more than our due, perhaps: "Ordinary least squares estimation is usually inapplicable because of autoregressive error.... Glass, Willson, and Gottman have assembled the best approach" (Donald T. Campbell).

But the early warm reception was followed by years of cool disregard. The interrupted time-series quasi-experimental design is probably the most powerful—in the causal demonstration sense—design available in almost countless situations, and yet it is probably the most under-utilized. Two reasons at least may account for this. Time-series experiments require some patience in data collection in order to establish a well behaved baseline stream of data from which to detect a deflection coincident with an intervention. This often runs afoul of the necessity to get on with things when one is executing dissertation research or responding to political pressure for quick results. But more importantly, perhaps, the complexity of the best statistical analysis raised a daunting obstacle to researchers who themselves were not deeply engrossed in the intricacies of ARIMA models. Researchers in several fields, particularly "behavioral analysis," invented bizarre and sub-optimal techniques for detecting interrupt effects. And worse, the misconception quickly arose—more as an excuse than anything else—that ARIMA analysis required a very long stream of data, say 50 or more points in time. As in so many other applications, advice about "sample size" must be qualified in a huge number of ways; and for ARIMA analysis, no one was much talking about the qualifications. Computer programs that perform interrupt effect estimation and testing are now common and friendly and should quiet some complaints about the difficulty of properly analyzing time-series experiment data. (SPSS permits the estimation and testing of intervention effects in ARIMA models, as does SAS. For the latter, see Brocklebank and Dickey, 2003.)

In spite of the under-utilization of the interrupted time-series design, several important applications have been published in the past thirty years. I illustrated some and cited some others in 1997 in a chapter in the American Educational Research Association volume on *Complementary Methods for Research in Education*. In 1992, Thomas Kratochwill and Joel R. Levin edited a book addressed to "single subject" design and analysis, which is the behavioral psychology nomenclature for the interrupted time-series experiment; it rose above the shortcomings of the typical treatments of the subject in that discipline's literature. And even today, disciplines far afield from Campbell and Stanley's original interest are calling attention to potential wide application of the time-series experiment (Biglan, Ary and Wagenaar, 2000).

The application of the interrupted time-series design for causal analysis in education may have been retarded more recently by ideologically inspired pronouncements from sectors of the federal government regarding "scientifically based research." The *No Child Left Behind Act of 2001*—the reauthorization of the Elementary and Secondary Education Act—called for "scientifically based research" as the foundation for education improvement. In 2002, Valerie Reyna, Deputy Director of the Department of Education's Office of Educational Research and Improvement spoke at a seminar of experts seeking some interpretation of what NCLB meant by "scientifically based research." She argued that only randomly controlled trials could produce "scientifically based evidence" for education reform: "This [the randomly controlled trial] is the only design that allows you to do that, to make a causal inference. Everything else is subject to a whole bunch of other possible interpretations."[1] It was clear that the federal government, the source of most financial support for education research, would privilege randomized experiments in its funding. That such research happened to favor short-term, easily executed studies supporting the government's favored reading program, Reading First, was not thought to be irrelevant to its

---

1 http://www.ed.gov/nclb/methods/whatworks/research/index.html

stand on "causal inference" by many observers. Suffice it to say that the adjudication by bureaucrats in the federal government of questions concerning what constitutes evidence for causal relationships in education research was unprecedented and intellectually unsupportable. When genuine philosophers of science turn their attention to the question of discovering or verifying causal relationships, the government's arguments are revealed as specious and one suspects that they were driven by ulterior motives. (See Michael Scriven's (2008) direct critique of the Department of Education's position, as well as the recent work of the British philosopher of science Nancy Cartwright, 2007, and of S. L. Morgan and Christopher Winship, 2007.) This dust-up over "scientifically based evidence" has done nothing to promote the intelligent pursuit of research in education; quite the contrary in fact. We could not do better in clearing the air after nearly a decade of ideologically controlled research than to return to the 1963 publication of the "Campbell-Stanley chapter" and read past the first 20 pages. It is our hope that the republication of this book supports the effort to restore reason and sense to arguments that were inappropriately politicized.

A balanced and rational attitude toward the discovery or verification of causal relationships in education and the social sciences should return attention to the art and science of quasi-experimental design. Although the sophistication of statistical analysis of interrupted time-series experiments continues to evolve, the principles of time-series experiment design explicated in the first five chapters of the current work remain relevant. The potential to extract useful conclusions about causes from existing data banks has never been greater, primarily because the number and depth of such data streams is so much greater. The subdividing of data streams and examination of interrupts often reveals patterns of effects that in themselves argue for stronger inferences about causes than even randomly controlled trials can produce. Consider Stephen D. Levitt's work reported in his recently published trade book with Stephen J. Dubner, *Freakonomics: A Rogue Economist Explores the Hidden Side of Everything* (2005). Levitt and Dubner pointed out that in the years following the *Roe v Wade* decision (January 1973), the number of abortions in the U.S. rose from three-quarter million to more than one-and-a-half million in 1980. By the early 1980s, one abortion was being performed for every 2.25 live births. Look at this another way: nearly a third of all pregnancies were terminated by abortion in the early 1980s. And that segment of society that was obtaining abortions shifted significantly as a result of legalization. Formerly, abortions were an expensive option chosen by the wealthy and upper-middle classes. After *Roe v Wade*, they became more affordable, didn't involve travel expenses, and were more available to young and poor women. The "hidden side" of the legalization of abortion (to which the authors refer in their subtitle) is that 15 to 20 years after *Roe* the U.S. crime rate showed a remarkable decline. Levitt and Dubner attribute this decline in crime to the decline in the population share of young, crime prone males. Their reasoning rested on a fine-grained analysis of the data subdivided by states. States that had legalized abortion shortly before *Roe* was upheld by the Supreme Court showed an earlier decline in violent crime 15 to 20 years later than states that legalized it after *Roe*. Moreover, states with higher abortion rates showed greater decreases in crime two decades later.

Finally, a note on typography of this text is in order. The heavy mathematical load in the later chapters of the book presented a daunting prospect for typesetters and copy editors (not to mention authors) alike. And the investment of time in producing mathematical manuscripts was driving up costs of books substantially in the early 1970s. Many such books were being set into letter press type in Europe where publishers had gone in search of cheaper labor (a circumstance that caused some chagrin to my father who was a long-time member of the US-based International Typographical Union). A conversation with Patrick Suppes in the late stages of our manuscript preparation sent us down a different path. Pat pointed out that many books and journals in specialized technical fields were going directly from type-writer manuscript to final manuscript without the intervening hot metal type-setting. It was faster and cheaper. We chose that path and saved ourselves time and buyers money. Modern desktop publishing makes such considerations irrelevant today, but it is worth noting that books that routinely sold for $35 in 1975 would cost more than $140 today. The 1975 version of this book sold for about $15.

Finally, I wish to express my thanks to George F. Johnson, President of Information Age Publishing, whose idea it was to bring back selected texts from the history of education research and make them readily available again, even though the prospect of great profits to the company is remote.

~ Gene V Glass
July 2008

REFERENCES

Bickman, L. (Ed.) (2000). *Research Design: Donald Campbell's Legacy, Vol. 2*. Thousand Oaks, CA: Sage.

Biglan, A., Ary, D., & Wagenaar, A. C. (2000). The value of interrupted time-series experiments for community intervention research. *Prevention Science, 1*(1), 31–49.

Brocklebank, J., & Dickey, D. (2003). *SAS for Forecasting Time Series*, Second Edition. NY: SAS Press and John Wiley Sons Inc.

Cartwright, N. (2007). *Hunting Causes and Using Them: Approaches in Philosophy and Economics*. Cambridge, UK: University Press.

Glass, G.V (1997). Interrupted Time-series Quasi-experiments. In R. M. Jaeger (Ed.), *Complementary Methods for Research in Education* (2nd ed., pp. 589-609). Washington, DC: American Educational Research Association.

Kratochwill, T. R., & Levin, J. R. (Eds.) (1992). *Single-Case Research Design and Analysis: New Directions for Psychology and Education*. Hillsdale, NJ: Erlbaum.

Levitt, S. D., & Dubner, S. J. (2005). *Freakonomics: A Rogue Economist Explores the Hidden Side of Everything*. NY: William Morrow.

Morgan, S. L., & Winship, C. (2007). *Counterfactuals and Causal Inference: Methods and Principles for Social Research*. Cambridge, England: Cambridge University Press.

Scriven, M. (2008). A summative evaluation of RCT methodology: And an alternative approach to causal research. *Journal of MultiDisciplinary Evaluation, 5*(9), 11-24. Retrieved July 24, 2008 from http://survey.ate.wmich.edu/jmde/index.php/jmde_1/article/view/160/186.

CHAPTER ONE

TIME-SERIES EXPERIMENTS AND THE

INVESTIGATION OF CAUSAL CLAIMS

The "pretest-posttest" experimental design has never been highly regarded as an experimental technique in the behavioral and social sciences, and for good reasons. The simple pattern of "observation-treatment-observation of change" which worked so well in the physical sciences is seldom equal to the difficult task of demonstration of causal relationships in systems of human behavior. In such systems observations must be made repeatedly both before and after the intervention, i.e., introduction of the "treatment" or assumed cause. The change from immediately before to immediately after intervention can then be judged as either the effect of the intervention or merely the regular progression of an evolving and dynamic process unaffected by the intervention. The assessment of a causal claim can be made more reliably by an extension of the pretest-posttest design known as the time-series experimental design.

The most basic time-series experimental design involves some number of repeated observations, O, of an outcome variable across time with an intervention, I, introduced between two observations: An abrupt change in some property of the observations which coincides with I may be the effect of I on the outcome variable. When

1

properly implemented and carefully interpreted, the time-series experiment is a sensitive tool for the investigation of causal claims in the behavioral and social sciences.

The time-series design has been utilized infrequently in the study of individual and group behavior, but the technique has figured prominently in the methodology of operant conditioning in psychology. Nonetheless, the formal problems encountered in implementing and analyzing time-series experiments have received little attention. Campbell and Stanley (1963) drew attention to the technique, christened it "the interrupted time-series quasi-experiment," and discussed the difficulties of its statistical analysis (also see Campbell, 1963). Box and Tiao (1965) contributed greatly to the analysis of time-series experiment data, though apparently unaware of the interest in the method which was then kindling in the social sciences. The utility of the time-series design has been endorsed in numerous textbooks and articles since 1963, but the design has been less often applied. Its infrequent applications include studies of revised automobile speeding laws (Campbell and Ross, 1968; Glass, 1968), detection of drunken drivers (Ross, Campbell, and Glass, 1970), the revision of German divorce laws (Glass, Tiao, and Maguire, 1971), the formation of the Common Market (Caporaso and Pelowski, 1971), Sino-Indian relations (Smoker, 1969), and the effects of self-monitoring of talk in classrooms (Gottman and McFall, 1972). The most extensive and stimulating exposition of the time-series experimental methodology since 1963 is due to Campbell (1969). Gottman (1973) discussed applications of the time-series design in research on psychotherapy. Kazdin (1972) reviewed several "single-subject" designs prevalent in operant psychology. The principal work on the statistical analysis of data from time-series experiments has been pursued by Box and Tiao (1965), Sween and Campbell (1965), Gottman, McFall, and Barnett (1969), Glass and Maguire (1968), Jones, Crowell and Kapuniai (1969), and Kepka (1972).

This paper extends past work on the methodology of time-series experimental designs in several directions: some new concepts in the design of time-series experiments are offered as aides in judging the validity of applications of the design; several variations on the basic paradigm are identified, illustrated with data, and evaluated; sources of invalidity in the time-series experiment are identified; existing statistical analytic techniques due to Box and Tiao are extended to cover a variety of special estimation problems arising in various applications of the time-series design. The work of Box and

Jenkins (1970) in forecasting and control is built upon in the derivation of statistical analytic models for time-series experiments.

Uses of the Time-Series Design

The time-series experiment can often be used as an unplanned experiment to evaluate governmental or institutional reform; such post hoc experiments are by-products of archival record-keeping. A planned time-series experiment may be the method of choice when the simultaneous experimental comparison of two or more treatments is impossible or impractical. Even when the traditional randomized, "true" comparative experiment is feasible, the perspective on intervention effects (their immediacy, duration, changing character across time) afforded by the time-series design can be illuminating. Finally, the time-series design permits the study of an experimental effect on a single person or experimental unit.

Campbell (1967, 1969) argued compellingly that the post hoc time-series analysis of archival data can be useful in evaluating the effects of interventions by governmental agencies and established institutions. He saw the time-series design as an important tool of the social scientist in the "experimenting society" studying "reforms as experiments."

Advantages Over Simultaneous Comparison of Interventions

When the researcher experiments at his own volition, not waiting for society to reform, the time-series design may avoid certain problems arising from the simultaneous comparison of treatments in a randomized design. Experimental units may be "linked" (or "mutually dependent") in such a way that a treatment effect on one set of units works an increase or decrease on other units. In this instance the consequences of universal application of the treatment would possibly not be correctly inferred from the simultaneous comparison of two different treatments. For example, suppose that a psychologist discovers a projective test which predicts felonious behavior with a multiple correlation coefficient of .95. Suppose further that the U.N. institutes a program of testing and deporting potential criminals. In the ten "experimental" countries, the crime rate drops precipitously but continues to rise in the ten "control" countries; because units are "linked," country A's crime rate goes down partly at the expense of country B's crime rate going up. The

4

U.N. then recommends universal adoption of the procedure, not realizing that there will be no.place for the bad guys to go when everyone deports their felons.

Cross-contamination may arise in the simultaneous comparison of multiple treatments as philosophy, methods, techniques, etc. spread from one treatment to another. For example, the presence of a flashy individualized instruction program in a school could have a beneficial effect on the instruction given "control" classes in the same school since teachers may have shared teaching tips or even materials.

The interpenetration of treatment effects poses a problem for some experimental research. The experimental units assigned to treatment A may be affected by treatment B. This is particularly troublesome in communications research. For example, suppose a randomized experiment is designed to compare the poster vs. the handbill medium of educating teen-agers in Chicago about the transmission of venereal disease. Census tracts are randomly assigned to one treatment or the other. The dependent variable is measured by interviewing teen-agers in the respective census tracts and finding the rate of certain understandings about venereal disease. Unfortunately it would be difficult to determine whether a particular teenager acquired his knowledge via a poster or via a handbill (or via personal experience); and the subject himself may be a highly unreliable authority on the question of the genesis of his knowledge. The time-series design offers one means of resolving in part each of the above difficulties in implementing simultaneous comparative experimental designs.

The most important advantage of the time-series design is not that it offers an alternative when a traditional, randomized comparative experimental design is not feasible, but that it offers a unique perspective on the evaluation of intervention (or "treatment") effects. Simultaneous comparative designs in the Fisherian tradition may blind the experimenter to important observations when such designs become a thoughtless habit of mind. The Fisherian design which has so captured the attention of social and behavioral scientists was originally developed for use in evaluating agricultural field trials. The methodology was appropriate to comparing two or more agricultural methods with respect to their relative yields. The yields were crops which were harvested when they were ripe; it was irrelevant in this application whether the crops grew slowly or rapidly or whether they rotted six months after harvest. For social systems, there are no planting and harvest times. Interventions into societies and institutions do not have merely "an effect" but "an effect pattern" across time. The value of an intervention is properly judged not by whether the effect is observable at the fall harvest, but by whether the effect occurs immediately or is delayed, whether it increases or decays, whether it is only temporarily or constantly superior to the effects of alternative interventions. The time-series design provides a methodology appropriate to the complexity of the effects of interventions into social organizations or with human beings. The importance of the longitudinal perspective on experimental interventions has been repeatedly emphasized in the work of Chassan (1960, 1961, 1965, and with Bellak, 1965) in his discussion of the "intensive design." Chassan argued for the use of time-series designs for "$\underline{N}$-of-one" research in assessing the effects of psychotherapy. The advantages of such research in the context of psychotherapy were discussed by Gottman (1972).

Levels of Causal Inference in Time-Series

The ultimate objective of early physical science was to classify events and to establish causal connections between classes of events. The law of causality can be stated as, the initial state of a system plus its dynamic forces determine all subsequent states. Newton was the first scientist to express dynamic forces mathematically. Today, three centuries after Newton's formulation of the law of causality, quantum mechanics indicates that the law of causality has utility only "in the large." Heisenberg's "uncertainty relations" make it impossible in principle to simultaneously pinpoint the position and momentum of a particle. Expressed by Bohr as the Principle of Complementarity, this means that "a rigorous space-time description and a rigorous causal sequence for individual processes cannot be realized simultaneously—the one or the other must be sacrificed." (D'Abro, 1951, p. 951.) Bohr's principle is based on the impossibility of simultaneously reducing measurement error in both the initial state (position) and dynamic forces (momentum) of a system. Therefore, modern physics has rejected the law of causality as an ultimate objective of science. It remains, however, an important working principle "in the large," that is, for physical systems far larger than the atom. But in the social sciences the law of causality remains a useful working hypothesis.

Concomitant Variation

The most primitive level of causal inference comes from describing the fluctuations of a system over time and searching for concomitant variation. Figure 1 is an illustration of the concomitant variation in thunderstorms in Siberia and sunspot activity during the same time period. These two series exhibit nearly parallel concomitant variation. By studying this covariation, it is possible to generate hypotheses of causal connection. At this point in the development of the social sciences it is wise to consider this stage of causal inference as exploratory data analysis. These analyses yield the most information in the negative case: If two series are uncorrelated it is unlikely that they are causally connected. It is true that concomitant variation does not necessarily imply causation, but it is also true that "neither does anything else," i.e., no other set of observations is sufficient evidence of a causal relationship. Causal connection is never demonstrated; rather, rival hypotheses which militate against confidence in a causal claim are successively eliminated.

An excellent example of the use of concomitant variation in time-series is provided by Fisher's (1921) analysis of wheat yields. Edwards and Cronbach (1952) discussed the logic of Fisher's analysis:

> [Fisher] found that after he controlled variety, and fertilizer, there was considerable variation from year to year. This variation had a slow up-and-down cycle over a seventy-year period. Now Fisher set himself on the trail of the residual variation. First he studied wheat records from other sections to see if they had the trend; they did not. He considered and ruled out rainfall as an explanation. Then he started reading the records of the plots and found weeds a possible factor. He considered the nature of each species of weed and found that the response of specific weed varieties to rainfall and cultivation accounted for much of the cycle. But the large trends were not explained until he showed that the upsurge of weeds after 1875 coincided with a school-attendance act which removed cheap labor from the fields, and that another cycle coincided with the retirement of a superintendent who made weed removal his personal concern.

Economists search for connections between time series in the hope of finding "lead indicators." A lead indicator is a series whose fluctuations are predictors of the fluctuations of another series; for

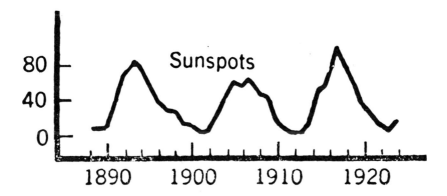

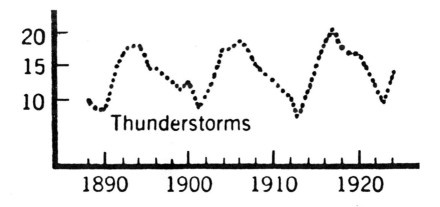

Figure 1. Sunspot numbers compared with thunderstorms in Siberia (adapted from Huntington, 1945, p. 520).

example, wholesale prices are a lead indicator of retail prices. One way of studying the concomitant variation between series is by the use of a technique called "transfer functions." A transfer function is a linear equation which relates the past of one time series to the present or future of another time series (see Box and Jenkins, 1970, pp. 402-412). The logic of experimental inference using transfer functions among time-series is closely related to the quasi-experimental techniques of "cross-lag panel correlations," which is due to Campbell and Stanley (1963) and "path analysis" which is being developed within mathematical sociology.

Ex Post Facto Experiments

The second level of causal inference comes from generating post hoc hypotheses to account for the fluctuations of a system by using an historical log or journal of events assumed to be causal in nature and scanning for shifts in the series. Granger and Hatanaka (1964) analyzed the responses of stock price indices to strikes, wars, and major non-recurring events (such as the stock market crash). Figure 2 is an indication of the hypotheses they generated by pairing a log of events assumed to be causal and by scanning for shifts in the series.

In a program for potential high school dropouts, teachers assumed they had made major breakthroughs in treatment following a long, emotional, intimate talk with a student. There were three instances of this event. Time-series analysis on three behavioral indicators, however, showed that each of the students significantly avoided the teacher subsequent to the talk, did not improve in academic performance, and significantly increased classroom participation in a disruptive manner (Gottman, 1971).

In Figure 3 are recorded the skin temperature reactions of a young nurse during an interview with a psychiatrist, coupled with an historical log of events during the interview. This graph permits many hypotheses to be generated. For example, the psychiatrist's entry twice results in a similar drop in skin temperature, and the slope of the drops are the same.

Another illustration may be helpful in understanding the benefits in generating hypotheses for the design of interventions. Figure 4 is a presentation of ten years of the Dow Jones Industrial Average annotated with certain critical incidents. We can divide up the series into fairly homogeneous parts and sort the events related

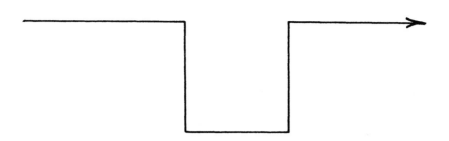

The effect of a strike to stock price indices is to add a curve like the above to the time-series.

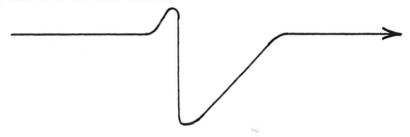

The effect of major non-recurring crises such as the stock market crash is to add a series like the above.

The effect of war is to add a series like the one above.

Figure 2. Granger and Hatanaka's (1964) conceptualization (empirically based) of the effects of strikes, market "crashes" and wars on the stock price index.

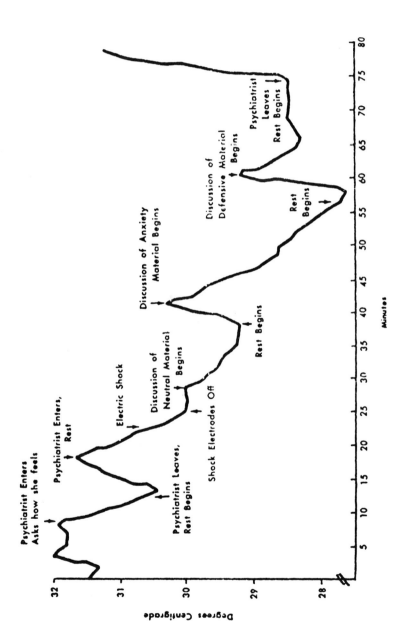

Figure 3. Changes in finger skin temperature of a subject during a psychiatric interview.

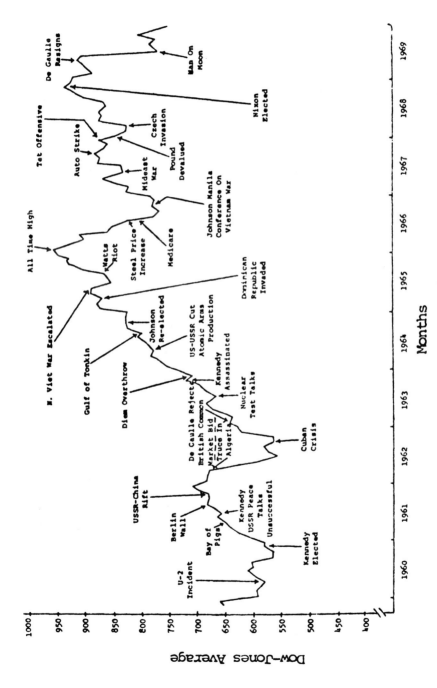

Figure 4. A ten-year segment of the Dow-Jones Industrial Average with post hoc "explanations" of changes in level.

to shifts. Gottman and Clasen (1972) discussed these data and generated hypotheses using these critical incidents.

Scanning for shifts in the series is accomplished by considering the series to be an interrupted time-series experiment. It becomes difficult to generalize from one such quasi-experiment without cross-validation. Even when several similar events can be associated with similar shifts in the series, strong causal inferences are impossible without the use of planned experimentation.

Planned Experiments

In a real sense the previous levels of causal inference are similar to Johannes Kepler's search for empirical relationships in the motions of the planets. The post hoc nature of the analysis of variation and concomitant variation is appropriate in astronomy or macroeconomics where little experimental control is possible over the system being studied.

Series of observation of a variable across time are important data in many fields of inquiry. Each of the sciences using time-series data encounters a different range of experimental control possibilities. The astronomer tries to decompose incoming electromagnetic radiation from stars into components which reveal the structure of the stars. In economics, more control is possible for both micro- and macro-systems; the economist also attempts to decompose time-series such as the Dow Jones Industrial Average into components which generate models for economic systems; for example, he is interested in determining periods of business cycles of major importance. The economist also determines the effects of various classes of events over which he has little control (strikes, wars, natural catastrophies) as well as the effects of planned interventions (changes in interest rates, wage and price freezes, changes in governmental spending). The geophysicist studying the structure of the earth may exert control by detonating explosives, examining time-series seismographic recordings, and decomposing them on the basis of pre-established response characteristics of various geological layers he assumes to be present.

Campbell and Stanley (1963, p. 205) stated that "the task of theory-testing data collection is therefore predominantly one of rejecting inadequate hypotheses." We can assume that the uses of time-series discussed above serve the important function of generating hypotheses about causal connection. However, convincing tests of the hypotheses generated must occur _via_ the use of planned intervention. A variety of experimental design options, to be presented in Chapter Two, makes it possible to eliminate different rival hypotheses and clarifies the discovery of causal relationships.

Notation

As before, $\underline{O}$ represents the observation of one or more dependent variables, and $\underline{I}$ designates an intervention into a sequence of observations. Both $\underline{O}$ and $\underline{I}$ may be subscripted; to designate time in the former case and distinctness in the latter. The data resulting from the observation process will be denoted by $\underline{z}$, subscripted to denote time. For example, a basic time-series experiment in which three pre- and post-intervention observations are taken on a dependent variable would be designated as follows:

Design	Data
$O_1\,O_2\,O_3\,I_1\,O_4\,O_5\,O_6$	$z_1\,z_2\,z_3\,z_4\,z_5\,z_6$

Where more than one unit of observation (person, group, geographical unit, etc.) is involved, their relationship to each other in terms of whether they are randomly or nonrandomly equivalent will be denoted by a preceding $\underline{R}$ in the former case and a separating line of dashes in the latter:

$$R \quad O_1\,O_2\,O_3\,I_1\,O_4\,O_5\,O_6 \qquad O_1\,O_2\,O_3\,I_1\,O_4\,O_5\,O_6$$
$$\text{------------}$$
$$R \quad O_1\,O_2\,O_3\,I_2\,O_4\,O_5\,O_6 \qquad O_1\,O_2\,O_3\,I_2\,O_4\,O_5\,O_6$$

Whenever multiple groups are involved, the possibility exists of either random or nonrandom assignment of experimental units to the groups. In diagrams and illustrations we shall depict the nonrandomly equivalent groups designs since they are more frequently encountered. It should be kept in mind that random assignment of experimental units to groups is to be preferred when it is feasible.

Any two symbols which are aligned vertically denote simultaneous activities. For example, in the above two designs the randomization, the identically numbered observations, and the interventions occur at the same time.

A final notational consideration is important since it has tradi-
tionally been understated—or overlooked entirely—in time-series
experiment methodology and because it has important implications for
the problem of characterizing in advance of data analysis an anticipated intervention effect. An intervention may occur once in a series
and not be maintained, or it may be applied continuously over several
points in time. For example, a voter registration appeal could be
televised once on the fifteenth day of the month, or it could be televised daily from the fifteenth to the thirtieth. The expected intervention effect could be different in these two circumstances: In the
former, there might be a peak response (voter registration) on the
sixteenth and seventeenth days which rapidly decays thereafter; in
the latter, the response might grow or remain constant across the last
half of the month. The two designs could be diagrammed as follows:

Continuous Intervention

$$\cdots \; O_{13} \; O_{14} \; O_{15} \; I \; O_{16} \; I \; O_{17} \; I \; O_{18} \; \cdots$$

Temporary Intervention

$$\cdots \; O_{13} \; O_{14} \; O_{15} \; I \; O_{16} \; O_{17} \; O_{18} \; \cdots$$

Although we shall allow this distinction to slide by for notational convenience—except later in "Monitoring Interventions"—it
bears in fundamental ways on the problem of attributing changes in a
time-series to interventions. For example, in Figure 5 we illustrate
how the behavior of the same series may constitute strong evidence
for an intervention effect if the intervention is temporary and weak
evidence if it is continuous.

Unit-Repetition vs.
Unit-Replication

The organism, person, group, political unit, etc., which is
"treated" and observed in the time-series experiment is termed the
experimental unit. If the experimental unit is a single, intact body
observed at several successive points in time, the design is unit-
repetitive. For example, a single child might be observed interacting
with his classmates each day for sixty days, or an intact group of
thirty students might be observed at the end of the school year from

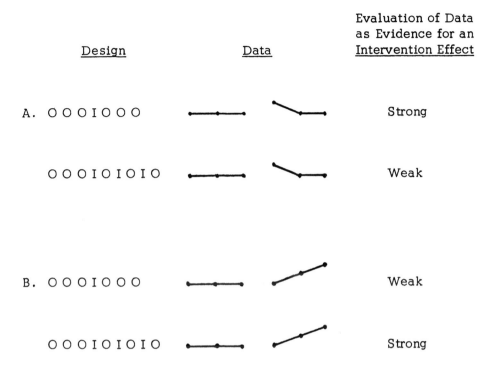

Figure 5. Illustration of how consideration of temporary vs. continuous interventions mediates the strength of the inference from data to a conclusion that an intervention effect exists.

Kindergarten through Grade 12; in these instances, observations are repeated on the same experimental unit. In contrast, the measurement of student performance on the "second grade" in a particular school district at the end of each year for twenty successive years might more properly be spoken of as replication of observation of an experimental unit which is defined conceptually and not be reference to specific individuals.

The annual measurement of the birth rate for the United States is unit-replicative in the strictest sense, because the "U.S. population" is an abstract unit comprising different individuals from year to year. However, many persons would be measured repeatedly in an annual assessment of the "U.S. population." Many designs will present a similar situation: Some individuals are repeated in the unit, others are not.

The concept of unit-repetitive vs. unit-replicative time-series designs has important implications for design validity, measurement and statistical analysis. The degree to which a design is unit-repetitive will be an important consideration even though the design cannot be classified as purely unit-repetitive. For example, since the composition of the "U.S. population" is relatively stable from year to year—it might be 96 percent "unit-repetitive"—attributing large shifts in a time-series to a change in composition of the experimental unit rather than an intervention may be illogical.

The methodological implications of this distinction are numerous. The unit-replicative design may often be more prone to invalidity due to an alteration in the nature of the individuals comprising the experimental unit which is coincident with the intervention. For example, if the unit is the "second grade" in a particular school district, and the intervention whose effect is to be assessed is coincident with the entrance into grade 2 of the first fully racially integrated class of students in the history of the district, the intervention effect would be confounded with the abrupt shift in the composition of the experimental unit. Such an invalidation of a design would be impossible in a unit-repetitive design in which the same thirty pupils were measured repeatedly across several years.

The unit-replicative design may be far less subject to a type of "Hawthorne" or "reactive" effect which could possibly arise in a unit-repetitive design in which the subjects perceived the experimental manipulation as a contrast with the baseline conditions under which they were first observed. This year's second grade class in a unit-replicative design would likely be unaware that past second grades had received a different type of instruction.

"Practice effects" of testing are not at issue in the unit-replicative design, though they may confound or complicate a particular unit-repetitive design. Problems of multiple-intervention interference effects (to be discussed in Chapter Four) arise in a unit-repetitive design but not one in which the unit is replicated.

When the experimenter has the choice, he may frequently strengthen a particular design by attending to the unit-repetitive vs. unit-replicative distinction, both in the application of a treatment and the observation of the outcome variable. For example, rather than intervene in an entire school district and measure all pupils, it may be possible to randomly select at each point in time a sample of pupils who will both receive the treatment and be measured against the outcome variable.

We shall return to the unit-repetition vs. unit-replication distinction on two or three occasions in this text. However, although the distinction is not reflected in the symbolism adopted later to depict various time-series designs, it should be held in mind that the concept cuts across nearly every design we shall discuss. In particular instances, this distinction may be crucial for judging the validity of an interpretation of a time-series design.

Sampling Time Units for Measurement

The choice of what constitutes a "unit of time" in a time-series is often arbitrary. Should a school or classroom be observed each minute, each day, or each month? If an experimental unit is to be observed weekly, should the observation be made on Monday morning or Friday afternoon? The answers to such questions are as varied as the individual applications of the time-series design.

When the time continuum is sampled for measurement purposes, the arbitrary choice of when to sample can have important implications for the detection of an intervention effect. Most systems are quite complex, and an intervention may not work a uniform effect across all hours of a day or all days of a week, for example. In these cases, sampled measurement could overlook the portion of time when the intervention had its effect. For example, one would be ill-advised to sample Wednesdays to assess the effect on absenteeism of a new incentive program since absences are minimal in the middle of the week to begin with; the intervention should have its greatest effect on Mondays or Fridays. Of course, exhaustive measurement (e.g., total absences per week) would be advisable—if it were practical. However, exhaustive measurement could partially obscure the effect of an intervention if that effect was strong only at intermittent points on the time continuum.

Ross, Campbell and Glass (1970) presented data which illustrate the importance of the sampled measurement concept. The British Road Safety Act was instituted on October 9, 1967, and was directed toward apprehension of drunken drivers. In Figure 6 appear graphs of the number of traffic fatalities in England under two different sampled measurement plans. Series A is based on the number of fatalities per month which occurred during hours when workers were commuting between home and work, viz., each day of the week

between 7 and 10 a.m. and 4 and 5 p.m. Series B is based on the
number of fatalities per month which occurred on weekend nights,
viz., Thursday midnight to 4 a.m. Friday; Friday midnight to 4 a.m.
Saturday; Saturday 10 p.m. to midnight. The intervention effect is
apparent in Series B but not in Series A. A sampled measurement
plan based on traffic fatalities during daylight hours would have com-
pletely overlooked the intervention effect.

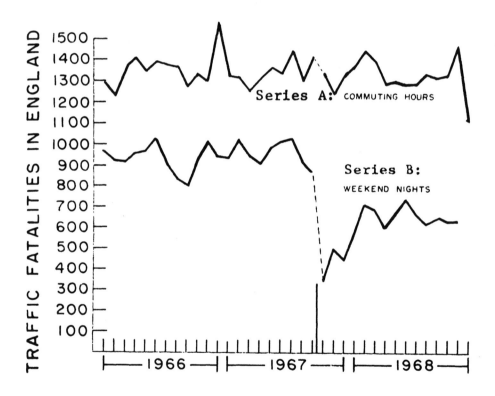

Figure 6. Illustration of dependence of an intervention effect on the
sampling of time units for measurement of the outcome variable (data
adapted from Ross, Campbell, and Glass, 1970).

CHAPTER TWO

VARIATIONS ON THE BASIC TIME-SERIES
EXPERIMENTAL DESIGN

In this chapter, several variations on the basic time-series experimental design are specified and illustrated. The unique features of these various designs and their implications for causal inference are discussed.

In Figure 7, a variety of modifications of the basic time-series experiment design is presented. The half-dozen or so basic types of design in Figure 7 immediately suggest numerous other variations constructed by combining features depicted in the figure. For example, the "sequential multiple-group—single-I," the "sequential reversal," or the "stratified 'interaction'" designs come readily to mind and could be depicted in an obvious manner. The purpose of Figure 7 is to illustrate fundamental variations on the simplest design, not to capture the inexhaustible variety of designs which ingenuity and the exigencies of a specific experimental problem can create. Depending on particular circumstances of subjects, processes, interventions, measurement procedures, etc., one of these variations may enjoy a greater measure of validity than all others. In the remainder of this chapter we shall illustrate these various designs and consider the special circumstances bearing on their validity.

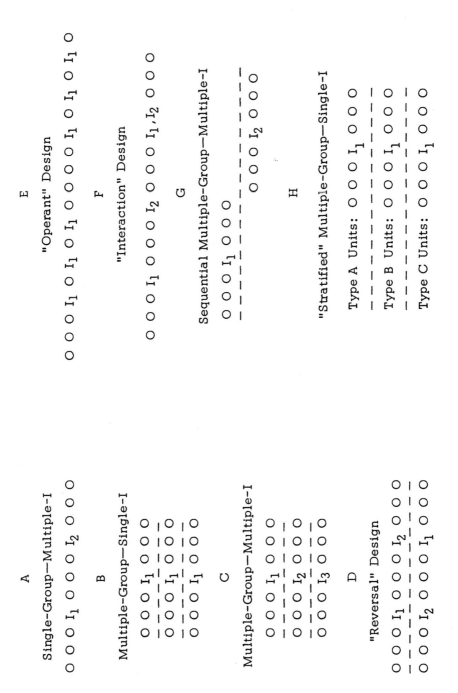

Figure 7. Variations on the basic time-series experimental design.

We must emphasize, however, that there are definite limits to the utility of discussing design validity in the abstract. Although abstract features of designs are of some importance, usually the validity of a particular experiment hinges upon special circumstances and contingencies which no theory can anticipate. So-called "weak designs" may be quite appropriate in a specific setting; putative "strong designs" may not be equal to the task they are intended to accomplish. More properly, there are no "strong" or "weak" designs, only more or less valid applications of designs. The designs and their features which we discuss here are intended to aid the experimenter in making his own judgments about the validity of his experiments; they cannot be used to render that judgment for him.

Single-Group—Multiple-I Design

Holtzman (1963) presented data due to Mefferd which illustrates the "single-group—multiple-$\underline{I}$" design (see Figure 8). In this instance the "group" is a single schizophrenic patient observed for 240 successive days. The patient's "perceptual speed" was observed for 60 days under baseline conditions; on the 61st day the patient was placed on chlorpromazine, a first generation tranquilizer; on the 121st

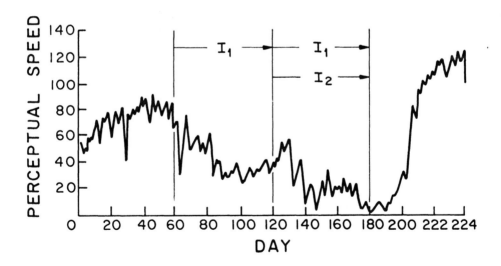

Figure 8. Effects of a tranquilizer (chlorpromazine) —I_1—electro-shock—I_2—on the perceptual speed of a single schizophrenic patient.

day electroshock treatment was added to the chlorpromazine treatment; both treatments were suspended on the 181st day and baseline conditions reinstated for the final 60 days. The exact design employed by Mefferd is slightly more complex than the paradigmatic "single-group—multiple-$\underline{I}$" design. Using the concept of continuous intervention and symbolizing simultaneous interventions by a columnar arrangement of $\underline{I}$-symbols, the design can be depicted as follows:

$$O_1 \cdots O_{60} \; I_1 \; O_{61} \; I_1 \; O_{62} \cdots I_1 \; O_{120} \; \begin{matrix} I_1 \\ I_2 \end{matrix} \; O_{121} \; \begin{matrix} I_1 \\ I_2 \end{matrix} \; O_{122} \cdots \begin{matrix} I_1 \\ I_2 \end{matrix}$$

$$O_{180} \; O_{181} \cdots O_{240}.$$

The data in Figure 8 seem to show decrements in perceptual speed coincident with both interventions, although the picture is clouded by a great deal of random error which needs to be dealt with by appropriate statistical methods.

In general, the "single-group—multiple-$\underline{I}$" design is characterized by the successive introduction of two or more interventions into a process assessed on one experimental unit. This experimental unit could be a person, group of persons, socio-political unit, etc. In any case, the logic of the causal inference is that any abrupt change in level or direction of the time-series coincident with an intervention is the effect of that intervention.

An attractive feature of the "single-group—multiple-$\underline{I}$" design is one that is shared with all "within-subject" designs: economy. A single subject can afford the testing of several causal hypotheses — a distinct advantage, for example, in cases of treating rare diseases or bizarre psychopathologies. This design has an obvious application in those instances (see Campbell, 1969) in which simultaneous comparison of treatments is politically impossible. However, one trades off at least one strength of "between-subjects" designs to achive this economy. Causal inferences in the "single-group—multiple-$\underline{I}$" design may be confounded by the "multiple-intervention interference" effect, which Campbell and Stanley (1963) discussed (under the name "multiple-treatment interference") in connection with other types of "within-subject" design. Briefly, an experimental unit (organism or social unit) may respond differently to $\underline{I_2}$ because it was preceded by $\underline{I_1}$ than if $\underline{I_2}$ were encountered in isolation from $\underline{I_1}$ or before it. (See the "reversal design" below for a means of controlling for multiple-intervention interference.) For example, in the illustration, the decrease in perceptual speed after day 120 (if it is real and not random) could be due to the effect of electroshock or to the effect of electroshock with a person already receiving chlorpromazine. In Chapter Four we shall discuss the problem of multiple-intervention interference at greater length.

The validity of the "single-group—multiple-$\underline{I}$" design is also related to the distinction between temporary and continuous intervention. If the interventions are abrupt and are "applied" for one unit of time, then the threat of multiple-intervention interference may be lessened. In this case the "interaction design" (see below) may shed light on the separate and combined effects of the interventions.

The "single-group—multiple-$\underline{I}$" design can be easily fortified against such dangers as multiple-intervention interference, repeated testing effects, and certain instrumentation errors when the experimental unit is a large group of interchangeable subunits. In these instances, it is often advisable to sample at random a small number of units from the larger group at each point in time for either measurement, exposure to the intervention, or both. For example, in evaluating the effect of a "student governmental decentralization" in a large high school, it might be advisable to sample a different group of students each week rather than to form a "panel" of students and measure them repeatedly. In the latter case ("unit repetition"), the panel could be sensitized to the occurrence of the intervention (the decentralization) and react as they perceive the experimenter wishes them to.

Multiple-Group—Single-$\underline{I}$ Design

The intervention of one treatment into separate time-series being observed on two or more experimental units not distinguished by type is the essence of the "multiple-group—single-$\underline{I}$" design. This design is simply the simultaneous application of the simplest time-series design to more than one experimental unit without any attempt to characterize the various experimental units as to type.

The "multiple-group—single-$\underline{I}$" design represents an attempt to deal with generalizability ("external validity") of an intervention effect. The aggregation of data from several subunits into a group average may mask differences in the response of individual units to an intervention. At the very least, the "multiple-group—single-$\underline{I}$" design permits an examination of the pervasiveness of the intervention effect, and more importantly, may lead to the characterization—a typology—of units which react differently to an intervention (see "stratified multiple-group—single-$\underline{I}$" design below.)

Hilgard (1933) presented data on the effect of intensive training in digit memory on the digit spans of each of two twins (see Figure 9). Although his purpose was to demonstrate the futility of premature training, Hilgard's data illustrate the replication of an intervention effect on two experimental units. It is apparent from inspection of Figure 9 that twin 1's digit memory was enhanced by training, while twin 2 serving as twin 1's control showed no change during the same period of time. The effects are reversed during the phase of training for twin 2. It is important to note that twin 2 was not measured between week No. 1 and week No. 14; it is conceivable, though unlikely, that twin 1's growth from week No. 1 to week No. 12 was due to the act of measurement per se and not to training. The design could have been more tightly controlled if twin 2 had been measured but not trained from week No. 1 to week No. 14.

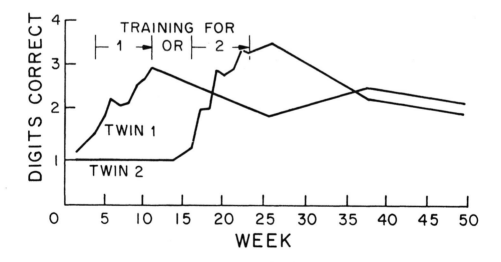

Figure 9. Effects of intensive training on the digit memory of two twins. (After Hilgard, 1933.)

Hilgard's design featured sequential rather than the simultaneous interventions of the same treatment. This design can be called a "time-lagged control" design (Gottman, 1971). Such a staggering of interventions could often enhance the "multiple-group—single-$\underline{I}$" design by demonstrating that the effect is general across time and not a mere historical coincidence. This design provides both a control group for a limited time and an independent replication of the effect. Such a design may also ameliorate the ethical concerns of withholding an intervention to those presumed to be in need of it; the intervention is withheld from some only for a time and is administered when it has been shown to be effective (as in the "delayed-treatment control-group" design used in psychotherapy outcome research). However, if experimental units "interact" with the intervention, i.e., have differential reactions to it, the sequential feature of the "time-lagged control" design confounds the historical and the interaction explanations of why one unit showed an interaction effect and a second unit did not.

Morris (1972) utilized the "multiple-group—single-$\underline{I}$" design in an interesting study of organizational behavior. In Morris's study, the "group" was an individual; three researchers in an educational research and development organization were observed weekly for a year on three variables: percent of time spent in a) conducting research, b) in reviewing the literature, and c) in visiting schools. Midway through the experiment the three individuals were appointed to the policy board of the organization. Morris found differential responses of the individuals to this intervention. He was able to relate post hoc the nature of the individual's response to being appointed to the policy board to the individual's former position and responsibilities in the organization. The oldest, highest-ranking member was unaffected by the appointment as was the youngest man, who regarded himself as a "pure scientist" unwilling to sully his hands with administrative business; the appointment significantly affected the behavior of the third researcher who was of middle status in the organization before the appointment and aspired to a loftier spot. Morris's study illustrates an important principle: It may be advisable not to aggregate data from several time-series experiments for fear of obscuring possibly meaningful individual differences in intervention effects.

Multiple-Group—Multiple-$\underline{I}$ Design

In the "multiple-group—multiple-$\underline{I}$" design, two or more different interventions occur in an equal number of distinct time-series.

The design is analogous to the "multiple-group—single-I" design (and many of the same considerations apply) with the exception that different interventions occur in the separate groups.

Data from Glass (1968) illustrate the "multiple-group—multiple-I" design. On December 23, 1955, Governor Abraham Ribicoff of the State of Connecticut took unprecedented executive action to reduce traffic fatalities. Ribicoff announced that as of January 1, 1956, persons convicted of speeding would have their licenses suspended for thirty days at the first offense, for sixty days at the second offense, and for an indefinite period at the third offense. Data on Connecticut traffic fatalities before and after the Connecticut crackdown on speeding can be supplemented with a similar data stream from the State of Massachusetts to form a "multiple-group—multiple-I" design; I_1 is the Connecticut crackdown on speeding occurring in January 1956, and I_2 is the absence of such measures to reduce fatalities in Massachusetts. (In actuality, three other nearby states—Rhode Island, New York, and New Jersey—were used by Glass (1968) as additional control states in assessing the effect of the Connecticut crackdown; thus the full design involved five "groups" and two types of intervention: I_1 the crackdown in Connecticut and I_2 "no crackdown" in the four control states.) The data in Figure 10 for the two states are in the form of seasonally (monthly) adjusted* fatalities per 100,000,000 driver miles for the sixty months prior to and the forty-eight months after January 1, 1956. (See Campbell and Ross, 1968, and Glass, 1968, for analyses and interpretations of the "Connecticut experiment.")

The "multiple-group—multiple-I" design enjoys a large measure of validity. Problems of multiple-intervention interference do not arise because it is based on a "between groups" rather than "within-groups" comparison of intervention effects. The design is greatly enhanced by the random assignment of experimental units to interventions or an attempt to match units receiving different interventions. Such matching or randomization was not performed, of course, in the Connecticut illustration, and the selection bias in the study clouds the apparent finding that the Connecticut crackdown reduced traffic fatalities.

---

*A cyclic seasonal trend in the data was removed by deviating each January figure around the mean for all months of January in the series, each February figure around the February mean, etc.

27

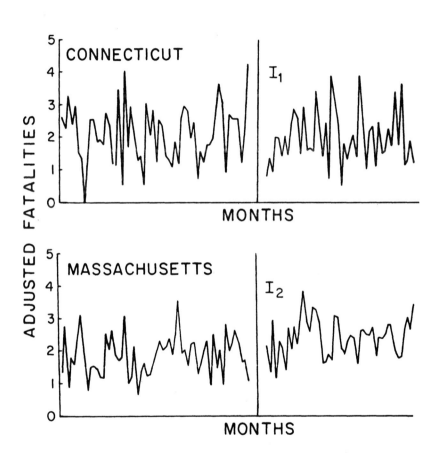

Figure 10. Fatalities/100,000,000 Driver Miles Minus Monthly Average Plus 2 for Connecticut (upper) and Massachusetts (lower) before and after the January 1956 crackdown on speeding in Connecticut.

Random assignment of heterogeneous experimental units to the
different interventions is less desirable than a careful matching when
there are few units. Essentially each group in the design is a single
experimental unit with distinctive characteristics which may interact
with the particular intervention it receives. Random assignment does
little to "equate" the multiple groups when there are so few of them,
just as random assignment of four subjects to two levels of a factor
in an experiment does little to equate the comparisons on uncontrolled, antecedent variables (a fact which is properly reflected in the
enormous differences required for statistical significance in a two-
group experiment with two subjects per group). A deliberate attempt
to match experimental units is generally preferable to random assignment when the units cannot be subdivided into smaller units for the
purposes of the experiment. For example, a random selection of control states that resulted in Texas, Idaho, California, and North
Dakota would have produced decidedly poorer design to assess the
Connecticut crackdown than the premeditated selection of
Massachusetts, Rhode Island, New York, and New Jersey as controls.

However, when the groups in the "multiple-group—multiple-I"
design comprise several smaller units, e.g., three groups of twenty
persons each, the random assignment of the smaller units to groups
which then receive distinct interventions has obvious advantages.

"Reversal" Design

In the "reversal" design, two groups are observed under baseline conditions for some number of points in time; intervention I_1 is
introduced into group 1, followed at a later time by I_2. The order of
introduction of the two interventions is reversed in group 2. The
design permits assessment of two intervention effects with control
over the multiple-intervention interference problem.

Gottman and McFall (1972) utilized the "reversal" design in an
experiment on the effects of self-monitoring on speech production of
high-school sophomores. The experiment timeline, which extended
over one semester, was divided into the following periods: Eight
weeks for a baseline, one week for the first self-monitoring experimental period and one week for the second self-monitoring period
during which the interventions for the two groups were reversed. The
baseline period consisted of forty days of observations. On the
forty-first day of class, the self-monitoring experiment was initiated
by giving the students the following instructions: "I would like to

ask your help in an experiment to find out two things: How often you
talk in the class discussion, and how often you would like to talk in
the class discussion but do not. I am passing out pink and green
index cards. Those of you with pink cards [five male, three female]
should make a check each time you talk, whether it is a long comment
or a very short one. If you say something, and someone else says
something, and then you say something again—that would call for two
checks. Those of you with green cards [six male, three female]
should put down a check each time you would like to talk but, for any
reason, do not."

The first set of experimental instructions was in effect for four
days. The second experimental period, which covered the next five
school days, was initiated by simply reversing the instructions to the
two experimental groups.

Each student's rate of oral class participation was observed for
thirty minutes daily and recorded. Throughout the thirty-minute
observation period, every three minutes was designated as a talk
unit. An observer recorded a check for each student who spoke during
each three-minute interval. From these data, each subject was given
a talk score, which was equal to the total number of checks he
received in each three-minute segment; thus, each subject received
ten talk scores per day. The data from the experiment appear in
Figure 11. For a detailed analysis of the data see Gottman and
McFall (1972).

The "reversal" design is actually two simultaneous "single-
group—multiple-$\underline{I}$" designs with the order of intervention switched.
It affords control of the multiple-intervention interference effect
which threatens the simpler "single-group—multiple-$\underline{I}$" design. For
example, the fact the $\underline{I}_2$ works its effect only after or in the presence
of $\underline{I}_1$ is apparent in the following diagram of hypothetical data from a
"reversal" design:

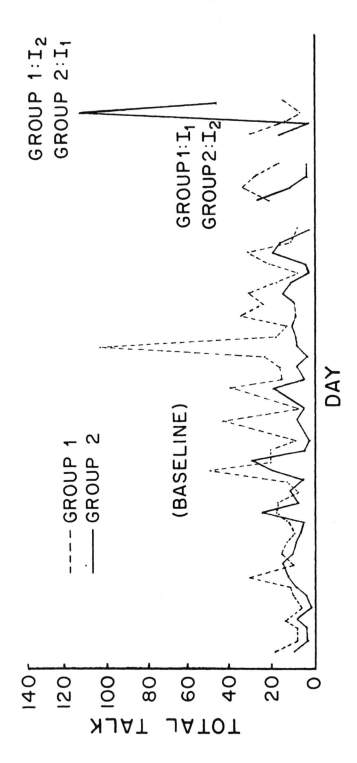

Figure 11. Effect of self-monitoring on total group talk; I_1: talk monitoring, I_2: non-talk monitoring.

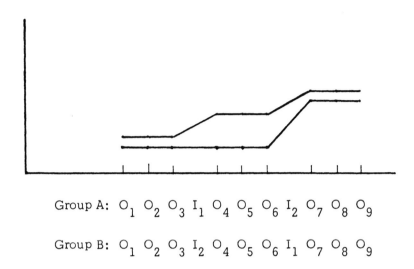

Group A: O_1 O_2 O_3 I_1 O_4 O_5 O_6 I_2 O_7 O_8 O_9

Group B: O_1 O_2 O_3 I_2 O_4 O_5 O_6 I_1 O_7 O_8 O_9

In a common variation on the "reversal" design, no baseline is established before the first intervention:

$$I_1 \ O \ O \ O \ I_2 \ O \ O \ O$$
$$\text{-----------}$$
$$I_2 \ O \ O \ O \ I_1 \ O \ O \ O$$

Tyler and Brown (1968) employed such a design to compare the effects of contingent and noncontingent token reinforcement on the academic performance of delinquent boys. For the first seventeen days, nine boys (group 1) received varying amounts of money which increased as their score increased on a ten-item multiple-choice test over the content of the previous night's Huntley-Brinkley news broadcast; group 2, six boys, received 21¢ per day for the first seventeen days for completing the test, regardless of their score. On the eighteenth day, the reinforcement schedules were reversed. The data appear as Figure 12.

It should be noted that in using the abbreviated "reversal" design, one forgoes any opportunity to assess the effects of $\underline{I}_1$ and $\underline{I}_2$ in isolation or without possible confounding from a multiple-intervention interference effect. Without the initial baseline observation period, one cannot assess the initial appearance of $\underline{I}_1$ and $\underline{I}_2$, as opposed to their occurrence after subjects have been exposed to the other intervention. In most instances, the complete, unabbreviated "reversal" design affords more information at little additional cost.

Quite obviously the "reversal" design can be extended to include J interventions which would require J! groups to evaluate all possible orders of intervention. For example, three interventions (A, B, and C) would require 3! = 6 groups in each of which one of the six possible orderings of interventions A, B, and C would appear. Group 1 would receive A, followed by B, followed by C; group 2 would receive A, then C, then B; etc. Fractions of a complete design would have to be employed for even modest numbers of interventions since, for example, 5! = 120.

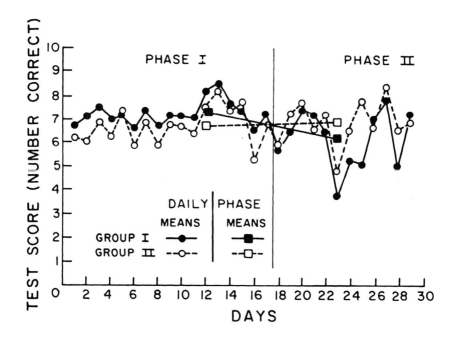

Figure 12. The effect of contingent and noncontingent token reinforcement on true-false test performance.

"Operant" Design

The unique feature of the "operant" design is that it adds a
"return to baseline" and reconfirmation of the intervention effect to
the simplest one-group—one-intervention design. The evidence for
the intervention effect is considerably stronger if the effect can be
brought about at will twice instead of once. The intent of the
"operant design" is commendable. The initial "no treatment" condition establishes a baseline for the variable being observed. If the
level of the series changes when the treatment is applied, the change
is attributed to the intervention. This attribution is based on the
assumption that the series would have remained at baseline level in
the absence of the intervention. It is precisely this assumption
which is checked when the treatment is subsequently removed and
one sees whether the untreated subject again operates at the baseline
level. If anything, the logic of the operant design is too stringent.
As will be seen in Chapters Five and Six, many processes—those
called "nonstationary"—have no baseline, in effect. However, in
such cases, one would be justified in concluding that an intervention had an effect even if the process did not return to "baseline"
when the intervention was removed.

In the "operant" design the intervention or "treatment" is
repeatedly applied for several points in time; the response of the
organism is assumed to be tied to the presence of this "treatment" so
that the intervention effect disappears (the organism "returns to baseline") when the intervention is removed. Hence, an intervention
effect is present when I is present, and absent when I is absent. The
intervention effect is assumed to be reversible. Clearly the design
is not feasible when the effect of the intervention cannot be reversed.
For example, if the intervention teaches a subject to drive a car, it
is hardly possible for him to "return to baseline."

Broden, Hall, and Mitts (1971) employed the "operant" design
in a study of the effect of self-monitoring on the study behavior of an
eighth-grade girl. The percent of ten-second intervals in an hour-
long daily history class during which the girl engaged in "study
behavior" was recorded for seven days under baseline conditions. On
the eighth day, the pupil was instructed to record her own study
behavior on a recording sheet at intermittent times during the hour;
this self-monitoring continued for five days at which time baseline
conditions were reinstituted for five days followed by a second nine-
day phase of self-monitoring. The data from the study appear in
Figure 13.

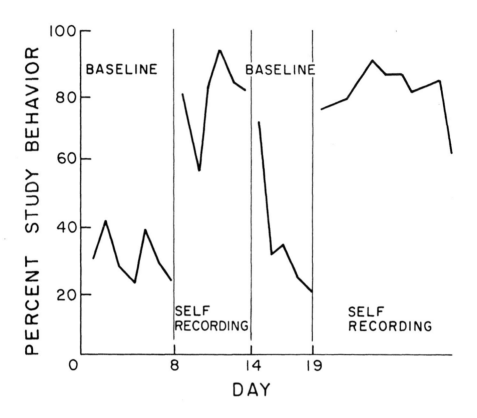

Figure 13. Effects of self-monitoring on the study behavior of a single student (after Broden et al., 1971).

"Interaction" Design

The "interaction" design is, in one sense, the time-series counterpart of a factorial experimental design. The four possible combinations I_1 and not-I_1, I_2, and not-I_2 all appear in the design:

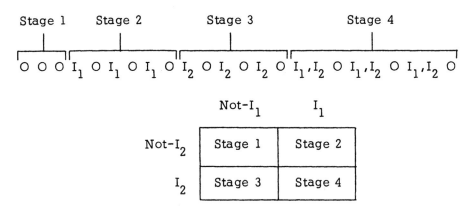

Hence, it is possible to estimate the independent ("main") and inter-active effects of two different interventions. Essentially the design represents a 2^2 factorial design strung out sequentially. Obviously a 2^k factorial design can be similarly constructed by extending the series to include all 2^k combinations of presence and absence of k different interventions.

Unlike the typical 2^k factorial experimental design, the time-series "interaction" design presents the problem of order of introduc-tion of interventions. There are $4! = 24$ possible orders in which the combinations of presence and absence of two interventions can be arranged. Where more than one experimental unit can be observed across time there are obvious advantages to varying the order of interventions in an "interaction reversal" design:

Unit No. 1: O O O I_1 O O O I_2 O O O I_1,I_2 O O O

— —

Unit No. 2: O O O I_2 O O O I_1 O O O I_1,I_2 O O O

— —

Unit No. 3: O O O I_1,I_2 O O O I_1 O O O I_2 O O O

For analysis purposes it is important to make several specific hypotheses concerning how the intervention effects should operate. For example, it will be necessary to answer the questions in connec-tion with the simple "interaction" design whether the effect of inter-vention I_1 will disappear when I_1 is removed, whether the effect of I_2 will disappear or be maintained when I_2 is removed and the combined I_1,I_2 is instituted, etc. These assumptions will determine the nature of the statistical model used to estimate and test the main and inter-action effects. (We shall illustrate in a later chapter the statistical analysis of multiple-I designs; the analysis of the "interaction" design parallels them almost exactly.)

Broden, Hall and Mitts's investigation of the study behavior of an eighth-grade girl, which was described under "operant" design above, also utilized an "interaction" design to investigate the sepa-rate and combined effects of "self-monitoring" and "praise by teacher." In Figure 14 are presented the four phases of this time-series experiment in which appear the four combinations of presence

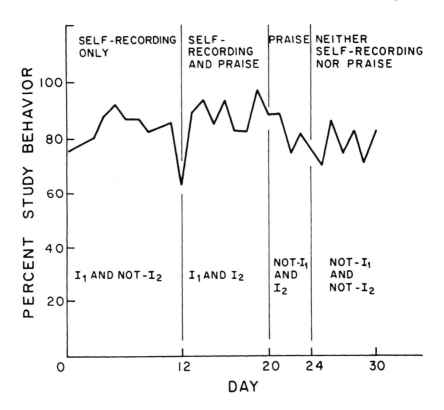

Figure 14. Effects of combined and separate self-monitoring and teacher praise on the study behavior of a single student (after Broden et al., 1971).

and absence of "self-monitoring" of study behavior and "teacher praise for study behavior" which constitute a 2^2 factorial design.

Sequential Multiple-Group—
Multiple-I Design

This design is analogous to the "multiple-group—multiple-I" design; the difference is that in this design the individual interrupted time-series are run sequentially.

Brown (1961) presented data adapted from Deese and Carpenter which illustrate the "sequential multiple-group—multiple-I design." One group of rats, Group A, was deprived of food for twenty-two hours (high-drive) before each of twenty-four trials involving running a short alley for food; for the final eight trials, these rats were fed for one hour (low-drive) before each trial. For Group B, the high-drive and low-drive states were reversed for the first twenty-four and last eight trials. The outcome variable observed was "latency" defined as the time between when the rat was placed in the apparatus and when he began to traverse the alley.

The data, starting speeds (or "latencies") expressed as the reciprocal of the average of the logs of the latencies, from this study are depicted in Figure 15. For convenience the data have been coalesced by graphing them with respect to "trials" within each experiment rather than "time" across experiments. (For a detailed analysis of the data in Figure 15, see Maguire and Glass, 1967.)

In general, the sequential design is logically weaker than the simultaneous multiple-group—multiple-I design. The possibility that the difference in the intervention effects is the result of an historical "accident" coincident with I_2, say, is slightly greater in the sequential design than in its simultaneous counterpart (i.e., the "multiple-group—multiple-I" design). However, in experimentation with large, reactive social systems, the difficulties of instituting alternative interventions at the same point in time—since they may be considered unfair or discriminatory by those who presume to know in advance which intervention will be more effective—may require that the "sequential multiple-group—multiple-I" design be used. In many cases, this design will be preferable to the "single-group—multiple-I" design because the latter design faces problems of multiple-intervention interference (q.v., Chapter Four).

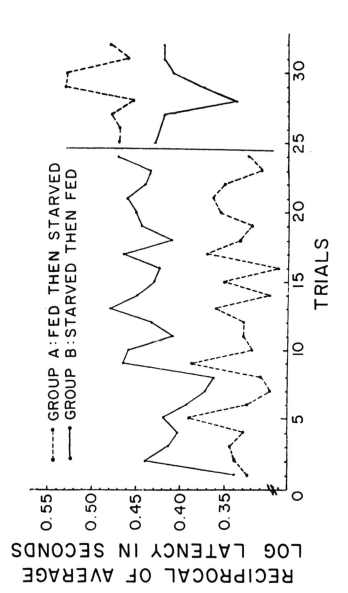

Figure 15. Starting speeds for two groups of rats before and after reversal of deprivation schedule (after Brown, 1961).

Stratified Multiple-Group—
    Single-I Design

This design is an extension of the "multiple-group—single-I"
design. In the stratified design, the groups are distinguished with
respect to type of experimental unit; in the simple multiple-group—
single-I design the experimental units are distinguished, but not by
type. The stratified design permits the investigation of differential
effects of the same intervention applied to different types of experimental unit. Rather than examining an aggregate intervention effect,
the experimenter stratifies the experimental units to investigate
whether boys, for example, respond differently to the intervention
than girls. Stratification of the experimental units represents a more
refined experimental question and should be greatly encouraged.

Data from a study of the effect of alteration in the divorce laws
of Germany in 1900 illustrate the "stratified multiple-group—single-
I" design (see Glass, Tiao, and Maguire, 1971). In Figure 16 appear
graphs of the petition for reconciliation* rate (per 100,000 inhabitants) in German states under three different types of legal code prior
to and for fourteen years after institution of the new Civil Code of the
German Empire on January 1, 1900.

The new Civil Code brought about a general "tightening up" of
divorce laws. Under the law beginning in 1900, divorce was to be
granted only in the case of guilty misconduct. The new Civil Code
was uniform across the German states, whereas divorce laws in
effect in the various states prior to 1900 were of three general types.
Approximately eight states were under the divorce laws of the
Prussian General Code prior to 1900 (see curve A in Figure 16). The
Prussian Code was the most lenient as regards divorce. Divorces
were granted in cases of misconduct, mutual agreement, and even on
grounds of "insuperable aversion" of one party for the other. In contrast to the lenient Prussian Code, the German "common law"
embodied ecclesiastical law concerning divorce. Catholics could not
divorce, and only grave misconduct was grounds for dissolution of a
Protestant marriage. German common law was in effect in twelve
states prior to 1900. Similar in practice to the German common law

---

*A "petition for reconciliation" was a mandatory first step in
divorce proceedings both before and after 1900. It was the initial,
public pronouncement of the disruption of a marriage.

40

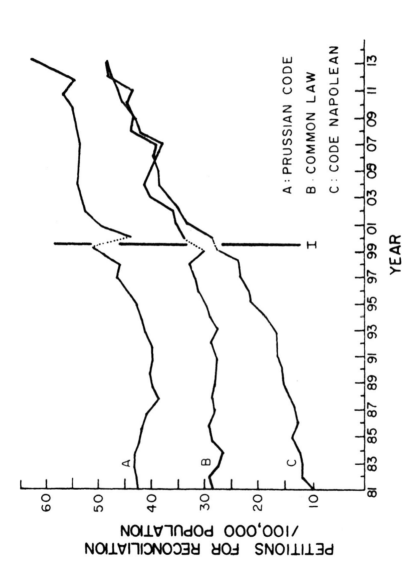

Figure 16. Effects of the 1900 revision of German divorce law on the petition for reconciliation/100,000 population rate in German states under three different types of pre-1900 law (after Glass, Tiao, and Maguire, 1971).

was the Code Napoleon, which was in effect in approximately four states. Divorce was granted only in cases of guilty misconduct; disruption of a marriage constituted insufficient grounds for divorce.

Analysis of the data in Figure 16 revealed an interesting pattern of differential intervention effects (see Glass, Tiao, and Maguire, 1971). The institution of uniform divorce laws in 1900 produced a significant decrement in the petition for reconciliation rate in the Prussian Code states, a significant increment in the Common Law states, and had no significant effect on the reconciliation rate in the Code Napoleon states. Thus, the effect of the intervention on the petition for reconciliation rate depended upon the type of state within the German Empire into which the intervention was made.

CHAPTER THREE

INTERVENTIONS AND INTERVENTION EFFECTS

An intervention into a time-series may affect the series in many ways. It may abruptly change the level of the series, or change the level after a short delay; it may change the level of the series permanently, or only temporarily; the intervention may sharply deflect a series formerly drifting downward, causing it to drift upward; it may make a highly variable series more stable, or *vice versa*. To complicate matters further, an intervention may work a combination of effects on a time-series, e.g., a downward drifting, highly variable series may show an abrupt change in level followed by a highly stable upward drift coincident with an intervention. The experimenter must scrutinize the data carefully, keeping his mind open to a variety of possible intervention effects while guarding against the false attribution of significance to random error. To assist with the assessment of significance we offer the variety of inferential statistical procedures in Chapters Five and Six; to assist with describing the form of the intervention effect, we present the typology of basic intervention effects in Figure 17.

The two basic types of intervention effects depicted in Figure 17 are level changes and direction changes. The abrupt change in level in response to an intervention is often found with single organisms or with interventions which are quickly and easily

44

implemented. A direction-change intervention effect can occur when the intervention is complex and must be implemented gradually. Consider an immunization campaign designed to eliminate a communicable disease; suppose that the program is implemented by vaccination of five-year-olds upon entering school. Approximately 2 percent of the population turns five each year; hence, at the end of post-intervention year 1, 2 percent of the population will have been "treated"; at the end of year 2, 4 percent; at the end of year t, $(2 \cdot t)$ percent of the population will have been vaccinated. Thus, one might hypothesize a linear downward shift in direction of the disease

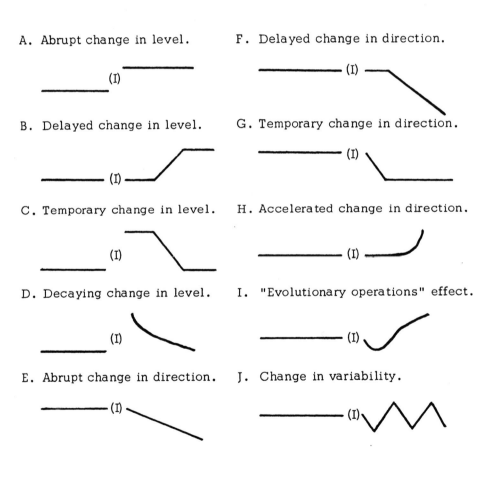

A. Abrupt change in level.

B. Delayed change in level.

C. Temporary change in level.

D. Decaying change in level.

E. Abrupt change in direction.

F. Delayed change in direction.

G. Temporary change in direction.

H. Accelerated change in direction.

I. "Evolutionary operations" effect.

J. Change in variability.

Figure 17. Varieties of intervention effects in the time-series experiment.

index starting at the point of initial intervention. An automobile safety law requiring seat-belts on all new cars would similarly be expected to bring about an abrupt change in direction of the fatality rate instead of an immediate change in level.

The correct anticipation of the intervention effect is important for at least two reasons: 1) it enables the postulation of an appropriate statistical model, resulting in a sensitive data analysis—e.g., to apply an analytic model based on the assumption of an immediate change in level of the time-series, when in fact the change is delayed, may result in a substantial underestimation of the change; 2) it raises the data analysis to a confirmatory plane, safely above the dangers of mis-interpreting random fluctuations as intervention effects.

Intervention effect type I in Figure 17 requires some explanation. An "evolutionary operations curve" (Box, 1967) is characterized by an initial extinction curve followed by a learning curve which elevates the series to a new level. This curve has been reported anecdotally in remedial reading where old habits must be unlearned before new habits are acquired. It is also the curve describing the successful survival of a species following an adaptive mutation (Box, 1967), where the ordinate is the population of the species at time t.

To this point we have considered only those effects on a series of an intervention which can be expressed in terms of constants related to the level or direction of drift of the series. Interventions may work more general or comprehensive effects on series, however. A particular intervention might alter the variance of errors, for example, of a series without affecting either the level or direction of drift. Less probably an intervention could modify the fundamental stochastic nature of the series, e.g., introducing an autoregressive component into an erstwhile simple moving-average process.

Holtzman (1963) presented data due to Mefferd which underscore the point that interventions introduced into a time-series may have complex and comprehensive effects. The data in Figure 18 depict a time-series of "word association relatedness scores" for a single schizophrenic patient; from day 1 to day 60 the patient received a placebo treatment; from day 61 to day 120 he was treated with chlorpromazine, an early tranquilizer; from day 121 to day 180 electroshock was combined with the chlorpromazine, after which the placebo was reinstated.

46

The measure of word-association relatedness appears to have been relatively unaffected by the switch from placebo during the first sixty days to the tranquilizer during the second phase of the experiment. However, the introduction of electroshock during the third phase seems to have influenced the word-association relatedness variable in complex ways.

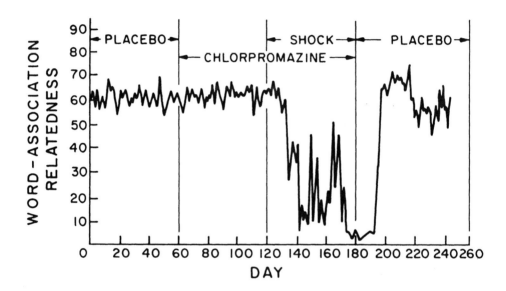

Figure 18. Effects of a tranquilizer (chlorpromazine) and electroshock on the word association-relatedness scores of a single schizophrenic patient.

Mefferd's design came close to being an "interaction design." If chlorpromazine had been withheld after day 180 and electroshock continued for sixty days (as it was, both were removed on day 180), it would have been possible to assess and compare the combined and separate effects of the two interventions. It appears from Figure 18 that electroshock affected "word association relatedness," but the question whether the effect appears only in the presence of the tranquilizer is open.

The introduction of electroshock therapy on day 120 appears to have affected the time-series in several ways: 1) the level of series dropped by nearly forty points on the average; 2) the series drifted precipitously downward for about the first twenty days after day 120; 3) the variance of the observations was increased; 4) the stochastic nature of the series itself appears to have been changed.

The experimenter must be alert not only to multiple effects from a single intervention, but he should expect to find different effects of the same intervention on different dependent variables. Holtzman (1963) also presented data on two other variables (one psychological and one biochemical) observed on a single schizophrenic patient over 240 days; the effects of the introduction of electroshock and a tranquilizer were quite different across the three dependent variables (see Figures 8 and 18 above and Figure 11.1 in Holtzman, 1963, p. 201). The "tightening" of the divorce laws throughout the German Empire in 1900 (see section entitled "Stratified Multiple-Group—Single-I Design" in Chapter Two above) produced an abrupt increase in the petition for reconciliation rate (the mandatory first step in divorce proceedings) and a decrease in the divorce rate in states formerly under the German Common Law prior to 1900 (see Figure 4 in Glass, Tiao, and Maguire, 1971).

Monitoring the Intervention

Interventions may be constant over time, or ephemeral, or of variable intensity. It is essential to monitor the intervention as well as the outcome (dependent) variable over time. In general, too little attention has been paid to describing the specific nature of the intervention. In some applications, interventions are contingent upon the dependent variable; an operant experiment consists of the administration of the reinforcement for successive approximations to the desired terminal behavior. Therefore, the intervention is contingent upon the operant and is a variable intervention. For example, in shaping initiative speech in autistic children (Lovaas et al., 1966), initially reinforcement is delivered for a response vaguely representing speech; later the same response does not receive reinforcement.

Broden, Hall, and Mitts (1971) instructed the eighth-grade history teacher in the study described under "Operant Design" in Chapter Two to praise the female subject for her study behavior whenever possible. This "teacher attention" intervention was to be introduced from the thirtieth to the forty-first days. The time-series

48

of the intervention appears in Figure 19 as a graph of the number of
times the teacher attended to (i.e., praised) the subject during each
class period. The importance of monitoring the intervention is evident in Figure 19. The mean number of instances of teacher attention
is not markedly different between the treatment and the baseline ses-
sions; one could question whether the intervention was ever fully
implemented and whether the study should be regarded as an adequate
test of the "teacher attention" intervention.

Of the variety of types of intervention, two general types are
prevalent and have important implications for analysis of time-series
experiments: <u>continuous</u> interventions and <u>temporary</u> (or "spiked")
interventions. The term "continuous intervention" denotes a treatment which is introduced at a point in time and is maintained across
time, e.g., a change in a law or a drug dosage administered daily.
A temporary or "spiked" intervention denotes a treatment which is
applied over a relatively short number of time units, e.g., a drug
administered once or a single televised political speech. The nature
of the intervention will often suggest whether the experimenter should
expect a permanent or lasting intervention effect, whether the appearance of the intervention effect is immediate or delayed, etc.

The Multiple Baseline Design

Risley and Baer (1969) presented a design developed in the field
of operant conditioning which represents a significant departure from
the design concepts heretofore encountered. The <u>multiple baseline
design</u> involves observing two (or more) "behaviors" (or variables)
across time on a single unit. The two variables are unobserved under
"control" conditions for sufficient time to establish baseline rates for
each. Then a treatment condition intervenes which is supposed to
affect only one of the variables.

Any change in the level of this behavior [the variable "treated"] is
compared with the level predicted for that behavior from the baseline measures. The accuracy of this prediction is assessed by
comparing this prediction with the continuing measures of the other
behavior(s). If, in fact, the level of the other behavior(s) remains
relatively constant, and to the extent that it can be assumed that
uncontrolled [influences], if they had occurred, would have similarly effected [sic] all of the behaviors measured, the baseline
prediction of the first behavior is supported. (Risley and Baer,
1969, pp. 5-6.)

49

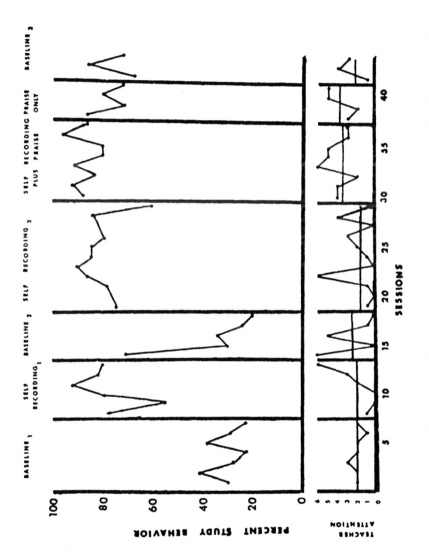

Figure 19. Time-series illustrating the monitoring of an intervention. (In this case the intervention is "teacher attention" which is supposed to begin on day 30 and terminate on day 41.)

Meichenbaum et al. (1968) employed the multiple baseline design in a classroom setting. A classroom of girls was observed over days on the two variables "attention to task during morning class" and "attention to task during afternoon class." After a baseline period of several days, rewards were given for attention to task during the afternoon only. Attention to task increased in the afternoon but not in the morning. Ross, Campbell and Glass (1970) employed the logic of the multiple baseline design in examining the results of a naturalistic time-series experiment on road safety (see Chapter One, Figure 6 and accompanying text). The British Road Safety Act of 1967 made the apprehension of drunken drivers the focus of efforts to reduce traffic fatalities. The decline in traffic fatalities was nonexistent during hours of commuting to and from work (variable 1) but was marked on weekend nights (variable 2), which was in accord with predictions from consideration of how the Road Safety Act should have worked its effect.

The multiple baseline design is an interesting variation of the time-series experiment paradigm with special potentialities and special problems. The design places a high premium on clear understanding of how variables interact in a particular system, which relationships among them are causal and which are spurious, etc. In practice, its logic may be assymetrical—which is hardly an indictment of uses of logic in the social and behavioral sciences: if the anticipated pattern of changes was observed, the intervention would be regarded as causing the effect on the target variable; however, if both variables showed an abrupt and marked change from baseline coincident with the intervention, we doubt that the investigator would regard his causal hypothesis concerning the target variable as being unsubstantiated. For example, if in the Meichenbaum et al. experiment, a simultaneous increase in both morning and afternoon "attention to task" could readily be rationalized as generalization (transfer, or spread) of the treatment effect.

Furthermore, two elements of the multiple baseline logic appear to work in opposition. Two outcome variables are to be selected which are somewhat functionally independent, i.e., the intervention should affect one but not the other. On the other hand, uncontrolled influences are to be recognized by the fact that they affect both variables equally. To the extent that the first condition (functional independence) is satisfied, the second condition (identical influence of uncontrolled conditions on both variables) would seem not to be satisfied.

However, as with all designs, utility will not be ajudged by theoretical second-guessing, but rather by the repeated application and analysis of the designs in actual research situations.

CHAPTER FOUR

SOURCES OF INVALIDITY IN

TIME-SERIES EXPERIMENTS

Changes in a time-series which coincide with the occurrence of
an intervention are presumed to be the effects of the intervention.
This causal claim may be invalid; events unrelated to the intervention
may cause the series to change abruptly at the point of intervention.
In addition, random variation in a time-series may be misinterpreted
as the effect of an intervention. No amount of general discussion of
invalidating influences in time-series experiments can replace the
need for the insight and cleverness one needs to judge the validity of
a particular application of a time-series experiment. However, a
half dozen or more common invalidating influences deserve special
attention because of their pervasiveness and generality.*

History

An event extraneous to the intervention but coincident with it
may produce an alteration of the series which is mistaken as an

---

*Campbell (1969) discussed sources of invalidity specific to
the (one-group) time-series experiment. We build upon and add to
his list here.

intervention effect. This is an example of <u>historical invalidity</u>. For example, a researcher may hypothesize that federally-funded compensatory education programs instituted in a school district in 1966 should have sharply reduced the "drop-out" rate. He compiles the data and observes an abrupt 58 percent decrease in the drop-out rate from 1966 to 1967, with no comparable shifts between any other successive years. He prepares to announce a major success for the compensatory education program when he recalls that the largest employer of unskilled labor in the area shut down its plant in February 1966. The decrease in the drop-out rate between 1966 and 1967 is uninterpretable; it could have been caused either by the special school program or the coincident demise of the largest employer of drop-outs. The study has been invalidated by an historical event coincident with the intervention being evaluated.

In <u>ex post facto</u> time-series experiments, the danger of historical invalidity is usually quite high. Intervention into complex social systems is generally multifaceted; it is no simple matter to sort out the effect of one intervention from the effects of many other simultaneous interventions targeted toward aspects of the same problem. To what would one attribute a decline in the school drop-out rate in New York City dating from 1956? Head Start? The Elementary and Secondary Education Act of 1965? Model Cities? Office of Economic Opportunity programs? Controlling for historical invalidity in such instances requires the most ingenious use of special measurement and data analysis techniques.

However, measurement and analysis cannot substitute for an exhaustive historical analysis of possible confounding interventions which may have nearly coincided with the intervention of primary interest. Ross, Campbell, and Glass (1970) illustrated this methodology in a study of the effect of the British Road Safety Act of 1967 on traffic fatalities in England. The focus of the Road Safety Act was the apprehension of drunken drivers; it represented an intervention based on a demonstrated correlation between drunkenness and traffic fatalities. Ross, Campbell, and Glass considered and dismissed seven coincident events which some observers purported to be the true causes of the abrupt decline in traffic fatalities which occurred when the Road Safety Act went into effect; these coincident events included 1) publicity for the Act (rejected because the fatality rate did not rise when the publicity stopped); 2) improvement in traffic controls (rejected because the improvements were gradual and the change in fatality rate was abrupt); 3) tire inspection (rejected because it produced a gradual increase in safe tires on vehicles); 4) decline in

two-wheeled vehicles (rejected because the decline was part of a
long-term trend and because the fatality reduction effect is also
apparent for four-wheeled vehicles only); 5) improved traffic law
enforcement in London (rejected since no one has ever demonstrated
a correlation between severity of conventional traffic law enforcement and the fatality rate); 6) declining rate of growth in British
highway traffic (rejected because though the growth rate is declining
the actual volume is increasing).

In planned time-series experiments, the threat of historical
invalidity is somewhat lessened. The experimenter can purposely
select the point of intervention least likely to coincide with any
extraneous event. It would seem to be inadvisable to select the
intervention point at random; little control is realized by random
intervention, and an unlucky draw may give too few time points before
or after intervention for a proper determination of intervention effects.
(As will be seen later—see the end of Chapter Nine—consideration of
the power of statistical analysis suggests that the best intervention
point is in the middle of the series.)

"Reactive" Interventions[*]

Interventions may come about as reactions to past or impending
changes in the system into which the intervention is made. Hence,
the intervention is confounded with a coincident change in the system; an abrupt change in the level or direction of the outcome series
may be due either to the intervention or other changes in the system
which brought about the intervention. For example, a school principal institutes a teacher-aide program in September in anticipation of
an influx of pupils from the families of employees of a recently
opened industry in the city. The reading performance of the pupils
tested the following May is six months above that obtained at the
same grade in previous years. Is the increase due to the intervention of the teacher-aide program or to the coincident shift in the

---

[*]In naming this source of invalidity, we were torn between the
appropriate connotations of "reactive interventions" and the risk of
confusion arising between this name and Campbell and Stanley's
(1966) "reactive arrangements." The latter refers to external
invalidity arising from novelty and surveillance effects in either
true or quasi-experiments, a concept quite distinct from what we
mean here by "reactive interventions."

composition of the student body? One cannot know without extensive
—and often impossible—auxillary analyses.

Particularly in complex, socio-political systems, an extreme
level of the outcome series is likely to precipitate the very intervention which is designed to affect the outcomes themselves. This
situation can create the impression of an intervention effect—indeed,
even a "statistically significant" effect—in the absence of a true
effect.

In January, 1955, Governor Abraham Ribicoff of Connecticut
took unprecedented executive action in an attempt to reduce traffic
fatalities; speeders had their licenses suspended for thirty days on
the first offense, sixty days on the second offense, and for an
indefinite period on the third offense. Ribicoff's action (taken on
December 23, 1955, and instituted on January 1, 1956) was brought
about in part by an alarming increase in the traffic fatality rate in
December 1955. The number of traffic fatalities per 100,000,000
driver miles in Connecticut for many months before and after
January 1, 1956 is graphed in Figure 10 in Chapter Three. It can be
seen that the December 1955 fatality rate which precipitated
Ribicoff's action was higher than at any time in the preceding sixty
months. If the series merely returned to its normal level in January
1956, there would appear to be a large decrement in the fatality rate
due to Ribicoff's crackdown. If one is monitoring a time-series
(formally or indirectly) and it suddenly jumps markedly in one direction, it can probably be expected to "regress" back toward its normal
level at the next point in time. After the tragic December of 1955,
Connecticut was the worst possible place for an immediate investigation of the effect of a crackdown on speeding. An experimentally
wise, but politically stupid, executive would have persuaded
Massachusetts to crackdown on its speeders in January 1956 for a
more valid assessment of the intervention!

The phenomenon of the return of a series to a normal level from
an aberrant or extreme observation is analogous to the regression
effect in the pretest-posttest experimental design. If one plots a
scatter diagram of z_t against z_{t-1}, i.e., the scatter diagram of pairs
of successive values in the time-series, one sees clearly that
extremely high or low values of the series tend to be followed by
less extreme values (see Figure 20). Whether or not any intervention
is made into a time-series, it will appear to change direction back
toward the normal level of the series after the series attains an
extreme location. Thus, when the intervention is partly or entirely

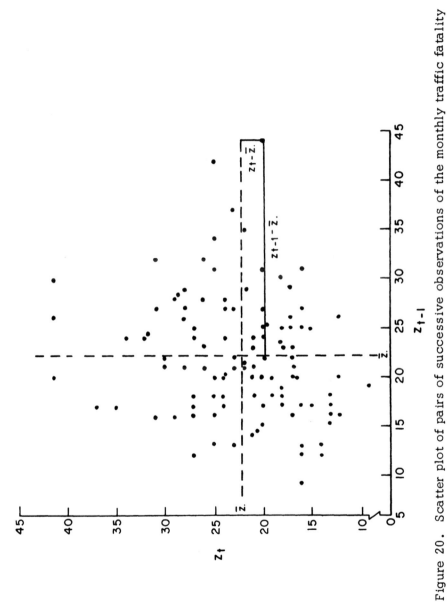

Figure 20. Scatter plot of pairs of successive observations of the monthly traffic fatality rate (deaths per 100,000,000 driver miles) in Connecticut from January 1951 through December 1959 (illustrating the "regression phenomenon" in time-series data).

induced by the fact that the series being monitored has deviated to an extreme position, the validity of the time-series experiment is accordingly compromised.

Multiple-Intervention Interference

Certain variations (see Figure 7) on the simple time-series design involve two or more interventions into the same time-series. In such cases, the second or later interventions can produce effects which are unique to experimental units which have been exposed to the preceding interventions. The false attribution of an effect to an intervention—when in fact it is due to the intervention and a previous intervention—is invalidation through multiple-intervention interference. Exactly the same problem has been discussed extensively in the psychological literature where it has taken the form of a concern with whether "within subjects" comparisons of treatments are equivalent to "between subjects" comparisons. (See Bracht and Glass, 1969, p. 456.)

As an example, suppose that an experimenter wishes to compare two methods of teaching the deciphering of cryptograms: rules-followed-by-examples and examples-followed-by-rules. After twenty cryptograms have been solved by a group of subjects, instruction is given in the "rules-followed-by-examples" format; twenty more cryptograms are solved after which "examples-followed-by-rules" instructions are given and twenty more cryptograms are solved. The experimenter concludes that the abrupt decrease in solution time between cryptograms No. 20 and No. 21—and the lack of any change between cryptograms No. 40 and No. 41—is evidence of the superiority of "rules-followed-by-examples" teaching. This conclusion might well be fallacious due to multiple-intervention interference. If the first intervention taught most of the relevant strategies for solving cryptograms which the subjects were capable of learning, there was no residual ignorance remaining for the second intervention to show an effect on.

The data in Figure 15 used to illustrate the "sequential multiple-group—multiple-I" design suggest a multiple-intervention interference effect. A group of rats suddenly shifted from a low-drive (food satiation) to a high-drive (food deprivation) state showed a marked increase in starting speed in running a short alley to obtain food. However, a second group of rats switched from a high-drive to a low-drive state did not show a correspondingly marked decrease in starting speed. Thus, high-drive state following low-drive state produces an effect different from an initial high-drive state. Brown (1961, p. 118) linked this dependence of the reversal effect on the order of drive-states to an associative theory of learning. (For Group B—see Figure 15—running is conditioned to a complex of internal cues while the rats are in the high-drive state, and many of these cues remain when the rats are switched to a low-drive state for the final trials.)

Instrumentation

Invalidation due to instrumentation refers to an abrupt change in a time-series due to a change in the method of observing the outcome variable, such change being coincident with the intervention being evaluated. The instrumentation effect is particularly important since reforms in large institutions or social systems are likely to involve some alterations of record-keeping procedures.

In 1959, Orlando Wilson, an internationally-known criminologist and authority on law enforcement, was appointed Chief of Police in the city of Chicago. Wilson immediately instituted many reforms in the Chicago Police Department, including techniques aimed at reducing crime and other techniques to improve crime detection and reporting. In Figure 21 appears the graph of "number of reported burglaries" in Chicago by year from 1942 through 1962. There is a huge, abrupt increase in the outcome variable coincident with Wilson's reform! More than likely, the increase reflects improved detection and better reporting of burglaries than any genuine increase in the number of such crimes. Other indices (e.g., murders and non-negligent manslaughters) show no evidence of Wilson's reform (Campbell, 1969).

The situation is more complex than simply writing off the data in Figure 21 as evidence against Wilson's reforms. The reformed practices could have effected a 10 percent decrease in actual burglaries and a simultaneous 9 percent increase in reporting and detection of burglaries; the net 1 percent decrease could hardly be discerned in the observed data.

Large city crime statistics showed a marked rise in the incidence of reported rape during the first half of 1972. In the opinion of police administrators the data reflected an increased willingness on

60

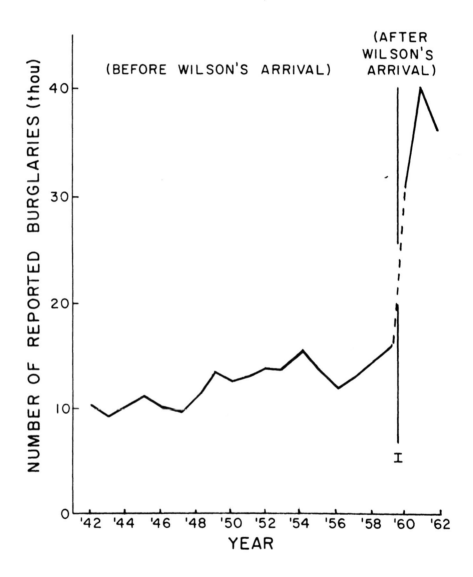

Figure 21. Number of reported burglaries in Chicago, Illinois, from 1942 to 1962. (Chicago police force was reorganized in 1959 by the newly-appointed Chief of Police, Orlando Wilson.) Source: Uniform Crime Reports for the United States, 1942-1962.

the part of women to report a rape rather than any increase in the actual occurrence of rape.*

Hahn (1970) presented interesting data on motor vehicle deaths which illustrate specific difficulties in the use of index numbers (ratios) to detect changes in phenomena over time. The number of motor vehicle deaths (MVD) in the United States nearly doubled between 1945 and 1967; however, the number of motor vehicle deaths per 100,000 population (MVD/P) changed very little over the same period of time. From 1915 to 1935, MVD and MVD/P rose rapidly at almost exactly the same rate; thereafter, MVD/P has shown no consistent increase, while MVD has risen sharply. A "safety" intervention in 1935 could have affected the safety of automobiles which would only be apparent in the rate of motor vehicle deaths per 100,000 population. Moreover, both the MVD and the MVD/P show an abrupt, but temporary, decrease from 1940 to 1945 which undoubtedly reflect the effects of gas rationing during World War II rather than the effect of a highway safety campaign beginning in 1940.

Instability

Instability refers to "statistical error"—i.e., unaccountable variation—in the time-series which may be mistaken for an intervention effect, but which is not improbably larger than other unaccountable fluctuations in the series between successive points in time. Instability is the source of invalidity against which the inferential statistical techniques developed in Chapters V and VI are designed to control. These techniques are addressed to the question, "Does the apparent shift of the time-series at the point of intervention represent a statistically significant shift or should it be regarded merely as a probable fluctuation in a series following its normal course?"

Lovitt and Curtiss (1969) applied operant conditioning techniques in an attempt to shape the academic performance of a single student. For nine days, the student's "academic responses"— defined as the number of times during an hour in which he engaged in several different types of study behavior—were observed under baseline conditions. For the next twelve days, academic responses were rewarded in accord with contingencies specified by the teacher (e.g., spelling eighteen words earned the student one minute of free time); for the next twenty-two days the student was rewarded in accord with

---

*Newsweek, 31 July 1972, p. 72.

his own schedule of response-reward contingencies (e.g., spelling ten words earned two minutes of free time). The teacher-specified contingencies were reinstated during the last seven days. The data appear in Figure 22.

Statistical analyses of the data in Figure 22 using the methods of Chapters Five and Six revealed no statistically significant effect of the three interventions into the time-series. Lovitt and Curtiss (1969, p. 52) interpreted the slight instability in the data to be the effects of the interventions:

> The data from [the experiment] indicated that, for this student, self-imposed contingencies were associated with an increased academic response rate. This was evidenced in [the experiment]; during Stage 2 . . . , the period of self-contingencies, the student's median performance was higher than during Stages 1 and 3, the periods of teacher-imposed contingengies.

Our experience leads us to believe that inferential statistical problems are of substantial importance in the interpretation of time-series experiments. In the social sciences, most researchers' inferential intuitions have been developed on problems involving comparisons among independent samples. These intuitions serve one poorly where dependent data are involved, as in the time-series experiment. We have often analyzed data from time-series experiments which did not appear to the naked eye to show a significant intervention effect but which gave highly statistically significant results when appropriately tested. Conversely, some effects which appear statistically significant prove not to be when analyzed appropriately.

Changes in Experimental
Unit Composition

When the experimental unit comprises a number of individuals (persons, geographical units, etc.), the composition of this group may change across time. The loss of several individuals from the experimental unit immediately before the intervention could cause the time-series to change its course abruptly, even though under other circumstances the intervention would not have altered the series. Incorrectly attributing a change in the series to an intervention when in fact the change is due to the loss or gain of subjects between time points n_1 and $n_1 + 1$ is invalidation due to a change in experimental unit composition.

63

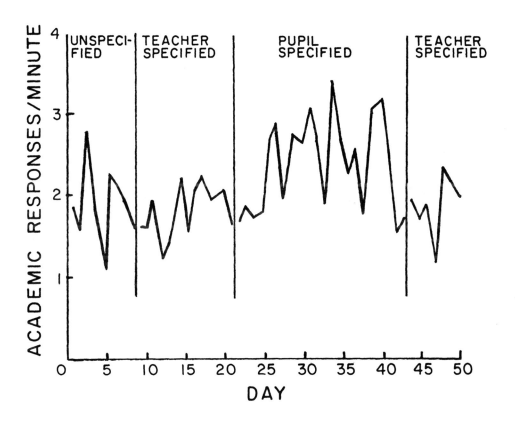

Figure 22. Daily academic response rate for a student under teacher-specified and self-specified response-reward contingencies.

Change in unit composition is an unlikely source of invalidity in small experiments where the experimenter chooses the point of intervention. However, in complex social systems, the same large complex of conditions which brings about the intervention may bring about a coinciding abrupt change in the nature of the group being treated and observed. For example, suppose a cohort of one hundred high school pupils is observed weekly from September until June, and the rate of discipline problems is recorded. Suppose the experimenter introduced a student-run discipline committee starting with the second semester. Conceivably, 10 percent of the cohort could be lost at the end of the first semester due to families moving, students "dropping out" of school, etc. The loss of 10 percent of the cohort could cause the rate of discipline problems to change abruptly in the absence of a true intervention effect. If the experimenter had kept records on individual pupils, he could correct for the loss of subjects by eliminating from the pre-intervention discipline rate all disciplinary acts involving students who eventually "dropped out." Then he need only worry about whether by their presence some of the "drop outs" encouraged some of the "persisters" to get into trouble during the pre-$\underline{I}$ period!

A more careful consideration of the change-in-unit-composition problem leads to the distinction between unit-replication and unit-repetition which was discussed in Chapter One.

Interaction of "Selection" and Other
Sources of Invalidity

Several of the time-series designs presented earlier involve the comparison of time-series on two or more groups of experimental units. Whenever these groups are not randomly constituted, a <u>selection</u> "bias" exists. This selection may interact with any one of the above sources of invalidity to confound the process of determining an intervention effect (or differential effects).

For example, the multiple-group—multiple-$\underline{I}$ design permits the assessment and comparison of the effects of I_1 and I_2. As a hypothetical example, suppose that the counties of Indiana constitute group 1, and the counties of Illinois, group 2. In a given year, the legislature of Illinois is reapportioned $(\underline{I}_1)$, but the Indiana legislature remains unchanged, I_2. A researcher observed the effects of these interventions on the "per-student expenditure for post-secondary education." A reduction in the expenditure rate of $10/student is observed for Indiana, but the rate drops $52/student in Illinois. The researcher concludes that the reapportionment of the Illinois legislature produced a decrease in the expenditure rate over and above the decreases in the rate produced by other influences (such as those represented in Indiana at the time). The researcher is unaware that the Illinois decrease is due to a change in the calculation of the per-student expenditure for post-secondary education rate; in Illinois, students in community and junior colleges were included in the expenditure rate for the first time after reapportionment. His conclusion was invalidated by the interaction of selection and instrumentation.

Relationship of Sources of Invalidity and
and Various Experimental Designs

In Table 1 are presented the logical relationships between various time-series experimental designs and sources of invalidity. The entries in the table indicate whether each source of invalidity is ("Yes") or is not ("No") a potential concern in judging the validity of a particular application of an experimental design. For example, "multiple-intervention interference" cannot possibly be a concern in the "multiple-group—single-I" design because there is only one intervention; "selection interacting with instrumentation" cannot be a concern in the randomized form of the "reversal" design because a selection bias is controlled by the randomization process. It cannot be emphasized too strongly that Table 1 should not be used to judge the validity of particular applications of a time-series experimental design; it merely indicates whether a particular factor is a possible invalidating influence. Judging the validity of particular applications is too complex a task, depending on too many specific circumstances to be accomplished with the aid of a checklist of finite length.

Postscript to Design Considerations

The authors believe that research methodology must arise from practice to be significant and that even the most elegant methods "must be tested in the crucible of application," to use Donald Campbell's words. We now present the abstract of a research report which illustrates several of the methodological considerations developed throughout these first four chapters.

Press (1972) studied the effect on crime of a 40 percent increase in the police force (from 212 to 298) in the 20th Precinct in New York City on October 18, 1966. Press first recognized several

Table 1

Relevance of Sources of Invalidity to Judging the Validity of
Various Time-Series Experimental Designs

Design	Source of Invalidity						
	History	Reactive Intervention	Multiple-Intervention Interference	Instrumentation	Instability	Change in Unit Composition	Interaction of Selection and Other Sources of Invalidity
Basic Design: O O O I O O O	Yes	Yes	No	Yes	Yes	Yes	No
A. Single-group—multiple-I	Yes	Yes	Yes	Yes	Yes	Yes	No
B. Multiple-group—single-I							
1. Randomized	Yes	Yes	No	Yes	Yes	Yes	Yes
2. Non-randomized	Yes	Yes	No	Yes	Yes	Yes	No
C. Multiple-group—multiple-I							
1. Randomized	Yes	Yes	No	Yes	Yes	Yes	No
2. Non-randomized	Yes	Yes	No	Yes	Yes	Yes	Yes

NOTE: A "Yes" indicates that the source of invalidity is a possible concern in judging the
validity of the design in question in particular circumstances. A "No" indicates that the source of
invalidity cannot possibly be a source of concern for the design in question because of formal
logical (definitional) reasons.

Table 1 (continued)

Design	Source of Invalidity						
	History	Reactive Inter-vention	Multiple-Inter-vention Inter-ference	Instru-men-tation	Insta-bility	Change in Unit Compo-sition	Interaction of Selec-tion and Other Sources of Invalidity
D. "Reversal"							
1. Randomized	Yes	Yes	Yes	Yes	Yes	Yes	No
2. Non-randomized	Yes	Yes	Yes	Yes	Yes	Yes	Yes
E. "Operant"	Yes	Yes	Yes	Yes	Yes	Yes	No
F. "Interaction"	Yes	Yes	Yes	Yes	Yes	Yes	No
G. Sequential multiple-group—multiple-I							
1. Randomized	Yes	Yes	No	Yes	Yes	Yes	No
2. Non-randomized	Yes	Yes	No	Yes	Yes	Yes	Yes
H. "Stratified" multiple-group—single-I	Yes	Yes	No	Yes	Yes	Yes	No

NOTE: A "Yes" indicates that the source of invalidity in question is a possible concern in judging the validity of the design in question in particular circumstances. A "No" indicates that the source of invalidity cannot possibly be a source of concern for the design in question because of formal logical (definitional) reasons.

difficulties arising in an attempt to attribute any changes across time in crime rates to the police manpower increase: "The proportion [of crimes] reported [italics added] may increase itself if police manpower increases"—instrumentation error; "if an area experiences basic sociological or economic changes [historical invalidation] such as might happen after an influx of low-income immigrants [unit-replication vs. unit-repetition and change in unit composition invalidation], patterns of crime might be expected to change independently of changes in police procedure." "If a 'crackdown on crime' is attempted in one area of the city and not in others, crime may decrease in that part of the city but increase in other parts as criminals merely rotate their activities"—linked experimental units.

"The decision was [made] to study crime on a weekly basis [from January 1, 1963 to December 31, 1967] because of unevenness in the incidence of crime over days of the week; more crime is committed on weekends"—sampling time units for measurement. "A group of precincts located in other parts of the city were selected as controls for the 20th Precinct, separately for each crime type, on the basis of how 'similar' they were to the 20th . . . "—multiple-group—multiple-I design (with an ingenious twist!).

Eight months before the intervention a central crime reporting bureau was established and "some of the definitions of what constitutes a reportable crime change"—instrumentation invalidity, but Press adjusted for it. "It was . . . reasoned that when a new system of reporting crime is instituted it takes some time for the police personnel to adapt to the new system. . . . It was reasoned that after a substantial change in police manpower in an area the residents might change their rate of reporting crime, and therefore the reported incidence of crime. . . . To allow, at least in part, for the short-run aspect of this adaptation effect, the first month of data after the manpower increase began was not used in the . . . analysis"—delayed intervention effect.

"Another possibility [for increasing experimental validity] might have been to increase police manpower (and then remove the additional force) several times in the 20th Precinct"—continuous vs. temporary interventions and the "operant" design. "Moreover, the 20th Precinct might have peculiarities not common to other precincts, and had several precincts been selected at random and the results averaged, results would have been more acceptable as representative of the City"—multiple-group—single I design, but we would prefer an attempt to group precincts into homogeneous strata (the "stratified" multiple-group—single-I design) rather than averaging.

The change in crime rates between the 20th Precinct and the seven "control precincts was evaluated on the following multiple dependent variables: robbery, grand larceny, burglary, auto theft, miscellaneous felonies, and miscellaneous misdemeanors." ". . . decisions were made about which net changes were larger than could be explained purely by chance, or sampling variation"—instability invalidation. Press's findings revealed a decrease in "outside crimes" (e.g., robbery, auto theft, and certain felonies and misdemeanors) but no decrease in rates of "inside crimes" (e.g., burglary and certain types of grand larceny)—different intervention effects on different variables.

Indeed, the concepts developed in the first four chapters in this text seem real and not mere fabrications of our over-stimulated imaginations.

CHAPTER FIVE

OUTLINE OF TIME-SERIES ANALYSIS

In this chapter we will present the mathematical prelimi-
naries necessary for an understanding of the major contribution
of this book, namely, the testing of intervention effects. The
bulk of this chapter will review work for describing time-series
data. These descriptions are called "models," that is, equations which relate observations at time t to the previous history
of the series. Two kinds of model are widely used in sciences
concerned with observations over time. For continuous or
nearly continuous observations, a method called spectral analysis is usually used. Spectral analysis views a time-series as
a complex wave pattern composed of weighted simple waves.
The spectral analytic technique decomposes the time-series
into frequency bands which contribute significantly to the total
variance of the series. In spectral analysis a function is
defined called the spectrum. Just as the spectrum of light
coming from a distant star is a breakdown of light into major
colors or basic frequencies, the spectrum of a time-series is
defined as a function which has peak values at frequency bands
which contribute significantly to oscillations in the series. An
outline of spectral methods in time-series is presented in
Appendix A.

In this chapter, a general model will be discussed which is conceptually and mathematically equivalent to spectral models. The major difference lies in the language used to interpret model parameters. Part of the usefulness of this model lies in its application with data which contain fewer observations than the nearly continuous case usually considered in the spectral approach. This general model is called the AutoRegressive-Integrated-Moving-Average (ARIMA) model and is due to Box and Jenkins (1970). (See Nelson, 1973, and Aigner, 1971, for a relatively less mathematical treatment of the methods of forecasting developed by Box and Jenkins.)

The major issues in the sciences which have used both spectral and ARIMA models have been forecasting the future values of a series, causal inference via the search for predictors or "lead indicators," and theory construction.

Issues concerned with the effects of interventions in longitudinal processes are the major concern in this text. This use of time-series data for experimental purposes raises problems in statistical analysis which have usually been overlooked. Researchers have often simply applied an independent groups t-test to the pre- and post-intervention data. This method (and more sophisticated, but essentially similar, analysis of variance techniques) is inappropriate on two counts. First, as is clear in Chapter Three on "Interventions and Intervention Effects," the attribution of an effect to an intervention is not simply a matter of comparing pre- and post-intervention means. Obviously a time-series which drifts steadily upward but shows neither change in level nor in direction of drift coincident with I will show different pre-I and post-I means; a significant t-test between pre-I and post-I data is simply irrelevant to the assessment of an intervention effect. Moreover, an intervention which changes the upward drift of a series to a downward drift (in a triangular pattern with the abscissa) would yield a nonsignificant t-statistic. Second, inferential techniques based on the assumption of independent data cannot safely be applied to time-series data which typically show dependence among the observations. Chassan (1967, p. 201) overlooked some relevant research (e.g., Scheffé, 1959, Chapter 10) when he suggested that "on the basis of some preliminary theoretical statistical analysis it appears that the standard t-test can be used with a reasonable validity even within a highly autocorrelated, dependent series."

Kelly, McNeil, and Newman (1973) were likewise heed-
less of the problems entailed by statistical dependence among
observations in a time-series when they presented a series of
"statistical models for research in behavior modification."
Their proposed techniques, based on the general linear model
with assumptions of independence of "errors," are, in large
part, equivalent to techniques devised previously in econometrics (e.g., Johnston, 1966, pp. 227 ff.; Kmenta, 1971,
pp. 419-425). Kelly et al. (1973) confused "random sampling"
with "statistical independence" in stating the assumptions of
the normal theory general linear model, and thus obscured the
issue to which the bulk of the remainder of this text is
addressed. The "robustness" literature which they cited does
not support their disregard of statistical dependence. Furthermore, these authors committed the common error of assuming
that problems of "repeated measures" designs are adequately
resolved if "persons," upon whom measures are repeated
across trials or treatment conditions, is included as a random
factor in the model and interactions of persons with other fac-
tors are used as error terms. Such inclusion is necessary, but
not sufficient to resolve the difficulties with repeated measures.
Gentile, Roden, and Klein (1972) presented an analysis-of-
variance model for use in operant experiments; their model is
equivalent to one of the models presented by Kelly et al. (1973).
Gentile et al. (1972) were more careful in explicating the
necessary assumption of statistical independence, and they
acknowledged that it would be violated in most instances in
which their method would be employed. They attempted to deal
with the violation by arguing that dependence would tend to bias
their F-test in a negative direction. Such would often be the
case, though biases in the opposite direction can also occur.

Finally, the methods presented by Kelly et al. and Gentile
et al. do not handle adequately the problem of nonstationary
time-series (i.e., those which do not possess any fixed level
across time). The practical significance of this failure to deal
with nonstationary series is that the proposed methods will
reject null hypotheses with high power even when the series
evidences no abrupt intervention effect.

If a series of observations were assumed to be independent observations sampled from a normally distributed population,
then the problem of assessing the effects of an intervention is

easily solved. Shewart (1951) solved this problem and it forms the basis of the use of industrial quality control charts. Suppose the task is to monitor the diameter of ball bearings manufactured by a particular machine. In the baseline bands are drawn two standard deviations above and below the mean diameter. If successive observations drift outside this Shewart band, then a significant change has occurred. Some processes are best described by such Shewart processes, namely, those which oscillate randomly about a fixed mean and in which the history of a series up to time $t-1$ adds no reduction in uncertainty about the next observation at time t.

However, unfortunately, most time series do not consist of independent observations. The t-th observation, z_t, is predictable to some degree from the previous observations, z_{t-1}, z_{t-2}, . . . or from previous random shocks, a_{t-1}, a_{t-2}, . . . , which entered the system. These two types of dependence, i.e., upon previous observations or previous random shocks, correspond to the two basic types of time-series process: autoregressive and moving averages.

Autoregressive and Moving Averages Processes

The observations z_1, . . . , z_n are made of a time-series process on occasions $t=1$, . . . , n. Although no observation of z is made at time $t=0$, it will be assumed that the level of the series at that time is L, an unknown parameter. Models of the autoregressive type describe a process in which the observation at time t is predictable to a greater or lesser extent from previous observations. For example, in a first-order autoregressive process, the observation z_t is predicted from the observation z_{t-1}, thus the series is regressed upon itself one time-point in the past. It is mathematically convenient to express z as deviations from L, so the mathematical model for the first-order autoregressive process becomes

$$z_t - L = \phi_1(z_{t-1} - L) + a_t, \qquad (5.1)$$

where

ϕ_1 is the autoregressive coefficient which lies between -1 and $+1$,

and

a_i is independently and normally distributed with mean 0 and variance σ^2, i.e.,

$$a_i \sim NID\,(0, \sigma^2).$$

In a second-order autoregressive process, z_t depends on both z_{t-1} and z_{t-2}:

$$z_t - L = \phi_1(z_{t-1}-L) + \phi_2(z_{t-2}-L) + a_t. \qquad (5.2)$$

An alternative model for the dependence among the z's employs the concept of moving averages of the random shocks. For example, the observation z_t could be regarded as dependent upon the current random shock to the series, a_t, and a portion of the previous random shock, a_{t-1}:

$$z_t - L = a_t - \theta_1 a_{t-1}. \qquad (5.3)$$

The model in (5.3) is a _first-order moving averages_ process since only the immediately prior random shock, a_{t-1}, is involved in the current observation. (The minus sign for θ_1 is arbitrary and was selected for convenience later on.) Second and higher order moving averages models have obvious definitions. For example, the second-order moving averages model takes the form:

$$z_t - L = a_t - \theta_1 a_{t-1} - \theta_2 a_{t-2}. \qquad (5.4)$$

Autocorrelation

To describe the type of dependence among the observations of a time-series, the concept of autocorrelation must be introduced. For a set of observations z_1, z_2, z_3, . . . , we can plot the t-th observation against the $(t+1)$-st to produce a scatterplot. For the data 1, 2, 3, 4, 6, 8, 7, 9, a scatterplot would have pairs (z_t, z_{t+1}): (1,2), (2,3), (3,4), (4,6), (6,8), (8,7), and (7,9) plotted (see Figure 23). This scatterplot is called the "lag 1" scatterplot since pairs of observations are lagged by only one time unit. It is also possible to plot a

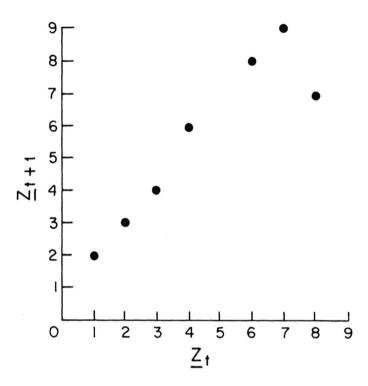

Figure 23. Scatterplot used to illustrate the concept of lag 1
autocorrelation.

lag 2 scatterplot by plotting pairs (z_t, z_{t+2}): $(1,3)$, $(2,4)$, $(3,6)$, $(4,8)$, $(6,7)$, and $(8,9)$. Each scatterplot defines a correlation coefficient, called the <u>autocorrelation</u>. The lag 1 scatterplot yields the lag 1 sample autocorrelation coefficient written r_1; the lag 2 scatterplot yields the lag 2 sample autocorrelation coefficient, written r_2. The plot of r_k as a function of the lag $\underline{k}$ is called the <u>correlogram</u> of the series. The equation of the lag $\underline{k}$ sample autocorrelation[*] is

$$r_k = \left(\sum_{t=1}^{N-k} (z_t - \bar{z}.)(z_{t+k} - \bar{z}.) \right) \Big/ \left(\sum_{t=1}^{N} (z_t - \bar{z}.)^2 \right). \qquad (5.5)$$

Examination of these lagged autocorrelation coefficients illuminates the structure of the time-series.

For the first-order autoregressive series in Equation (5.1), it can be shown that $\underline{r_1} = \phi_1$, $\underline{r_2} = \phi_1^2$, $\underline{r_3} = \phi_1^3$, and so on. The memory of the first-order autoregressive series is exponentially decaying if ϕ_1 is less than one. For a first-order moving averages model, the lag 1 autocorrelation will be nonzero and the autocorrelations for lags 2 and greater will be zero, within sampling error. The autocorrelations provide the key by which the model underlying an observed series is identified.

Consider again the issue of ignoring the autocorrelation of a series and treating it as a series of independent observations. Suppose an obtained series were actually well fit by the autoregressive model of Equation (5.1). Denote the mean of the series by μ. Suppose that $\underline{n}$ observations are made and that μ is estimated with the standard $100(1-\alpha)$ percent confidence interval,

$$\bar{z}. \pm {}_{1-\alpha/2}t_{n-1}s_z/\sqrt{n}.$$

Scheffé's (1959, pp. 338-339) findings imply that, for large $\underline{n}$, if we set α at .10 and assume a moderate autocorrelation of

---

[*]The value of r_k is usually regarded as a sample estimate of the population autocorrelation coefficient ρ_k which is defined in a later section of this chapter.

$\phi_1 = .40$, the 90 percent confidence interval actually has confidence coefficient .72; even for $\phi_1 = .3$ the actual coefficient is .76. As ϕ_1 becomes increasingly negative the actual level of confidence exceeds the nominal level. Gastwirth and Rubin (1971) found nearly identical results for small $\underline{n}$ using the same autoregressive model (cf. Padia, 1973). <u>Clearly, the effect of dependent observations on probability statements cannot be disregarded</u>, unlike considerations of normality and homogeneous variances (cf. Glass, Peckham, and Sanders, 1972). The purpose of methods presented in this and the next chapter is to account for the dependence in serial observations and correct for it so that intervention effects can be estimated and tested with standard techniques which assume independent observations.

Properties of Time-Series

In the Box-Jenkins system of Autoregressive Integrated Moving Averages (ARIMA) models, an observed time-series is regarded as having three basic properties: 1) the observed series is stationary or nonstationary, and if the latter, there exists a degree of "differencing" of the series required to produce stationarity; 2) the order of the autoregressive component of the model; 3) the order of the moving average component of the model. We shall discuss the property of stationarity-nonstationarity, then illustrate the orders of autoregressive and moving averages components before moving to the general problem of model identification.

Stationarity and Nonstationarity

As many as half of the time-series encountered in practice can be described by using <u>stationary</u> models. A stationary model is one in which the series remains in equilibrium around a constant mean level, although its oscillations around the mean need not be random. If the series is not stationary, successive differences are taken until the resulting series is stationary; for example, if the values of a series are 1, 3, 5, 7, 9, etc., there is a linear trend. First differencing reduces the series to 2 (= 3-1), 2 = (5-3), 2 (= 7-5), 2 (= 9-7) and the resulting series of all 2's is clearly stationary. If the values of a series are 1, 4, 9, 16, 25, 36, there is a quadratic trend. First differencing gives 3, 5, 7, 9, 11, and differencing again gives 2, 2, 2, 2. In general, first differencing eliminates linear trend, second differencing eliminates quadratic trend, and so on. To identify the degree of differencing needed, the autocorrelation function is used. If the estimated autocorrelation function does not die out rapidly, the series should be differenced and the function computed again. Some series are described by autocorrelations which tend to damp out and alternate in sign with increasing lag. Box and Jenkins (1970) wrote that "autocorrelations of this kind are not uncommon in production data and can arise because of 'carry-over' effects. In this particular example a high yielding batch tended to produce tarry residues which were not entirely removed from the vessel and adversely affected the yield of the next batch" (pp. 33-34). This kind of series is also typical of data on weight reduction where a weight loss on one day may result in the dieter overdoing it a bit on the next, then sharply cutting down again on the next, and so on.

If a series is nonstationary in level, it will oscillate around a mean level for a time and then drop or rise to a new temporary level. First differencing, $z_t - z_{t-1}$, will produce a stationary series. If a series is nonstationary in slope, it will drift in one direction for a time and then temporarily shift direction for a time. Second differencing, $(z_t - z_{t-1}) - (z_{t-1} - z_{t-2})$, is necessary to produce a stationary series in this case. Box and Jenkins (1970) wrote that "in practice d [the degree of differencing necessary to produce a stationary time-series] is normally 0, 1, or 2, and it is usually sufficient to inspect the first twenty or so estimated autocorrelations of the original series and its first and second differences" (p. 175). We shall cite some empirical data on this question at the end of this chapter.

Backward Shift and Difference
Operators

A shorthand notation will now be adopted for the discussion of time-series models. Two functions will be defined: 1) B, the backward shift operator; and 2) ∇ the first difference operator. The backward shift operator converts the observation z_t into the previous observation z_{t-1}: $B z_t = z_{t-1}$. This is the definition of B, and this equation is simply shorthand. It is a convenient shorthand because B applied twice is

$\underline{B}^2 \underline{z}_t = \underline{B}(\underline{B}\,\underline{z}_t) = \underline{B}(\underline{z}_{t-1}) = \underline{z}_{t-2}$, and so $\underline{B}$ applied $\underline{k}$ times is $\underline{B}^k \underline{z}_t = \underline{z}_{t-k}$. The first difference operator is defined by the equation $\overline{\underline{\nabla}} \underline{z}_t = \underline{z}_t - \underline{z}_{t-1}$. Note that this can be rewritten as

$$\nabla z_t = z_t - z_{t-1} = z_t - Bz_t = (1-B)z_t. \qquad (5.6)$$

This notation leads to an algebra of operators. The first-order autoregressive equation

$$z_t - L = \phi_1(z_{t-1} - L) + a_t ,$$

can be rewritten in terms of $\underline{B}$, the backward shift operator, as follows,

$$(z_t - L) = \phi_1 B(z_t - L) + a_t ,$$

or, transposing the opposite side,

$$(1-\phi_1)B(z_t - L) = a_t. \qquad (5.7)$$

For the $\underline{p}$th order autoregressive model, the backward shift notation yields

$$z_t - L = \phi_1(z_{t-1} - L) + \ldots + \phi_p(z_{t-p} - L) + a_t$$

$$(1-\phi_1 B - \phi_2 B^2 - \ldots - \phi_p B^p)(z_t - L) = a_t. \qquad (5.8)$$

The rather complex operator $(1-\phi_1\underline{B}-\phi_2\underline{B}^2 - \ldots)$ can be denoted by $\phi_p(\underline{B})$ to obtain a simplified autoregression notation:

$$\phi_p(B)z_t = a_t. \qquad (5.9)$$

The backward shift operator may also be used to simplify the notation for moving averages models. Recall that the first-order moving averages process has the form

$$z_t - L = a_t - \theta_1 a_{t-1},$$

which can be represented as

$$z_t - L = (1-\theta_1 B)a_t.$$

For the moving averages model of order $\underline{q}$,

$$z_t - L = a_t - \theta_1 a_{t-1} - \ldots - \theta_q a_{t-q},$$

which can be written

$$z_t - L = (1-\theta_1 B - \theta_2 B^2 - \ldots - \theta_q B^q)a_t. \qquad (5.10)$$

The backward shift terms in (5.10) constitute a polynomial in $\underline{B}$ of order $\underline{q}$, which we shall denote by $\theta_q(B)$. Thus (5.10) can be abbreviated to

$$z_t - L = \theta_q(B)a_t. \qquad (5.11)$$

TABLE 2

Representations of Autoregressive and
Moving Averages Models by
Operator Notation

Autoregressive of Order p	Moving Averages of Order q
$(1-\phi_1 B - \phi_2 B^2 - \ldots -\phi_p B^p)z_t = a_t$	$z_t = (1-\theta_1 B - \theta_2 B^2 - \ldots -\theta_q B^q)a_t$
$z_t = \phi_1 z_{t-1} + \phi_2 z_{t-2} + \ldots$	$z_t = a_t - \theta_1 a_{t-1} - \theta_2 a_{t-2} - \ldots$
$+\phi_p z_{t-p} + a_t$	$-\theta_q a_{t-q}$

The general equations are presented for an autoregressive model of order $\underline{p}$ and for a general moving average model of order $\underline{q}$. An interesting result that helps in model identification is that the correlogram of a purely autoregressive process is exponentially decaying (for ϕ's positive) but is abruptly truncated after $\underline{q}$ lags for the purely moving average process. We shall return to this important distinction between the two models later in this chapter.

The General ARIMA (p, d, q)
   Process

Many series observed in application are not stationary. That is, it may be necessary to apply the differencing operator, ∇, several times until the resultant series is stationary. The number of times ∇ must be applied to obtain a stationary series is denoted $\underline{d}$, the degree of differencing.

After differencing, a series can be both autogressive of $\underline{p}$ and moving averages of order $\underline{q}$. This most general class of models is given by the equation

$$\phi_p(B)\nabla^d(z_t - L) = \theta_q(B)a_t, \qquad (5.12)$$

where $\underline{L}$ is the true location of the series at time $\underline{t} = 0$,

$$\phi_p(B) = 1 - \phi_1 B - \phi_2 B^2 - \phi_3 B^3 - \ldots - \phi_p B^p,$$

$$\theta_q(B) = 1 - \theta_1 B - \theta_2 B^2 - \theta_3 B^3 - \ldots - \theta_q B^q,$$

and

$$\nabla^d = (1-B)^d.$$

Equation (5.12) represents an autoregressive integrated moving averages model of order (p, d, q).

Invertibility-Stationarity

In order that $\nabla^d \underline{z_t}$ be stationary, the weights $\phi_1, \ldots, \phi_p$ and $\theta_1, \ldots, \theta_q$ must separately satisfy a set of restrictions known as the invertibility-stationarity conditions. The form of these conditions depends upon the value of $\underline{p}$ (or $\underline{q}$). When $\underline{p} = 1$, the series is stationary when

$$-1 < \phi_1 < 1. \qquad (5.13)$$

Similarly for $\underline{q}=1$, the stationarity-invertibility condition is that

$$-1 < \theta_1 < 1. \tag{5.14}$$

When $\underline{p}=2$ or $\underline{q}=2$, the conditions on ϕ's or θ's are as follows:

$$-1 < \phi_2 < 1 \qquad\qquad -1 < \theta_2 < 1$$
$$\phi_1 + \phi_2 < 1 \qquad \text{or} \qquad \theta_1 + \theta_2 < 1 . \tag{5.15}$$
$$\phi_2 - \phi_1 < 1 \qquad\qquad \theta_2 - \theta_1 < 1$$

Graphically, these conditions imply, for example, that ϕ_1 and ϕ_2 (or θ_1 and θ_2) lie in the triangle with vertices at $(0,1)$, $(2,-1)$ and $(-2,-1)$:

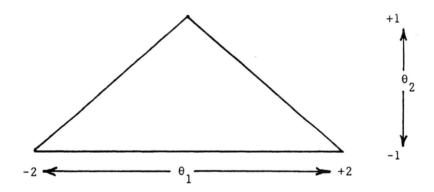

For example, if a second-order autoregressive model were constructed out of the values $\phi_1 = 2$, $\phi_2 = .5$, the series would rapidly "explode" in a positive or negative direction, evidencing radical nonstationarity.

For $\underline{p}=3$ (or $\underline{q}=3$) the invertibility-stationarity conditions become somewhat more complex:

$$\phi_1 + \phi_2 + \phi_3 < 1 \qquad\qquad \theta_1 + \theta_2 + \theta_3 < 1$$

$$-\phi_1 + \phi_2 - \phi_3 < 1 \qquad\qquad -\theta_1 + \theta_2 - \theta_3 < 1$$

$$\text{or} \qquad\qquad\qquad\qquad\qquad\qquad\qquad\qquad (5.16)$$

$$\phi_3(\phi_3 - 1) - \phi_2 < 1 \qquad\qquad \theta_3(\theta_3 - 1) - \theta_2 < 1$$

$$-1 < \phi_3 < 1 \qquad\qquad\qquad -1 < \theta_3 < 1$$

These conditions correspond to a complex graphic representation which we shall omit (see Box and Jenkins, 1970, p. 114).

The invertibility-stationarity conditions become important when values of ϕ and θ must be estimated prior to testing for intervention effects (in Chapters Six through Nine).

More About Some Specific Models

By specifying values of p, d, and q, the general model in (5.12) reduces to various specific time-series models. For example, the first-order autoregressive process has the form

$$(z_t - L) = \phi_1(z_{t-1} - L) + a_t. \qquad (5.17)$$

This model corresponds to (5.12) when p = 1, d = 0 and q = 0:

$$\phi_1(B)\nabla^0(z_t - L) = \theta_0(B)a_t,$$

$$(1 - \phi_1 B)(z_t - L) = a_t,$$

$$z_t - L = \phi_1(z_{t-1} - L) + a_t.$$

Thus, the first-order autoregressive model can be denoted by ARIMA (1, 0, 0). The reader may readily verify that ARIMA (0, 0, 0) denotes the "white noise" process: $z_t = L + a_t$.

We shall now develop in detail the mathematics of some of the more commonly encountered processes.

First-Order Moving Averages Model, ARIMA (0, 0, 1)

Suppose that a process is adequately represented by the ARIMA (0, 0, 1) model, i.e., the undifferenced data comprise no autoregressive components and one moving averages component

$$(z_t - L) = (1 - \theta_1 B) a_t ,$$

(5.18)

$$z_t = L - \theta_1 a_{t-1} + a_t ,$$

where L and θ_1 are parameters, $a \sim NID\,(0, \sigma^2)$, and $-1 < \theta_1 < 1$.

This process is called a moving averages model of order 1; it is stationary, always remaining in the vicinity of the location parameter L. A graph (simulated data) of a portion of this model with $L = 100$, $\sigma^2 = 1$, and $\theta_1 = -0.5$ appears as Figure 24.*

$$E(z) = E(L - \theta_1 a_{t-1} + a_t) = L.$$

(5.19)

A first-order moving averages process can be readily identified from the data by looking at the correlogram. The variance of z is

$$\mathrm{Var}(z) = E[z - E(z)]^2 = E(z - L)^2 = E[-\theta_1 a_{t-1} + a_t]^2 = \sigma^2 (\theta_1^2 + 1).$$

(5.20)

The covariance of z_t with the immediately prior observation z_{t-1} (i.e., the lag 1 autocovariance) is given by

---

*The raw data used in illustrations of analyses throughout the text are listed in Appendix B.

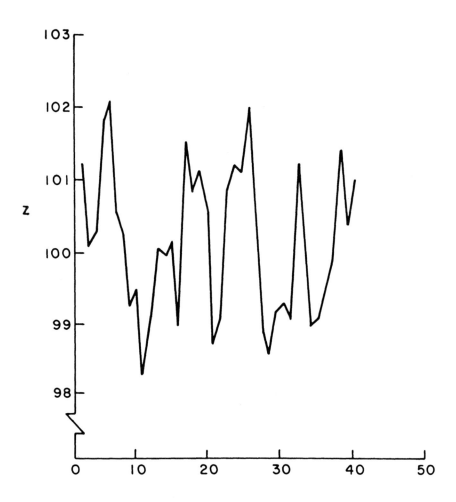

Figure 24. ARIMA (0, 0, 1) Data ($\underline{n}$ = 40).

$$\text{Cov}(z_t, z_{t-1}) = E\left[(z_t - L)(z_{t-1} - L)\right]$$

$$= E\left[(-\theta_1 a_{t-1} + a_t)(-\theta_1 a_{t-2} + a_{t-1})\right]$$

$$= E\left[\theta_1^2 a_{t-1} a_{t-2} - \theta_1 a_{t-1}^2 - \theta_1 a_{t-2} a_t + a_t a_{t-1}\right]$$

$$= -\theta_1 \sigma^2. \tag{5.21}$$

Hence, the lag 1 autocorrelation coefficient is

$$\rho_1 = \frac{-\theta_1 \sigma^2}{(\theta_1^2 + 1)\sigma^2} = \frac{-\theta_1}{\theta_1^2 + 1}. \tag{5.22}$$

Lagging the data by more than one time unit gives zero auto-covariance. Thus

$$\rho_k = 0 \quad \text{for} \quad k \geq 2. \tag{5.23}$$

One could, therefore, expect a moving averages process to have autocorrelations that truncate to zero (within sampling error) after a lag greater than the order of the process. For the data in Figure 24, $r_1 = .45$, $r_2 = .08$, and $r_3 = -.16$.

First-Order Autoregressive Model, ARIMA (1, 0, 0)

The first-order autoregressive process is of the form

$$z_t - L = \phi_1(z_{t-1} - L) + a_t, \tag{5.24}$$

where $a \sim \text{NID}(0, \sigma^2)$ and $-1 < \phi_1 < 1$ to insure stationarity. Figure 25 is a graph of forty simulated observations of a first-order autoregressive process with parameters $L = 100$, $\phi_1 = 0.6$, and $\sigma^2 = 1$. Notice that the series never wanders far from the location parameter $L = 100$. The correlogram of an ARIMA (1, 0, 0) process is important in identifying the series. For a first-order autoregressive process,

88

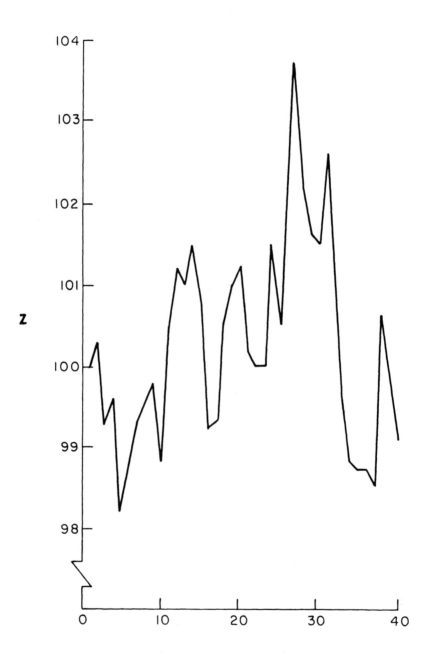

Figure 25. ARIMA (1, 0, 0) Data ($\underline{n}$ = 40).

$$z_1 - L = a_1,$$

$$z_2 - L = \phi_1(z_1 - L) + a_2 = \phi_1 a_1 + a_2,$$

$$z_3 - L = \phi_1(z_2 - L) + a_3 = \phi_1^2 a_1 + \phi_1 a_2 + a_3,$$

$$\vdots$$

$$z_t - L = \phi_1(z_{t-1} - L) + a_t = \phi_1^{t-1} a_1 + \phi_1^{t-2} a_2 + \ldots + \phi_1 a_{t-1} + a_t. \quad (5.25)$$

To derive the correlogram we need to calculate the variance and autocovariance of the series $\underline{z}_t$. One can see that

$$\text{Var}(z_t) = \sigma^2\left(\phi_1^{2(t-1)} + \phi_1^{2(t-2)} + \ldots + \phi_1^4 + \phi_1^2 + 1\right). \quad (5.26)$$

The lag 1 autocovariance of a first-order autoregressive series is given by

$$\text{Cov}(z_t, z_{t-1}) = \text{Cov}\left[L + \phi_1^{t-1} a_1 + \phi_1^{t-2} a_2 + \ldots + \phi_1 a_{t-1} + a_t,\right.$$

$$\left. L + \phi_1^{t-2} a_1 + \phi_1^{t-3} a_2 + \ldots + \phi_1 a_{t-2} + a_{t-1}\right]$$

$$= \sigma^2\left(\phi_1^{2t-3} + \phi_1^{2t-5} + \ldots + \phi_1^3 + \phi_1\right). \quad (5.27)$$

Hence, the lag 1 autocorrelation of $\underline{z}$ is equal to

$$\rho_1 = \frac{\text{Cov}(z_t, z_{t-1})}{\text{Var}(z_t)} = \frac{\sigma^2 \phi_1(\phi_1^{2t-4} + \phi_1^{2t-6} + \ldots + \phi_1^4 + \phi_1^2 + 1)}{\sigma^2(\phi_1^{2t-4} + \phi_1^{2t-6} + \ldots + \phi_1^4 + \phi_1^2 + 1)} = \phi_1.$$

$$(5.28)$$

Similarly it can be shown that the lag $\underline{k}$ autocorrelation of a first-order autoregressive process is given by

$$\rho_k = \phi_1^k. \quad (5.29)$$

Therefore while an ARIMA (0, 0, 1) process has a correlogram which truncates after lag 1, the ARIMA (1, 0, 0) process has a correlogram which decays exponentially (for ϕ_1 positive). For the data in Figure 25, $r_1 = .67$, $r_2 = .40$, $r_3 = .28$, $r_4 = .15$, $r_5 = .03$.

Integrated Moving Averages Model, ARIMA (0, 1, 1)

Perhaps the most commonly encountered nonstationary process is known as the integrated moving averages model. From its signature, ARIMA (0, 1, 1), it is seen to contain no autoregressive term, and the first differences contain one moving averages term. Thus the general model (5.12) is specialized as follows:

$$(1-B)(z_t - L) = (1 - \theta_1 B)a_t,$$

$$z_t - z_{t-1} = a_t - \theta_1 a_{t-1}. \qquad (5.30)$$

The process (5.30) can be stated in mathematically equivalent form:

$$z_t = L + (1 - \theta_1) \sum_{i=1}^{t-1} a_i + a_t, \qquad (5.31)$$

where L is the true, but unobserved, level of the process at time $t = 0$. The integrated moving averages model can be interpreted as follows: random shocks, a_i, enter the system at full strength at time t; a portion, $1 - \theta_1$, of the shocks remain in the system indefinitely after their initial occurrence. A process such as (5.31) will evidence nonstationarity, i.e., it will wander away from any given level for long periods of time rather than oscillating around a single level as in the case of the stationary processes. A graph of over 6,000 observations of a particular ARIMA (0, 1, 1) model, with $\theta_1 = 0$, appears as Figure 26.

The ARIMA (0, 1, 1) process is recognizable in its correlogram. As a nonstationary process, the correlogram of z_t does not die out to zero either exponentially or abruptly; the autocorrelations of the undifferenced data remain large for large

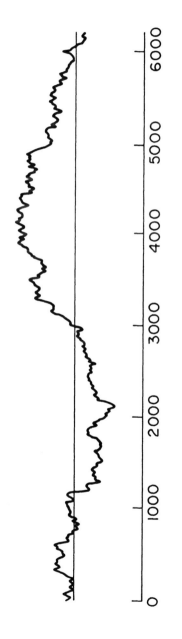

Figure 26. Graph of over 6,000 points in an ARIMA (0, 1, 1) process. (Adapted from Feller, 1957, p. 84.)

lags. However, the first differences of the data, $\underline{z}_t - \underline{z}_{t-1}$, are stationary. Furthermore, since they possess a first-order moving averages structure, their correlogram shows the moving averages property, i.e., the lag 1 autocorrelation is nonzero, but the autocorrelations for large lags are essentially zero. This property is apparent in the following formulations:

$$\text{Var}(z_t - z_{t-1}) = \text{Var}(a_t - \theta_1 a_{t-1}) = \sigma^2(1 + \theta_1^2).$$

$$\text{Cov}(z_t - z_{t-1}, \; z_{t-1} - z_{t-2}) = \text{Cov}(a_t - \theta_1 a_{t-1}, \; a_{t-1} - \theta_1 a_{t-2})$$

$$= 0 - 0 - \theta_1 \text{Cov}(a_{t-1}, a_{t-1}) + 0 = -\theta_1 \sigma^2.$$

Hence, the lag 1 autocorrelation of the first differences, i.e., the autocorrelation of $\underline{z}_t - \underline{z}_{t-1}$ with $\underline{z}_{t-1} - \underline{z}_{t-2}$, is

$$\rho_1 = \frac{-\theta_1}{1 + \theta_1^2} . \tag{5.32}$$

Examination of the above covariance formula shows readily that the lag 2 autocorrelation, i.e., the autocorrelation of $\underline{z}_t - \underline{z}_{t-1}$ and $\underline{z}_{t-2} - \underline{z}_{t-3}$, is zero, as well as the autocorrelation for all higher lags of the first differences.

In Figure 27 appears the graph of a nonstationary process which is stationary in the second differences, i.e., $\underline{d} = 2$. Notice that this process shows a variation in slope across time.

Model Identification

To identify the model we need to specify its order $(\underline{p}, \underline{d}, \underline{q})$ and to estimate the coefficients of each of the polynomials $\phi_p(B)$ and $\theta_q(B)$. As discussed above, the tools for specifying the order $(\underline{p}, \underline{d}, \underline{q})$ is the examination of the sample autocorrelation and sample partial autocorrelation functions.

Autocorrelations

To review, the autocorrelation is a function of the lag of observations $\underline{k}$ time units apart.

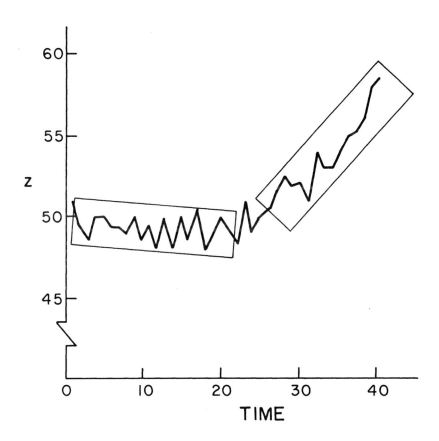

Figure 27. Forty observations of an ARIMA $(0, 2, 2)$ for which $L = 50$, $\theta_1 = 1.6$, $\theta_2 = -.7$, and $\sigma^2 = 1$.

$$\rho_k = \frac{Cov(z_t, z_{t+k})}{Var(z)} = \frac{E[(z_t-\mu)(z_{t+k}-\mu)]}{E[(z_t-\mu)^2]} . \qquad (5.33)$$

For an observed series of length $\underline{N}$, the estimated lag $\underline{k}$ auto-correlation coefficient is given by

$$r_k = \left(\sum_{t=1}^{N-k} (z_t-\bar{z}.)(z_{t+k}-\bar{z}.) \right) \Big/ \left(\sum_{t=1}^{N} (z_t-\bar{z}.)^2 \right). \quad (5.34)$$

The estimated autocorrelations lie on the interval -1 to $+1$. Box and Jenkins (1970) wrote that, "in practice, to obtain a useful estimate of the autocorrelation function, we would need at least fifty observations and the estimated autocorrelations r_k would be calculated for $k = 0, 1, \ldots, \underline{k}$ where $\underline{k}$ was not larger than say, $\underline{N}/4$" (p. 33).

It is useful to have a rough check on whether ρ_k is effectively zero beyond a certain lag. For this purpose a test by Bartlett (1946) is recommended (see "Identifying $\underline{p}$ and $\underline{q}$" below).

Partial Autocorrelations

The partial autocorrelation function is more complicated to define. It is calculated by fitting autoregressive processes of order $\underline{p}$ to the stationary process $\nabla^d \underline{z}_t$ and varying $\underline{p}$. We write $\underline{w_t} = \nabla^d \underline{z}_t$ as an autoregressive process of order $\underline{p}$,

$$w_t = \phi_1 w_{t-1} + \phi_2 w_{t-2} + \ldots + \phi_j w_{t-j} + a_t$$

and vary $\underline{j} = 1, 2, \ldots, \underline{p}$. If we denote the last, or $\underline{j}$th coefficient of the process as ϕ_{jj}, we can plot ϕ_{jj} versus $\underline{j}$ and this plot is called the sample partial autocorrelation function. It is obtained by solving the Yule-Walker equations which will be defined below. Multiplying through by $\underline{w_{t-k}}$ and taking expected values gives (when expressed in terms of autocorrelations)

$$E\left[w_{t-k}w_t\right] = E\left[\phi_1 w_{t-k}w_{t-1} + \phi_2 w_{t-k}w_{t-2} + \cdots \right.$$

$$\left. + \phi_j w_{t-k}w_{t-j} + a_t w_{t-k}\right],$$

or

$$\rho_k = \phi_1 \rho_{k-1} + \phi_2 \rho_{k-2} + \cdots + \phi_j \rho_{k-j} \qquad j = 1, 2, \ldots.$$

The Yule-Walker equations take the following matrix form:

$$
\begin{bmatrix}
1 & \rho_1 & \rho_2 & \cdots & \rho_{k-1} \\
\rho_1 & 1 & \rho_1 & \cdots & \rho_{k-2} \\
\cdot & \cdot & \cdot & & \cdot \\
\cdot & \cdot & \cdot & & \cdot \\
\cdot & \cdot & \cdot & & \cdot \\
\rho_{k-1} & \rho_{k-2} & \rho_{k-3} & \cdots & 1
\end{bmatrix}
\cdot
\begin{bmatrix}
\phi_{k1} \\
\phi_{k2} \\
\cdot \\
\cdot \\
\cdot \\
\phi_{kk}
\end{bmatrix}
=
\begin{bmatrix}
\rho_1 \\
\rho_2 \\
\cdot \\
\cdot \\
\cdot \\
\rho_k
\end{bmatrix}.
\qquad (5.35)
$$

After substituting sample for population autocorrelations, the Yule-Walker equations are solved successively for $k = 1, 2, \ldots$, for the $\hat{\phi}_{jk}$ and the coefficients $\hat{\phi}_{kk}$ are obtained. The $\hat{\phi}_{kk}$ alone can be obtained directly from the following equations:

$$\hat{\phi}_{11} = r_1,$$

$$\hat{\phi}_{22} = \frac{\begin{vmatrix} 1 & r_1 \\ r_1 & r_2 \end{vmatrix}}{\begin{vmatrix} 1 & r_1 \\ r_1 & 1 \end{vmatrix}},$$

$$\hat{\phi}_{33} = \frac{\begin{vmatrix} 1 & r_1 & r_1 \\ r_1 & 1 & r_2 \\ r_2 & r_1 & r_3 \end{vmatrix}}{\begin{vmatrix} 1 & r_1 & r_2 \\ r_1 & 1 & r_1 \\ r_2 & r_1 & 1 \end{vmatrix}} ,$$

$$\hat{\phi}_{44} = \frac{\begin{vmatrix} 1 & r_1 & r_2 & r_1 \\ r_1 & 1 & r_1 & r_2 \\ r_2 & r_1 & 1 & r_3 \\ r_3 & r_2 & r_1 & r_4 \end{vmatrix}}{\begin{vmatrix} 1 & r_1 & r_2 & r_3 \\ r_1 & 1 & r_1 & r_2 \\ r_2 & r_1 & 1 & r_1 \\ r_3 & r_2 & r_1 & 1 \end{vmatrix}} . \tag{5.36}$$

Box and Jenkins (1970) provided a recursive method due to Durbin (1960) for solving for estimates of the ϕ_{jj}. They caution that the estimates "become very sensitive to rounding errors and should not be used if the values of the parameters are close to the nonstationary boundaries" (p. 65). Our own experience reinforces this recommendation. The estimates obtained from (5.36) are generally quite poor. They frequently assume illegitimate values outside the interval -1 to +1. Perhaps only the first two or three autocorrelations can be adequately estimated from (5.36) with even relatively long series (n = 50 to 100). For $\hat{\phi}_{kk}$, the matrix in the denominator in (5.36) is a symmetric matrix with ones on the main diagonal and ρ_j on the jth diagonal above (or below) the main diagonal; the matrix in the numerator is identical to the denominator matrix with the exception of the last column which contains $\rho_1, \rho_2, \ldots, \rho_k$.

The theoretical partial autocorrelations are used to identify an autoregressive process. If $\underline{z}$ follows an autoregressive model of order $\underline{p}$, then only the first $\underline{p}$ partial autocorrelations (i.e., $\phi_{11}, \ldots, \phi_{pp}$) will be nonzero. Thus an abrupt cut-off in the graph of the partial autocorrelations is indicative of an autoregressive process. We shall return to this important point in "Identifying $\underline{p}$ and $\underline{q}$" below.

Identifying d

To identify $\underline{d}$, the correlograms of successive differences of a series are compared. If the correlogram neither damps out or truncates for a given $\underline{d}$, but instead remains large, then non-stationarity at that level of differencing is indicated. The correlograms of successive differences should be inspected ($\underline{d} = 1, 2, 3, \ldots$) until a plot approximating stationarity is observed; that is, differencing of the data is performed until the correlogram either shows a damping to zero (indicating an autoregressive component) or an abrupt drop to zero (indicating a moving averages component).

Identifying p and q

Once $\underline{d}$ has been identified, identification of $\underline{p}$ and $\underline{q}$ may be made. What we need to use Table 3 for is a way of estimating when population autocorrelations and partial autocorrelations are effectively zero. A test for the significance of the sample autocorrelations was given by Bartlett (1946). For the variance of the estimated autocorrelations, r_k, at lags $\underline{k}$ greater than a given value $\underline{q}$, beyond which the theoretical autocorrelation function is assumed to be zero,

$$\sigma^2_{r_k} \cong \frac{1}{N} \left\{ 1 + 2 \sum_{i=1}^{q} \rho_i^2 \right\}, \quad k > q. \quad (5.37)$$

In practice, the estimated autocorrelations r_k ($\underline{k} = 1, 2, \ldots, \underline{q}$) are substituted for the ρ_k.

TABLE 3

Identification of the Autoregressive and Moving Averages
Components of an ARIMA (p, 0, q) Series

Model	Autocorrelation	Partial Autocorrelation
ARIMA (p, 0, 0)	Dies out slowly	Cuts off after lag p
ARIMA (0, 0, q)	Cuts off after lag q	Dies out slowly
ARIMA (p, 0, q)	Dies out slowly	Dies out slowly

If the process is purely autoregressive ($q = 0$) and of order p, the variance of the "later" partial autocorrelations, given by Quenouille (1949), is

$$\sigma^2_{\hat{\phi}_{jj}} \cong \frac{1}{N} \quad \text{for} \quad j > p + 1. \quad (5.38)$$

The ρ_k die out exponentially for $k \leq p$ (see Table 2), or form a damped sine wave. The partial autocorrelation function cuts off abruptly after lag p.

If the process is purely ($p = 0$) moving average of order q, then the autocorrelation function cuts off abruptly after lag q (see Table 3), and the partial autocorrelation dies out gradually.

For mixed models both the autocorrelation and the partial autocorrelation die out slowly.

Table 4 summarizes the theoretical autocorrelations for selected autoregressive, moving average and mixed ARIMA models.

In Table 3, a summary is presented of identification procedures using the autocorrelation function and the partial autocorrelation. This table makes it possible to identify autoregressive and moving averages components in any given series. To illustrate these guides to model identification, Figure 28 is a plot of the autocorrelations and partial autocorrelations of the data of Figures 24 and 25 respectively. These graphs were

TABLE 4

Theoretical Autocorrelations for Autoregressive Models and the $\underline{d}$th Difference of Integrated Moving Average Models of Order (p, d, q)

Lag of Auto-correlation	Order of Autoregression (p) and Order of Moving Average (q)				
	First-Order Auto-regressive $p=1$; $q=0$	First-Order Moving Average $p=0$; $q=1$	Second-Order Autoregressive $p=2$; $q=0$	Second-Order Moving Average $p=0$; $q=2$	Mixed First-Order Autoregressive and Moving Average $p=1$; $q=1$
1	$\rho_1 = \phi_1$	$\rho_1 = \dfrac{-\theta_1}{\theta_1^2+1}$	$\rho_1 = \dfrac{\phi_1}{1-\phi_2}$	$\rho_1 = \dfrac{-\theta_1(1-\theta_2)}{\theta_1^2+\theta_2^2+1}$	$\rho_1 = \dfrac{(1-\theta_1\phi_1)(\phi_1-\theta_1)}{1+\theta_1^2-2\theta_1\phi_1}$
2	$\rho_2 = \phi_1^2$	$\rho_2 = 0$	$\rho_2 = \phi_2 + \dfrac{\phi_1^2}{1-\phi_2}$	$\rho_2 = \dfrac{-\theta_2}{\theta_1^2+\theta_2^2+1}$	$\rho_2 = \phi_1\rho_1$
3	$\rho_3 = \phi_1^3$	$\rho_3 = 0$	ρ_3^*	$\rho_3 = 0$	$\rho_3 = \phi_1\rho_2$
4	$\rho_3 = \phi_1^4$	$\rho_4 = 0$		$\rho_4 = 0$	$\rho_4 = \phi_1\rho_3$
. . .	. . .	. . .	. . .	. . .	. . .

*See Box and Jenkins (1970, p. 59, Equation 3.2.20).

100

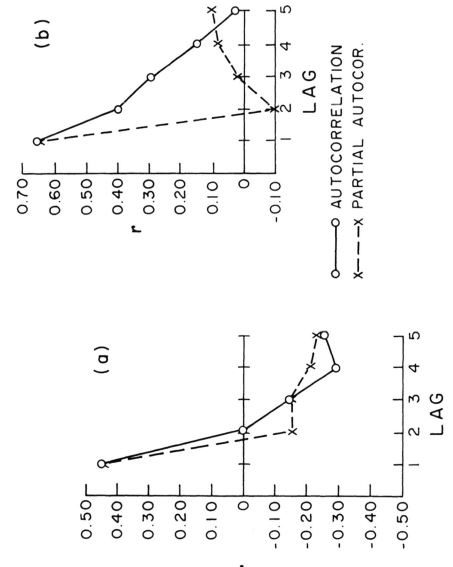

Figure 28. Autocorrelations and partial autocorrelations for (a) Figure 24 and (b) Figure 25.

computed for the original data (zero differencing). For the graph of Figure 24, the standard error of the autocorrelation coefficient is .16 for lag 1, .19 for lag 2, and .19 for lag 3. Hence the autocorrelation coefficient is effectively zero, or truncates after lag 1. This suggests an ARIMA (0, 0, 1) process. On the other hand, the data of Figure 25 show a gradually decaying autocorrelation function. The standard error is .16 for lag 1, .22 for lag 2, and .24 for lag 3. The partial autocorrelation function truncates after lag 1. This suggests an ARIMA (1, 0, 0) process.

Model Estimation

After $\underline{d}$, $\underline{p}$, and $\underline{q}$ have been identified, the parameters θ_1, θ_2, . . . , θ_q and ϕ_1, ϕ_2, . . . , ϕ_p must be estimated from the observed time-series. Since the ARIMA model was written in Equation (5.12) as

$$\phi(B)\nabla^d z_t = \theta(B)a_t,$$

then it can be rewritten

$$a_t = \theta^{-1}(B)\phi(B)(1-B)^d z_t.$$

Then the log likelihood for ϕ and θ is a linear function of the sum of squares

$$SS(\phi, \theta) = \sum_{i=1}^{N} \hat{a}_i^2.$$

In practice the $\underline{a}_i$'s are estimated and calculated recursively. For example, if we were fitting the model $(1-\phi_1 \underline{B})(1-\underline{B})\underline{z}_t = (1-\theta_1 \underline{B})\underline{a}_t$, then we could write

$$\hat{a}_t = \theta_1 \hat{a}_{t-1} + z_t - (1+\phi_1)z_{t-1} + \phi_1 z_{t-2}.$$

Knowing the $\underline{z}$'s we can calculate $\hat{\underline{a}}_{t-1}$, and so on. To start the series we can set $\hat{\underline{a}}_1$ equal to its expected value of zero, pick a value of θ_1 and ϕ_1 and calculate $\underline{SS} = \Sigma\hat{\underline{a}}_i^2$. The minimum $\underline{SS}$ determines the maximum likelihood estimates of θ_1 and ϕ_1.

A $(1-\alpha)$-percent confidence region is given by

$$SS_{(1-\alpha)}(\phi, \theta) = \left[SS_{\text{Calculated Minimum}}\right]\left[1 + \frac{\chi_\alpha^2(p+q)}{N}\right]. \qquad (5.39)$$

If we adopt a Bayesian viewpoint, then with a prior distribution

$$p(\phi, \theta, \sigma) = \frac{1}{\sigma} p(\phi, \theta)$$

the posterior distribution of ϕ and θ is

$$p(\phi, \theta | z) = (\text{constant}) SS^{-(N/2)}(\phi, \theta) p(\phi, \theta).$$

The posterior distribution for a locally uniform reference prior is obtained by plotting $\underline{SS}^{-N/2}$, which, when scaled to unit area, is equivalent to the likelihood function $\underline{h}(\phi, \theta | z)$. (See Box and Jenkins, 1970, pp. 212-213.)

The estimation of ϕ and θ is combined with the estimation of intervention effects and is developed in Chapter Six. To check the fit of the model to data, the autocorrelation of residuals $\hat{\underline{a}}_t = \underline{z}_t - \hat{\underline{z}}_t$ is computed and the correlogram of these residuals is inspected. If the correct model has been fitted to the data, the residuals should be uncorrelated. This may be checked by constructing confidence intervals about $\rho_k = 0$. If the residuals exhibit a pattern similar to a known model, however, then the model should be fit to the residuals, equivalent to fitting the combined model to the original data. Box and Jenkins (1970) derive approximate confidence regions for model parameters (pp. 228-229).

A real danger of overfitting of models to data exists, since additional error is introduced into the fit, and artificial correlation may be induced into the data. A random walk process, for example, is nonstationary. It is described by the drunkard who starts walking away from a lamppost. His every step is a random event and is described by

$$z_t = \sum_{i=1}^{t} a_i.$$

A sum of random terms may be introduced by over-differencing the data beyond its stationary value of $\underline{d}$.

Illustrations

The Ireland Data

In Figure 29 appears the graph of the percentage of students in Ireland who passed the intermediate and senior level examinations for the years 1879-1924 (see Airasian et al., 1972). (During this period, payments were made to Intermediate Boards of Education depending on the number of pupils attempting and passing the nation-wide examination.)

Inspection of the time-series suggests some slight non-stationarity. The series originates in the 60- to 70-percent region and appears to wander down to the 50- to 60-percent. This downward "drift" is not so severe as to suggest a deterministic drift. Instead the downward movement might well be explained as "probabilistic drift" to a new level, a phenomenon consistent with the interpretation that the first differences of the data follow a moving-average model. A more refined identification of the model makes use of the autocorrelations and partial autocorrelations.

In Table 5 appear the autocorrelations and partial auto-correlations for the data in Figure 29 and for the first and second differences of these data. The autocorrelations for the original data ("zeroeth" difference) remain relatively large for several lags, suggesting some nonstationarity in the series. The autocorrelations of the first differences, $\nabla \underline{z}$, show an abrupt drop to nonsignificance after the lag 1 autocorrelation, suggesting that the model may be an "integrated moving average" process of order ARIMA $(0, 1, 1)$, i.e., the first differences of $\underline{z}$ follow a first-order moving average model.

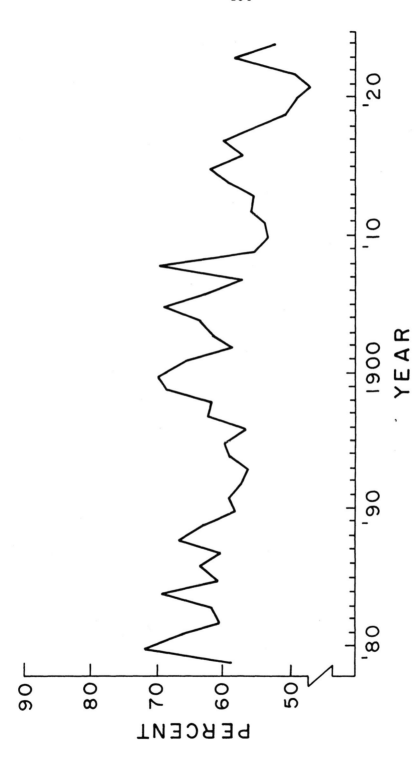

Figure 29. Percent of students passing intermediate and senior level examinations in Ireland (1879–1924).

TABLE 5

Autocorrelation and Partial Autocorrelation Coefficient for the Ireland Examination Data

(N = 46)

Autocorrelations and Their Standard Errors

Data		Lag											
		1	2	3	4	5	6	7	8	9	10	11	12
z		.536	.390	.316	.230	.086	.052	.062	.131	.119	.037	.046	-.073
σ_r		.15	.19	.20	.21	.22	.22	.22	.22	.22	.22	.22	.22
∇z		-.316	-.136	-.002	.074	-.110	-.033	-.042	.076	-.107	-.121	.120	-.106
σ_r		.15	.16	.17	.17	.17	.17	.17	.17	.17	.17	.17	.17
$\nabla^2 z$		-.507	.015	-.011	.069	-.040	-.009	-.017	-.023	.167	-.191	.165	-.109
σ_r		.15	.19	.19	.19	.19	.19	.19	.19	.19	.19	.19	.20

Partial Autocorrelations and Their Standard Errors

Data	$\hat{\phi}_{11}$	$\hat{\phi}_{22}$	$\hat{\phi}_{33}$	$\hat{\phi}_{44}$	$\hat{\phi}_{55}$	$\hat{\phi}_{66}$
z	.536	.143	.059	.092	.088	.042
∇z	-.316	-.262	-.173	.066	-.113	-.032
$\nabla^2 z$	-.507	-.325	-.246	.141	-.074	-.008

$$\sigma \hat{\phi}_{kk} = .147$$

However, the picture here is not crystal clear, and rarely is in any analysis. It could also be argued that the correlogram of the original ("undifferenced") data seems to show something resembling an exponential decay as the lag increases; however, the decrease in the autocorrelations is not rapid enough for the exponential decay implied by $\rho_k = \phi_1^k$. It also appears that there is an abrupt drop between the first and second partial autocorrelations of the original data, $\underline{z}$. These observations suggest that the data follow a first-order autoregressive model; in particular that $(\underline{z}_t - \underline{L}) = .536(\underline{z}_{t-1} - \underline{L}) + \underline{a}_t$.

This ambiguity between an autoregressive model in $\nabla^{\underline{d}}\underline{z}$ and an integrated moving average process in $\nabla^{\underline{d}+1}\underline{z}$ is not uncommon (see Box and Jenkins, 1970, p. 186). We can write the model

$$(1-B)z_t = \theta(B)a_t$$

as an ARIMA $(0, 1, \underline{q})$ model or as an ARIMA $(1, 0, \underline{q})$ with $\phi_1 = 1$.

Assuming that the model underlying the data in Figure 29 is ARIMA $(0, 1, 1)$, the parameter θ_1 can be estimated via

$$SS(\theta_1 \mid z) = \sum_{i=1}^{46} \hat{a}_i^2$$

by setting $\hat{\underline{a}}_1 = 0$, calculating the remaining $\hat{\underline{a}}_i$ from $\hat{\underline{a}}_t = \underline{z}_t - \underline{z}_{t-1} + \theta_1 \hat{\underline{a}}_{t-1}$, and repeating this process for values of θ_1 along the interval -1 to $+1$. The graph of $\underline{SS}(\theta_1 \mid \underline{z})$ against θ_1 appears as Figure 30. The minimum on the curve appears above a value of θ_1 of $.4$. Thus, the best estimate of the model for the data in Figure 29 is

$$z_t - z_{t-1} = a_t - \theta_1 a_{t-1} = a_t - .4a_{t-1}.$$

The New York Traffic
Fatalities Data

In Figure 31 appears the graph of the number of traffic fatalities per $100,000,000$ driver miles in the state of New York for the one hundred months from January 1951 to April 1960. The

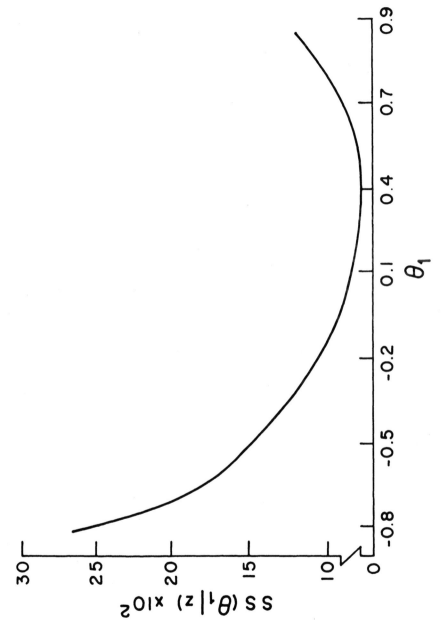

Figure 30. Sum of squared residuals as a function of θ_1 for the data in Figure 29.

108

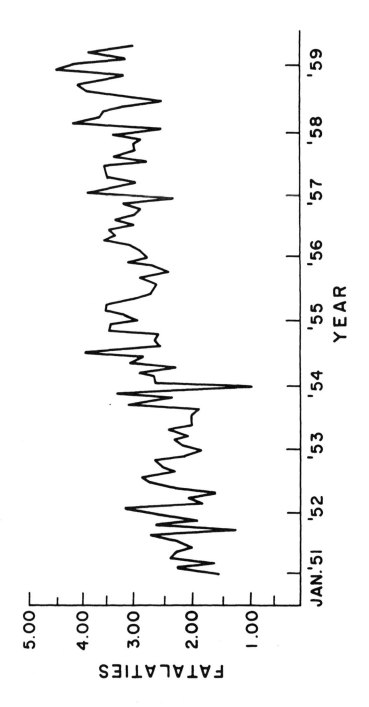

Figure 31. Seasonally adjusted traffic fatalities for New York State from January 1951 to April 1960. (Adjustment made by deviating monthly fatalities around average fatalities for like months and adding 3 to eliminate negative values.)

data have been "seasonally adjusted" to remove natural annual cycles in the data (i.e., the figure for each month has been deviated around the average for all like months in the total series; the resulting deviation scores have been increased by 3.0 to eliminate negative scores).

Examination of the graph of the time-series in Figure 31 indicates nonstationarity of the process. The series appears to drift probabilistically for some periods of time, but the drift is not consistent enough to suggest that a model for the data should include a parameter for deterministic drift.

In Table 6 appear the autocorrelations and partial auto-correlations of the undifferenced and first, second and third differences of the data in Figure 31. The autocorrelations cal-culated on $\underline{z}$, the undifferenced data, confirm the impression of nonstationarity; they show no tendency to die out even through the lag 15 coefficient. The autocorrelations for the first differ-ences (i.e., $\nabla \underline{z}_t = \underline{z}_t - \underline{z}_{t-1}$) show a definite moving average pattern. Specifically, the lagged autocorrelations abruptly fall to essentially zero after lag 1; each of the autocorrelations from lag 2 through lag 15 is not significantly different from zero. Since stationarity is thus achieved in the first differences of the series, it is unnecessary to go beyond this order of differencing to consider the second, third, etc., differences.

The pattern of partial autocorrelations (viz., a slight tailing off for $\nabla \underline{z}$) is somewhat consistent with the conclusion that the process is first-order moving average in its first dif-ferences; however, the evidence in the partial autocorrelations is not as clear and unambiguous as one might wish.

Assuming that the model underlying the data in Figure 31 is ARIMA (0, 1, 1), the parameter θ_1 can be estimated via inspection of $\underline{SS}(\theta_1 | \underline{z})$. The quantity $\underline{SS}(\theta_1 | \underline{z})$ is plotted against values of θ_1 from -1 to $+1$ in Figure 32. Inspection of the graph indicates that the best estimate of θ_1 is approximately .88. The best estimate of the model for the data in Figure 31, then, is as follows:

$$z_t - z_{t-1} = a_t - \theta_1 a_{t-1} = a_t - .88 a_{t-1}.$$

TABLE 6

Autocorrelation and Partial Autocorrelation Coefficients for the New York Traffic Fatalities Data

$(N = 100)$

Autocorrelations and Their Standard Errors

Data		1	2	3	4	5	6	7	8	9	10	11	12	13	14	15
													Lag			
z		.48	.53	.39	.47	.46	.40	.32	.42	.36	.37	.27	.26	.38	.27	.27
σ_r		.10	.12	.14	.15	.17	.18	.19	.19	.20	.21	.21	.22	.22	.23	.23
∇z		-.55	.17	-.19	.08	.04	.04	-.18	.11	-.01	.08	-.07	-.11	.18	-.09	.02
σ_r		.10	.13	.13	.13	.13	.13	.13	.14	.14	.14	.14	.14	.14	.14	.14
$\nabla^2 z$		-.72	.33	-.20	.11	-.02	.07	-.15	.12	-.06	.06	-.03	-.10	.17	-.11	.01
σ_r		.10	.14	.15	.15	.16	.16	.16	.16	.16	.16	.16	.16	.16	.16	.16
$\nabla^3 z$		-.80	.45	-.25	.14	-.07	.08	-.13	.12	-.07	.05	-.01	-.09	.14	-.09	.01
σ_r		.10	.15	.17	.17	.17	.17	.17	.17	.17	.17	.17	.17	.17	.17	.17

Partial Autocorrelations and Their Standard Errors

Data	$\hat{\phi}_{11}$	$\hat{\phi}_{22}$	$\hat{\phi}_{33}$	$\hat{\phi}_{44}$	$\hat{\phi}_{55}$	$\hat{\phi}_{66}$
z	.48	.39	.06	.18	.46	.32
∇z	-.55	-.20	-.23	.11	.00	.06
$\nabla^2 z$	-.72	-.39	-.13	.26	-.21	.19

$$\sigma_{\hat{\phi}_{jj}} = .10$$

111

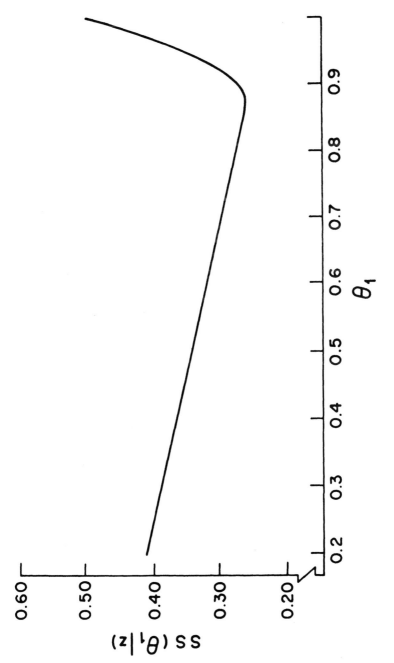

Figure 32. Sum of squared residuals as a function of θ_1 for the data in Figure 31.

Suggestions on Model Identification

Identifying the indices ($\underline{p}$, $\underline{d}$, $\underline{q}$) of an autoregressive integrated moving average model is a complex process. Fortunately the process is tolerant of errors of judgment in certain known directions; furthermore, identification of a model is only a provisional commitment that can easily be amended if subsequent analyses indicate changes would be wise. In this section, we offer some practical suggestions for identifying ARIMA ($\underline{p}$, $\underline{d}$, $\underline{q}$) models. The suggestions grow both out of the theory sketched above and out of personal experience in attempting to identify a couple of hundred actual series.

1. It will be quite difficult to identify most processes with any confidence when fewer than about fifty time points are available. Occasionally a particularly well-behaved series will show its true nature in thirty-five or forty observations.

    If seasonal (cyclic) processes are encountered, the $\underline{N}$ requirement could be much greater than fifty, depending on $\underline{p}$, $\underline{d}$ and $\underline{q}$ and the length of the cycles. The necessity of long series has nothing to do with the statistical power of tests of intervention effects. Large sample size (with respect to time points) is required for knowledge of $\underline{p}$, $\underline{d}$ and $\underline{q}$ so that the dependence among observations can be properly accounted for in statistical tests of intervention effects.

2. It is probably more important to identify $\underline{d}$ correctly than it is to make a correct identification of $\underline{p}$ and $\underline{q}$. Either underdifferencing or overdifferencing is bad. The former leaves dependence in the series which should have been removed; the latter introduces dependence into the data that should not be there.

    We doubt that real examples will be found for which $\underline{d}$ exceeds 2. When $\underline{d} = 0$, the series is stationary, i.e., fluctuates around a fixed level. When $\underline{d} = 1$, the series will change its level randomly, appearing to be stationary around one level for a while, then drifting off to become stationary around a different level for a time. When $\underline{d} = 2$, the series will drift (show a trend) for a while then drift in a different direction for a time.

The proper $\underline{d}$ is that value for which most of the autocorrelations (with the exception of a few at the lowest lags) drop to statistical insignificance, e.g., drop to within two standard errors of zero. We suspect that there is a tendency arising from inexperience to identify $\underline{d}$ as being slightly larger than it should be, e.g., setting $\underline{d}$ at 2 when it would be better to take it to be 1. This tendency probably arises from taking too seriously one or two "large" (more than one standard error from zero) autocorrelations at "odd" places in the correlogram, e.g., at lags 6, 11, etc., when there is no obvious reason why no zero autocorrelation would occur at that point.

Counting the percent of autocorrelations outside of two standard errors—see Equation (5.37)—from zero and choosing $\underline{d}$ to be the value for which that percent falls to 5 percent is not a bad rule of thumb. This rough-and-ready significance testing procedure can be augmented by the use of a chi-square test of whether a series comprises only white noise, i.e., $\underline{z}_t = \underline{L} + \underline{a}_t$. (See Box and Jenkins, 1970, pp. 290-293.)

Inspecting the graph of the series for stochastic changes in level $(\underline{d} = 1)$ or stochastic drifts $(\underline{d} = 2)$ is also quite helpful.

3. As was pointed out earlier, there are some formal equivalences among models which are worth noting. For example, the model (1, 0, 1), i.e.,

$$(1-\phi_1 B)z_t = (1-\theta_1 B)a_t,$$

becomes (0, 1, 1) when $\phi_1 = +1$, i.e.,

$$(1-B)z_t = (1-\theta_1 B)a_t.$$

It is , in general, preferable to take the higher level of differencing in this case, since estimates of parameters can become quite unstable near the extremes (e.g., ± 1).

However, confusing an ARIMA (1, 0, 1) when $\phi_1 = .9$ with an ARIMA (0, 1, 1) would not be a serious error, since the two are nearly equivalent.

4. A series may evidence a drift (consistent rise or fall, but not both) which persists far beyond what could reasonably be expected of the stochastic (probabilistic) drift of the $\underline{d} = 2$ process. (Such stochastic drift would change its course after a while.) When such drifting is not plausibly explained on purely probabilistic grounds, it is termed <u>deterministic drift.</u> One can generally find an explanation of deterministic drift, e.g., an index not corrected for population growth is observe, or a learning or decay curve has been encountered. Often, by redefining the variable (e.g., school drop-outs per 100,000 average daily attendance), the deterministic drift can be removed. Such redefinition is generally desirable. However, if for some reason (e.g., absence of a base rate measure) the variable is left in its original form with deterministic drift, the methods of Chapter Nine (which incorporate the drift into a nonzero mean for $\underline{a}_t$) should be employed.
    The question of whether deterministic drift exists in a series can be resolved in part by inspecting the mean of $(1-B)^{\underline{d}}\underline{z}$ and testing the significance of its deviation from zero. (See Box and Jenkins, 1970, pp. 119-120.)

5. Seasonal or cyclic data require special consideration. It almost goes without saying that the series must be observed for several time points (four or five times as many as the cycle length ?) before seasonal cycles can be identified confidently. Most data reported by months, weeks or days will show yearly cycles. Cyclic series are identifiable by the presence of non-zero autocorrelations of lag $\underline{s}$, where $\underline{s}$ is the length of the seasonal cycle. (See Box and Jenkins, 1970, Chapter 9, for identification of seasonal series.)
    We shall take up briefly the problem of estimating and testing intervention effects for a few seasonal models in Chapter Nine.

6. The nature of a process may change in the course of its being observed for unknown reasons. A process that has been consistently stationary may suddenly become nonstationary or vice versa. The value of $\underline{d}$ may not only change, but the value of $\underline{p}$ and $\underline{q}$ may change as well. This shift is particularly likely to occur coincident with a known intervention into the series. Indeed, it could be regarded as a type of intervention effect (to be added to those already identified in Chapter Three), though admittedly it leaves one with a somewhat perplexing conclusion (viz., "the intervention converted an ARIMA (0, 1, 1) process into an ARIMA (0, 2, 0) process"!).

A shift in the indices of an ARIMA $(\underline{p}, \underline{d}, \underline{q})$ process does present some problems for the estimation and testing of intervention effects. One is tempted to discard the offending observations if it is clearly a case of a few scores at the beginning or end of the series accounting for the problem. (We have on occasion submitted to the temptation and suffered no regrets.) A more rigorous treatment of this problem is considered in Chapter Nine.

Model identification is a judgmental procedure involving a degree of arbitrariness, but this is not to say that it is in any way capricious. (We remind the reader that some of his favorite statistical techniques may be equally arbitrary-judgmental, e.g., factor analysis, experimental design, step-wise regression, multidimensional scaling and even simple significance testing.) Experienced judges show a high degree of agreement in identifying $(\underline{p}, \underline{d}, \underline{q})$ from autocorrelations and partial-autocorrelations, particularly when the series is sufficiently long (e.g., 50 to 75 points). The first author and one of his students made independent judgments on 85 series of varying lengths (from $\underline{N} < 20$ to $\underline{N} > 200$) with agreement approaching 80 percent. Moreover, most of the disagreements were insignificant due to model ambiguity, discussed under No. 3 above.

The results of a large empirical study in which two judges attempted to identify over 100 series will help indicate the values of $\underline{p}$, $\underline{d}$ and $\underline{q}$ likely to be encountered in practice. A total of 116 series of social or behavioral indices were collected. The series varied in length from $\underline{N}$ less than 20 to $\underline{N}$

greater than 200. The series reflect a variety of things observed (e.g., a person, a city, a nation) and a varied range of applications: alpha brain waves, crime rates, examination scores, stock prices, word-association test scores, students' time spent studying, learning curves, etc. Most of the data were taken from published research reports. The two judges (the first author and one of his students) independently identified each series as one of the ARIMA ($\underline{p}$, $\underline{d}$, $\underline{q}$) class. In cases of disagreement, the series was double checked by both judges working together and a consensus was reached.

Of the 116 series, 21 were identified as being seasonal. Hence they possess no simple expression in terms of the basic (nonmultiplicative) ARIMA model. This figure of approximately 20 percent of the series being seasonal should not be taken to reflect on the rate at which cyclic series are likely to be encountered in practice; rather it merely reflects on one of the ad hoc properties of an unrepresentative group of series available to the authors.

The remaining 95 series were each identified, i.e., values of $\underline{p}$, $\underline{d}$ and $\underline{q}$ were selected from analysis of the autocorrelations and partial autocorrelations. The results are presented as Table 7. As an illustration of how Table 7 is read, consider the 21 entries in the cell at the junction of row 2 and column 1. This figure indicates that 21 of the 95 series were identified as $\underline{p}=1$, $\underline{d}=0$, and $\underline{q}=0$, i.e., 21 series were stationary ($\underline{d}=0$) with one autoregressive term ($\underline{p}=1$) and no moving averages term ($\underline{q}=0$). Stated symbolically, 21 series were of the form $(\underline{z}_t - \underline{L}) = \phi_1(\underline{z}_{t-1} - \underline{L}) + \underline{a}_t$.

Table 7 shows that in no case was differencing above the second order required to produce stationarity. In fact, the 95 series were roughly equally divided between stationarity ($\underline{d}=0$) and stationarity in the first differences ($\underline{d}=1$); only 6 cases required second-order differencing. The most often encountered processes where the first-order autoregressive (21 times) and the first-order integrated moving averages (22 times). Approximately 75 percent of the cases were covered by four models: The "white-noise" process (0, 0, 0)—16 cases; the first-order autoregressive process (1, 0, 0)—21 cases; "white-noise" after first differencing (0, 1, 0)—9 cases; the integrated moving averages process (0, 1, 1)—22 cases. Rarely did a model

TABLE 7

Results of Identification of Time-Series Models for Social-Behavioral Data

q	p	d = 0	d = 1	d = 2	Totals
0	0	16	9	2	
	1	21	1	0	q = 0: 51 p = 0: 71
	2	2	0	0	
1	0	10	22	2	
	1	0	0	0	q = 1: 34 p = 1: 22
	2	0	0	0	
2	0	2	4	2	
	1	0	0	0	q = 2: 8 p = 2: 2
	2	0	0	0	
3	0	0	2	0	
	1	0	0	0	q = 3: 2
	2	0	0	0	
Totals		51	38	6	95

require more than two moving average parameters or more than one autoregressive. However, the possibility of many moving average parameters—particularly in the physical sciences and engineering—being needed in a model cannot be discounted.[*]

A computer program, CORREL, for use in model identification has been developed and is available from the first author upon request. The program computes autocorrelations and partial autocorrelations for raw data and several differencings of the data. Partial autocorrelations are calculated via the Durbin algorithm and may lie outside the range -1 to +1 due to inaccuracy of the estimation procedure. Standard errors are also given for each coefficient. Means and variances of the original and differenced data are also printed. A chi-square test is performed of whether the series or differenced series is "white noise." In addition, a seasonal option is available in CORREL for identifying cyclic series; a known cycle length s̲ is entered into the program and differences corresponding to a multiplicative model (see Box and Jenkins, 1970, Chapter 9) are formed and autocorrelated.

---

[*]Gwilym Jenkins (personal communication) recounts one instance in engineering in which ten moving average parameters were not only indicated by the correlogram of the data but were interpretable in terms of physical processes. Also see Ames and Reiter (1961).

CHAPTER SIX

ESTIMATING AND TESTING INTERVENTION EFFECTS

In this chapter, methods are presented by which inferential statistical tests are made of the effects of intervention into various commonly encountered time-series models. Six of the ARIMA ($\underline{p}$, $\underline{d}$, $\underline{q}$) models will be examined in detail. These six models were chosen for special attention because they cover among them most real processes encountered in practice, and because they provide relatively clear illustrations of the theory of testing intervention effects. In Chapter Seven, a general formulation of the intervention effect estimation problem is given which subsumes the six cases developed here and extends the methods to all instances of non-cyclic processes encountered with real data.

The six models comprise two stationary processes and four nonstationary processes. These six models and their interrelationships are depicted in Figure 33.

The first-order moving average and autoregressive models are models of stationary time-series processes. They represent the two traditional methods of modeling stationary series. Their generalization is in the direction of adding terms lagged by two or more units in time (e.g., $z_t = L - \theta_2 a_{t-2} - \theta_1 a_{t-1} + a_t$). The

STATIONARY MODELS

ARIMA (0, 0, 1)

$$z_t = L - \theta_1 a_{t-1} + a_t$$

ARIMA (1, 0, 0)

$$(z_t - L) = \phi_1(z_{t-1} - L) + a_t$$

NONSTATIONARY MODELS

ARIMA (0, 1, 1)	ARIMA (0, 2, 1)
$z_t - z_{t-1} = a_t - \theta_1 a_{t-1},$	$z_t - 2z_{t-1} + z_{t-2} = a_t - \theta_1 a_{t-1},$
or, equivalently,	or, equivalently,
$z_t = L + (1 - \theta_1) \sum_{i=1}^{t-1} a_i + a_t,$	$z_t = L + (1-\theta_1) \sum_{i=1}^{t-1} (t-i)a_i + \sum_{i=1}^{t} a_i.$

ARIMA (0, 1, 2)	ARIMA (0, 2, 2)
$z_t - z_{t-1} = a_t - \theta_1 a_{t-1} - \theta_2 a_{t-2},$	$z_t - 2z_{t-1} + z_{t-2} =$
	$\qquad a_t - \theta_1 a_{t-1} - \theta_2 a_{t-2},$
or, equivalently,	or, equivalently,
$z_t = L + (1-\theta_1 - \theta_2) \sum_{i=1}^{t-2} a_i +$	$z_t = L + (1-\theta_1 - \theta_2) \sum_{i=1}^{t-1} (t-i)a_i +$
$\qquad (1-\theta_1)a_{t-1} + a_t.$	$\qquad (1 + \theta_2) \sum_{i=1}^{t-1} a_i + a_t.$

Figure 33.   Six basic time-series models.

general approach to estimating and testing intervention effects in these higher-order stationary models will be apparent after illustration on the simplest first-order model.

The four nonstationary models to be investigated represent the four combinations of two characteristics: 1) nonstationarity that is removed by either first- or second-order differencing; 2) moving-average processes of either the first or second order after differencing. For example, the ARIMA (0, 1, 2) process is such that the first differences $(z_t - z_{t-1})$ follow a moving average model of second order. It can be shown, incidentally, that ARIMA (0, 1, 1) is a special case of ARIMA (0, 1, 2)—when $\theta_2 = 0$—and that ARIMA (0, 2, 1) is a special case of ARIMA (0, 2, 2)—also when $\theta_2 = 0$. Thus redundancy in the models simplifies both the theoretical and practical labor of estimating and testing intervention effects.

Testing an Intervention Effect for a First-Order Moving Averages Process

Suppose that a variable z follows a first-order moving averages process, ARIMA (0, 0, 1), i.e.,

$$z_t = L - \theta_1 a_{t-1} + a_t, \qquad (6.1)$$

where $-1 < \theta_1 < 1$ and $a_i \sim NID(0, \sigma^2)$. We assume that this process holds for the n_1 points in time prior to the intervention, I. Further, it is assumed that the effect of the intervention on the process is to alter its level by an amount δ for the n_2 points in time following I:

$$z_t = L - \theta_1 a_{t-1} + a_t + \delta, \qquad t = n_1 + 1, \ldots, N. \qquad (6.2)$$

For a fixed value of θ_1 on the open interval -1 to $+1$, the model in (6.1) can be transformed into a variable y which has the form of the general linear model, i.e., y_t comprises a function of the first power of L and the random variable a_t and no other variable.

The observation z_1 already satisfies the conditions of the linear model* since errors, $\underline{a}$, associated with unobserved time points are assumed to be zero; hence, we take the first transformed observation to be the same as the first actual observation:

$$y_1 = z_1 = L + a_1. \tag{6.3}$$

Examination of the second observation reveals the term $-\theta_1 a_1$ which must be removed if $\underline{y}_2$ is to conform to the general linear model. The term can be removed by adding $\theta_1 \underline{y}_1$ to $\underline{z}_2$:

$$y_2 = z_2 + \theta_1 y_1 = L - \theta_1 a_1 + a_2 + \theta_1 L + \theta_1 a_1,$$

$$= (1 + \theta_1)L + a_2. \tag{6.4}$$

Since every $\underline{y}_{t-1}$ possesses only the error $\underline{a}_{t-1}$ and each $\underline{z}_t$ contains an unwanted $-\theta_1 \underline{a}_{t-1}$, the following recursive relationship for $\underline{y}_t$ is suggested:

$$y_t = z_t + \theta_1 y_{t-1}. \tag{6.5}$$

The transformation (6.5) will carry the ARIMA $(0, 0, 1)$ process over into the form of the general linear model. It is relatively simple to verify that for $\underline{t} \leq \underline{n}_1$

$$y_t = (1 + \theta_1 + \ldots + \theta_1^{t-1})L + a_t. \tag{6.6}$$

We now consider the addition of the intervention effect at time $\underline{t} = \underline{n}_1 + 1$. The transformed $\underline{y}$ will have the following form:

---

*A brief presentation of the fundamental notions involved in normal theory, least-squares analysis of the linear model appears as Appendix C to this text.

$$y_{n_1+1} = z_{n_1+1} + \theta_1 y_{n_1},$$

$$= L - \theta_1 a_{n_1} + a_{n_1+1} + \delta + \theta_1(1+\theta_1+ \ldots +\theta_1^{n_1-1})L + \theta_1 a_{n_1},$$

$$= (1 + \theta_1 + \ldots + \theta_1^{n_1})L + a_{n_1+1} + \delta.$$

Again it is straightforward to show that for $t > \underline{n}_1$,

$$y_t = (1+\theta_1+\ldots+\theta_1^{t-1})L + (1+\theta_1+\ldots+\theta_1^{t-(n_1+1)})\delta + a_t. \tag{6.7}$$

Equation (6.7) is of the form of the general linear model and can be readily identified as such when expressed in matrix form:

$$
\begin{bmatrix} y_1 \\ y_2 \\ \vdots \\ y_{n_1} \\ \hline y_{n_1+1} \\ \vdots \\ y_N \end{bmatrix}
=
\left[
\begin{array}{cc}
1 & 0 \\
1 + \theta_1 & 0 \\
\vdots & \vdots \\
1 + \ldots + \theta_1^{n_1-1} & 0 \\
\hline
1 + \ldots + \theta_1^{n_1} & 1 \\
\vdots & \vdots \\
1 + \ldots + \theta_1^{N-1} & 1 + \ldots + \theta_1^{n_2-1}
\end{array}
\right]
\begin{bmatrix} L \\ \delta \end{bmatrix}
+
\begin{bmatrix} a_1 \\ a_2 \\ \vdots \\ \vdots \\ \vdots \\ \vdots \\ a_N \end{bmatrix}. \tag{6.8}
$$

The least-squares estimators of $\underline{L}$ and δ are given by

$$\begin{bmatrix} \hat{L} \\ \hat{\delta} \end{bmatrix} = (X^T X)^{-1} X^T y. \tag{6.9}$$

The estimated errors, $\hat{a}_t$, are given by

$$\hat{a} = y - X\hat{\beta} \tag{6.10}$$

The values $\hat{a}$ are contingent upon particular values of $\hat{L}$ and $\hat{\delta}$ which are in turn contingent upon a value of θ_1. The sum of squared estimated errors for particular values of θ_1, $\hat{L}$ and $\hat{\delta}$ is denoted

$$SS(\theta_1 | z) = \hat{a}^T \hat{a}. \tag{6.11}$$

The value of θ_1, which is unknown, can be taken to equal that value on the interval -1 to $+1$ for which the quantity $\underline{SS}(\theta_1|\underline{z})$ is minimized.[*]

From normal distribution general linear model theory, we know that

$$\frac{\hat{L} - L}{s_a \sqrt{c^{11}}} \sim t_{N-2}, \tag{6.12}$$

and

$$\frac{\hat{\delta} - \delta}{s_a \sqrt{c^{22}}} \sim t_{N-2}, \tag{6.13}$$

where

$$s_a^2 = \frac{\hat{a}^T \hat{a}}{(N-2)}, \tag{6.14}$$

$\underline{c}^{jj}$ is the jth diagonal entry in $(\underline{X}^T\underline{X})^{-1}$, and

$\underline{t}_{N-2}$ is Student's $\underline{t}$-variable with $\underline{N}-2$ degrees of freedom.

The $100(1-\alpha)$ percent confidence interval on δ can be constructed from

---

[*]Minimizing $\underline{SS}(\theta_1|\underline{z})$ is equivalent to minimizing $\underline{s}_a^2$, the estimated residual error variance in the least-squares solution.

125

$$\hat{\delta} \pm {}_{1-\alpha/2}t_{N-2}\, s_a \sqrt{c^{22}}. \qquad (6.15)$$

Alternatively, hypotheses regarding $\underline{L}$ and δ can be tested using (6.12) or (6.13).

Illustrative Analysis Using the ARIMA (0, 0, 1) Model

A study by Hall et al. (1971) provides data for an illustration of testing intervention effects in an ARIMA (0, 0, 1) process. The disruptive "talking out" behavior of a second-grade class in a poverty area school was observed for 40 consecutive days, the first twenty days under baseline conditions and the second twenty days with praise and participation in a favorite activity contingent upon not talking out. The daily number of talking out episodes during the experimental period is graphed in Figure 34. The data are contained in the region of twenty to twenty-five episodes of "talking out" per day for the class prior to intervention. This feature would argue in favor of representing the series by a stationary model. It is not possible simply by inspecting the graph of the series to form any worthwhile notions regarding whether the series is autoregressive or moving averages; for this, the correlogram is required.

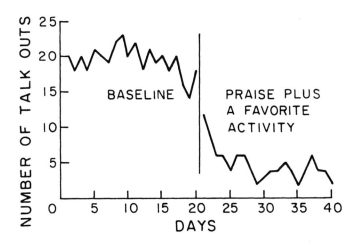

Figure 34. Daily frequency of "talking out" episodes in a second-grade classroom.

In order to identify an appropriate model, the correlograms must be computed separately for the pre-I and post-I series. A single correlogram should not be computed without regard to possible intervention effects. The presence of an intervention effect can greatly increase autocorrelation coefficients. The separate pre-I and post-I correlograms for the "talking out" data and the first and second differences of the original data, z, are as follows:

Lag		Pre-intervention			Post-intervention	
	z	$(1-B)z$	$(1-B)^2z$	z	$(1-B)z$	$(1-B)^2z$
1	.28	-.56	-.69	.46	.04	-.38
2	.29	.17	.35	.12	-.20	-.17
3	.09	-.10	-.19	.07	-.05	.13
4	.10	.07	.14	.08	-.12	-.04
5	-.05	-.11	-.18	.22	.09	-.16
6	-.01	.13	.24	.11	.37	.31
7	-.17	-.15	-.27	-.16	.03	.08
8	-.09	.13	.22	-.29	-.40	-.31

The standard errors for the above autocorrelations range from approximately .22 at lag 1 to about .30 at lag 8. It is apparent that not even first differencing is required to remove the latter nonzero autocorrelations in the original data. Thus, the series will be taken to be stationary ($d = 0$). It is problematic how one should proceed in combining the autocorrelation information from both pre-I and post-I. For our part, we shall average them:

Average Pre-I and Post-I Autocorrelations
For d = 0 (i.e., z)

Lag:	1	2	3	4	5.	6	7	8
r:	.37	.20	.08	.09	.08	.05	-.16	-.19

The autocorrelations fail to show the exponential decay characteristic of autoregressive terms, so we take $p = 0$. Only the first autocorrelation is significantly nonzero; thus q will be

taken as 1, and the model has been tentatively identified as
ARIMA (0, 0, 1).

Working on the assumption that the series is a first-
order moving average process, the intervention analysis outlined above was performed. Repeatedly for values of θ_1
between -1 and +1, the data were transformed by means of
Equation (6.5). A set of forty transformed y-values was then
subjected to least-squares analysis via (6.8) and (6.9), for
each value of θ_1 from -1 to +1 in steps of .02. Each of the
one hundred least-squares analyses produces a residual error
variance by which the maximum likelihood estimate of θ_1 may
be found. The relevant portion of the results, i.e., the region
in which error variance is minimized, is as follows:

θ_1	s_a^2	$\hat{L}$	$t(\hat{L})$	$\hat{\delta}$	$t(\hat{\delta})$
.	.	.	.	.	.
.	.	.	.	.	.
.	.	.	.	.	.
-.42	4.51	19.22	29.21	-14.25	-15.46
-.40	4.49	19.23	29.66	-14.26	-15.70
-.38	4.48	19.23	30.09	-14.27	-15.93
-.36	4.47	19.23	30.53	-14.28	-16.16
-.34	4.47	19.24	30.95	-14.29	-16.39
-.32	4.47	19.24	31.38	-14.30	-16.61
-.30	4.48	19.25	31.80	-14.32	-16.84
-.28	4.49	19.26	32.22	-14.33	-17.06
.	.	.	.	.	.
.	.	.	.	.	.
.	.	.	.	.	.

The minimum error variance criterion indicates that the
maximum likelihood estimate of θ_1 is approximately -.34.
Hence, the results of the least-squares analysis should be
inspected for $\theta_1 = -.34$. There it is seen that the estimate of
location of the series at $t = 0$ is 19.24, which is highly significantly different from zero ($t = 30.95$ with $df = 38$). But more
importantly, the least-squares estimate of the intervention
effect is -14.29 which is also quite significantly different from
zero ($t = -16.39$, $df = 38$). Hence, the series shows a

statistically significant drop starting on day No. 21 when restraint of "talking out" behavior began to be rewarded.

Testing an Intervention Effect for a
First-Order Autoregressive Process

Suppose that a variable $\underline{z}$ follows a first-order autoregressive model, ARIMA (1, 0, 0). For the $\underline{n}_1$ time points prior to intervention, the structure of $\underline{z}$ is as follows:

$$z_t - L = \phi_1(z_{t-1} - L) + a_t, \qquad (6.16)$$

where

$\underline{L}$ is the level of the series,

$\underline{a}_i \sim \text{NID}(0, \sigma^2)$, and

$-1 < \phi_1 < 1$.

The condition on ϕ_1 stated as an inequality keeps the process stationary; if ϕ_1 exceeds 1, the process will seem to "explode" in either a positive or negative direction. First, we shall find a transformation of $\underline{z}$ into a variable $\underline{y}$ which can be expressed in the form of the general linear model. We assume that the unobserved value $\underline{z}_0$ has associated with it an error of 0; hence, $\underline{z}_0 = L$, from which it follows that $\underline{z}_1 = \underline{L} + \underline{a}_1$. Since this expression conforms to the requirements of the linear model, we can associate the first value of $\underline{y}$ with it:

$$y_1 = z_1 = L + a_1. \qquad (6.17)$$

Consider $\underline{z}_2 = \underline{L} + \phi_1(\underline{z}_1 - \underline{L}) + \underline{a}_2$. By subtracting $\phi_1 \underline{z}_1$ from both sides, $\underline{z}_2$ assumes the form of the linear model:

$$y_2 = z_2 - \phi_1 z_1 = (1 - \phi_1)L + a_2. \qquad (6.18)$$

Equation (6.18) readily suggests the general expression for the transformation:

$$y_t = z_t - \phi_1 z_{t-1} = (1 - \phi_1)L + a_t. \qquad (6.19)$$

Consider the introduction of the intervention effect at $t = n_1 + 1$. The level of the series shifts to $L + \delta$; thus, the model becomes

$$z_t - (L + \delta) = \phi_1[z_{t-1} - (L + \delta)] + a_t. \qquad (6.20)$$

When z_{n_1+1} is transformed via (6.19), one obtains

$$y_{n_1+1} = (1 - \phi_1)L + \delta + a_{n_1+1}. \qquad (6.21)$$

Subsequent y's have the form

$$y_t = (1 - \phi_1)L + (1 - \phi_1)\delta + a_t, \qquad n_1 + 1 \lessgtr t \leq N.$$

Each of the equations (6.17), (6.18), (6.19) and (6.21) is in the form of the linear model and can be expressed jointly in matrix form as follows:

$$
\begin{bmatrix}
y_1 \\
y_2 \\
\vdots \\
y_{n_1} \\
\hline
y_{n_1+1} \\
y_{n_1+2} \\
\vdots \\
y_N
\end{bmatrix}
=
\begin{bmatrix}
1 & 0 \\
1 - \phi_1 & 0 \\
\vdots & \vdots \\
1 - \phi_1 & 0 \\
\hline
1 - \phi_1 & 1 \\
1 - \phi_1 & 1 - \phi_1 \\
\vdots & \vdots \\
1 - \phi_1 & 1 - \phi_1
\end{bmatrix}
\begin{bmatrix}
L \\
\delta
\end{bmatrix}
+
\begin{bmatrix}
a_1 \\
a_2 \\
\vdots \\
a_{n_1} \\
\hline
a_{n_1+1} \\
a_{n_1+2} \\
\vdots \\
a_N
\end{bmatrix}. \qquad (6.22)
$$

For a fixed value of ϕ_1, the least-squares estimates of L and δ are given by

$$\begin{bmatrix} \hat{L} \\ \hat{\delta} \end{bmatrix} = (X^TX)^{-1}X^Ty, \qquad (6.23)$$

where $\underline{X}$ is the $\underline{N}$-by-two design matrix in (6.22).

Under normal theory,

$$\frac{\hat{L} - L}{s_a \sqrt{c^{11}}} \sim t_{N-2}, \qquad (6.24)$$

and

$$\frac{\hat{\delta} - \delta}{s_a \sqrt{c^{22}}} \sim t_{N-2}, \qquad (6.25)$$

where

$$s_a^2 = \frac{(y-X\hat{\beta})^T(y-X\hat{\beta})}{(N-2)} = \frac{\hat{a}^T\hat{a}}{(N-2)}, \qquad (6.26)$$

and

$\underline{c}^{jj}$ is the $\underline{j}$th diagonal entry in $(\underline{X}^T\underline{X})^{-1}$.

Since ϕ_1 is unknown, Equations (6.23) and (6.26) are solved repeatedly for values of ϕ_1 between -1 and 1; ϕ_1 is assumed to be that value for which $\underline{s}_a^2$ is minimal. The estimates of $\underline{L}$ and δ corresponding to this value of ϕ_1 are tested and interpreted.

Illustrative Analysis for ARIMA
(1, 0, 0) Model

The data for illustration of the ARIMA (1, 0, 0) analysis come from a study of crime prevention in the city of Chicago. The rate of reported burglaries in the Hyde Park area of Chicago was observed for forty-eight months: for forty-one months prior to the intervention of Project Whistlestop and for seventeen months during the project (actually the year was divided into thirteen 28-day periods). The project involved distributing whistles to citizens which could be used to summon police when a crime was discovered in progress. The rate of reported burglaries is graphed as Figure 35.

The correlogram for the pre-intervention data (n_1 = 41) in Figure 35 and the first and second differences of the data is as follows:

Lag	z	(1-B)z	$(1-B)^2 z$
1	.52	-.15	-.49
2	.27	-.11	.02
3	.09	-.06	.14
4	-.05	-.34	-.37
5	.08	.24	.30
6	-.04	.11	.06
7	-.16	-.20	-.33
8	-.11	.20	.35
9	-.19	-.14	-.26
10	-.16	.05	.07
11	-.15	.13	.19
12	-.19	-.16	-.33
13	-.10	.20	.32

The estimated standard errors of the autocorrelations are approximately .23 for lags 3 and greater. It is apparent in the above results that the first three autocorrelations for z are almost exactly an exponential decay from a starting value of .52; moreover, the partial autocorrelations evidence the abrupt drop to nonsignificance characteristic of the first-order auto-regressive process: .52, .01, -.05, -.07, .12, -.02. Thus, the undifferenced data, z, can be assumed to follow a first-order autoregressive process: ARIMA (1, 0, 0). Differencing of the data merely introduced autocorrelation where there was none.

The analysis outlined in the section immediately above was performed. The unknown parameter ϕ_1 was varied from -1.00 to +1.00 in steps of 0.02. For each value of ϕ_1, the data were transformed to y via Equation (6.19) and the least-squares solution for $\hat{L}$ and $\hat{\delta}$ was obtained. The following portion of the results reveals how the minimum error variance is located and the results interpreted.

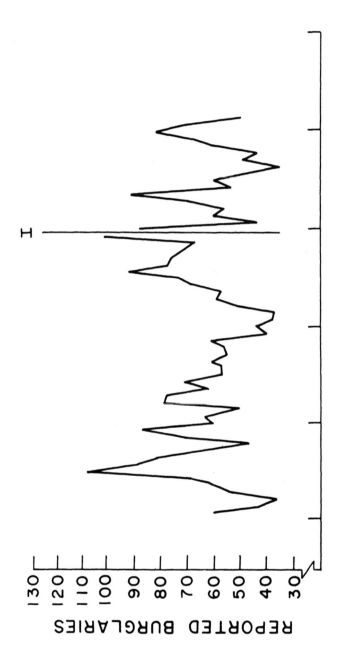

Figure 35. Reported burglaries by month for the Hyde Park section of Chicago (April 1969–September 1973). ($\underline{n}_1 = 41$, $\underline{n}_2 = 17$.)

ϕ_1	s_a^2	$\hat{L}$	$t(\hat{L})$	$\hat{\delta}$	$t(\hat{\delta})$
.	.	.	.	.	.
.	.	.	.	.	.
.	.	.	.	.	.
.44	206.70	64.47	16.60	−5.00	−.73
.46	206.11	64.49	16.09	−5.13	−.73
.48	205.75	64.50	15.58	−5.27	−.73
* .50	205.60	64.52	15.06	−5.41	−.72
.52	205.66	64.53	14.53	−5.57	−.72
.54	205.94	64.55	14.00	−5.75	−.72
.56	206.44	64.56	13.47	−5.94	−.72
.	.	.	.	.	.
.	.	.	.	.	.
.	.	.	.	.	.

The maximum likelihood estimate of ϕ_1 is approximately .50. For this value of ϕ_1, the estimated location of the series at time $t = 0$ is at 64.52 reported burglaries, which is highly significantly different from zero ($t = 15.06$, with $df = 46$). But more importantly, the estimated change in level of the series at the point of intervention is −5.41 reported burglaries per month, which is not at all significantly different from zero ($t = -.72$, with $df = 46$). (If desired, the standard error of $\hat{\delta}$ can be easily recovered from the t-statistic: $-5.41/-.72 = 7.51$.) Hence, there is no reason to believe that the post-I behavior of the series in Figure 35 represents anything other than the chance fluctuation of an ARIMA (1, 0, 0) process. Apparently, Project Whistlestop was not effective as a deterrent to burglary. However, the conclusions about reality are never quite so neat as the statistical analysis might lead one to believe. It is conceivable—though far-fetched, perhaps—that the intervention produced both a deterrent effect on burglaries, thus reducing the rate, and an increase in surveillance, thus increasing the reporting of burglaries. Such possibilities could not be assessed by means of the statistical analysis described here.

Testing an Intervention Effect for an
Integrated Moving Averages Process

The simplest nonstationary process is the ARIMA $(0, 1, 1)$, known as the <u>integrated moving averages</u> process. From the signature of the model, $(0, 1, 1)$, we can state its mathematical form:

$$z_t - z_{t-1} = a_t - \theta_1 a_{t-1}. \qquad (6.27)$$

Since all errors prior to $\underline{t} = 1$ are assumed to be zero, we know that

$$z_1 - z_0 = a_1 - 0,$$

whence

$$z_1 = z_0 + a_1.$$

The true location of the process at $\underline{t} = 0$ will be denoted by $\underline{L}$ so that

$$z_1 = L + a_1.$$

It follows that

$$z_2 = z_1 - \theta_1 a_1 + a_2 = L + a_1 - \theta_1 a_1 + a_2$$

$$= L + (1-\theta_1)a_1 + a_2. \qquad (6.28)$$

Continuing in this fashion, it is readily shown that

$$z_t = L + (1-\theta_1)(a_1 + \ldots + a_{t-1}) + a_t. \qquad (6.29)$$

The prior errors $(\underline{a}_1, \ldots, \underline{a}_t)$ are "integrated" into the value of $\underline{z}_t$, hence the name "integrated moving averages."

The model in (6.29) is assumed to hold for the process prior to the intervention. The familiar conditions are imposed upon the elements of the model: $-1 < \theta_1 < 1$ and

$a_i \sim NID(0, \sigma^2)$. We now seek a transformation of $\underline{z}$ in (6.29) into the form of the general linear model. It is clear that $\underline{z}_1$ is already in such form and $\underline{z}_2$ can easily be put into the desired form:

$$z_2 = L + (1-\theta_1)a_1 + a_2.$$

Hence,

$$y_2 = z_2 - z_1 + \theta_1 y_1$$

$$= L + (1-\theta_1)a_1 + a_2 - L - a_1 + \theta_1 L + \theta_1 a_1$$

$$= \theta_1 L + a_2.$$

In general, the difference between $\underline{z}_t$ and $\underline{z}_{t-1}$ will be of the form

$$z_t - z_{t-1} = a_t - \theta_1 a_{t-1}. \tag{6.30}$$

Since $\underline{y}_{t-1}$ will have been transformed into linear model form by the proper (as yet unspecified) transformation, it will contain the isolated error a_{t-1}. Thus, by adding $\theta_1 y_{t-1}$ to (6.30) all but the error a_t is removed from the transformed value. Hence, the desired transformation takes the form of the following recursive relationship:

$$y_1 = z_1,$$

$$y_t = z_t - z_{t-1} + \theta_1 y_{t-1}. \tag{6.31}$$

Manipulation of (6.31) and (6.30) reveals that $\underline{y}$ has the following form:

$$y_t = \theta_1^{t-1} L + a_t. \tag{6.32}$$

We assume that the effect of the intervention at time $t = n_1 + 1$ is an abrupt and constant change in level δ. Thus, for $\underline{t} = \underline{n}_1 + 1, \ldots, \underline{N}$,

$$z_t = L + (1-\theta_1)(a_1 + \ldots + a_{t-1}) + a_t + \delta. \tag{6.33}$$

Applying the transformation (6.31) to the post-$\underline{I}$ values in (6.33) produces

$$y_t = \theta_1^{t-1} L + \theta_1^{t-(n_1+1)} \delta + a_t. \tag{6.34}$$

The transformed $\underline{y}$'s are now in the form of the general linear model, and we may write $\underline{y} = \underline{X}\beta + \underline{a}$:

$$
\begin{bmatrix} y_1 \\ y_2 \\ \cdot \\ \cdot \\ \cdot \\ y_{n_1} \\ \hline y_{n_1+1} \\ \cdot \\ \cdot \\ \cdot \\ y_N \end{bmatrix}
=
\begin{bmatrix} 1 & 0 \\ \theta_1 & 0 \\ \cdot & \cdot \\ \cdot & \cdot \\ \cdot & \cdot \\ \theta_1^{n_1-1} & 0 \\ \hline \theta_1^{n_1} & 1 \\ \cdot & \cdot \\ \cdot & \cdot \\ \cdot & \cdot \\ \theta_1^{N-1} & \theta_1^{n_2-1} \end{bmatrix}
\begin{bmatrix} L \\ \delta \end{bmatrix}
+
\begin{bmatrix} a_1 \\ a_2 \\ \cdot \\ \cdot \\ \cdot \\ \cdot \\ \cdot \\ \cdot \\ \cdot \\ \cdot \\ a_N \end{bmatrix}
\tag{6.35}
$$

For a fixed value of θ_1, least-squares estimates of $\underline{L}$ and δ are obtained in the usual manner:

$$\begin{bmatrix} \hat{L} \\ \hat{\delta} \end{bmatrix} = (X^T X)^{-1} X^T y. \tag{6.36}$$

Under normal theory for the random variables $\underline{a}_i$, the distributions of the least-squares estimates are given by

$$\frac{\hat{L} - L}{s_a \sqrt{c^{11}}} \sim t_{N-2}, \tag{6.37}$$

$$\frac{\hat{\delta} - \delta}{s_a \sqrt{c^{22}}} \sim t_{N-2},$$

where

c^{jj} is the jth diagonal element of $(X^T X)^{-1}$,

$s_a^2 = (y - X\hat{\beta})^T (y - X\hat{\beta})/(N - 2)$,

and

t_{N-2} is Student's t-variable with $N - 2$ degrees of freedom.

Since θ_1 is not known, generally, one may solve (6.36) repeatedly for values between -1 and $+1$. That value for which s_a^2 is minimal is the maximum likelihood estimate of θ_1. At that point, one may test hypotheses about $\underline{L}$ and δ or establish confidence intervals on these two parameters.

Illustrative Analysis for the ARIMA (0, 1, 1) Model

Data to illustrate the testing of an intervention effect in the ARIMA (0, 1, 1) model come from a study by Mefferd (see Holtzman, 1963). A single schizophrenic patient's performance on a perceptual speed task was observed for 120 days: the first 60 days under baseline conditions, and the second 60 days while receiving chlorpromazine (an early tranquilizer). The graph of the data appears as the first 120 points in Figure 8 of Chapter Two.

The graph of the data shows some instability of level, suggesting nonstationarity. Nonstationarity of slope is not particularly evident though nonstationarity of level is suspected. A more refined analysis of the process depends on the results of the correlogram. Two correlograms, one for pre-$\underline{I}$ and one for post-$\underline{I}$, should be computed; an intervention effect, if present, could seriously confound a correlogram computed on the entire series. The following autocorrelations for the raw

data and first and second differences were obtained for pre-$\underline{I}$
and post-$\underline{I}$ data:

	Pre-intervention			Post-intervention		
Lag	$\underline{z}$	$(1-B)z$	$(1-B)^2z$	$\underline{z}$	$(1-B)z$	$(1-B)^2z$
1	.43	-.47	-.61	.62	-.47	-.71
2	.39	-.14	.03	.54	.17	.36
3	.47	.12	.14	.37	-.23	-.24
4	.40	-.05	-.13	.45	.03	.15
5	.43	.18	.23	.46	-.13	-.15
6	.24	-.26	-.29	.56	.14	.12
7	.35	.16	.19	.51	.08	.02
8	.27	.02	.05	.42	-.04	-.07
9	.17	-.25	-.31	.32	.06	.11
10	.32	.37	.42	.24	-.18	-.19
11	.11	-.23	-.28	.27	.14	.21
12	.15	.02	.08	.22	-.16	-.23
13	.15	.02	.02	.27	.20	.21
14	.09	-.06	-.11	.18	-.07	-.14
15	.18	.22	.27	.12	.07	.13

The standard errors of the autocorrelations above are
approximately .13 at lag 1 and rise to around .22 at lag 15.
The large autocorrelations for the undifferenced data, $\underline{z}$, indicate nonstationarity; thus first and, perhaps, second differences should be considered. Inspection shows that second
differences do not improve matters significantly (i.e., they do
not reduce any large autocorrelations in the first differences).
Hence, the model can be regarded as of the general form ARIMA
($\underline{p}$, 1, $\underline{q}$). Nothing in the correlogram suggests the exponential
decay associated with autoregressive terms; thus, $\underline{p}$ will be
taken to be zero. Finally, only the lag 1 autocorrelation of the
first differences appears significantly nonzero (for either pre-$\underline{I}$
or post-$\underline{I}$); therefore, the model which will be adopted will be
ARIMA (0, 1, 1), the integrated moving averages model. (To
our knowledge, no work has been done on how best to pool
information from the pre-$\underline{I}$ and post-$\underline{I}$ correlograms. If one
would simply average the first difference autocorrelations above,
the following aggregate correlogram would be obtained: -.47,
.01, -.05, -.01, .03, -.06, .12, -.01, ..., which shows

the pattern of ARIMA (0, 1, 1) autocorrelations. If n_1 and n_2 are unequal, some weighted average would be more appropriate.)

The process having been identified as ARIMA (0, 1, 1), the analysis for intervention effect outlined in the above section was performed. One hundred successive analyses were performed by varying θ_1 from -1 to +1 in steps of .02. For each value of θ_1, the observations were transformed into $\underline{y}$ via Equation (6.31). The $\underline{y}$ variable was then expressed as a special case of the linear model—Equation (6.35)—from which $\underline{L}$ and δ are estimated by least-squares analyses. Each of the one hundred least-squares analyses thus performed yielded a residual error variance, $\underline{s}_a^2$, from which the maximum likelihood estimate of θ_1 was found. The relevant portion of the one hundred iterations is as follows:

θ_1	s_a^2	$\hat{L}$	$t(\hat{L})$	$\hat{\delta}$	$t(\hat{\delta})$
.	.	.	.	.	.
.	.	.	.	.	.
.	.	.	.	.	.
.70	94.30	53.54	7.72	-20.82	-3.00
.72	93.80	53.66	7.98	-21.14	-3.15
.74	93.44	53.83	8.28	-21.48	-3.30
* .76	93.25	54.06	8.61	-21.83	-3.48
.78	93.29	54.37	9.00	-22.22	-3.68
.80	93.62	54.76	9.43	-22.63	-3.90
.82	94.34	55.26	9.94	-23.09	-4.15
.	.	.	.	.	.
.	.	.	.	.	.
.	.	.	.	.	.

The maximum likelihood estimate of θ_1 is approximately .76, since that value corresponds to the minimum residual error variance. For $\theta_1 = .76$, the estimated level of the series at "time 0" is 54.06, which is quite significantly different from zero ($\underline{t} = 8.61$, $\underline{df} = 118$). But more importantly, the estimated intervention effect is -21.83, also highly significantly different from zero ($\underline{t} = -3.48$, $\underline{df} = 118$, $\underline{p} < .001$). Hence, the introduction of the tranquilizer brought about a statistically significant downward shift in level of the series. A "naked eye" examination of Figure 8 would have seemed to have indicated such a shift, although the level of the series was dropping for about ten days prior to the intervention, and it is not obvious that the drop in the series after intervention is quite unexpected from an unaltered ARIMA (0, 1, 1) process. However, the statistical analysis demonstrates emphatically that the post-I level of the series is not the normal progression of the pre-I process.

It is interesting to note here that the results of the analysis are quite sensitive to the value of θ_1. If θ_1 were taken to be zero, the analysis would reduce to an independent groups t-test between the pre-I and post-I, for which $\hat{\delta}$ is -21.00 but the associated t-statistic fails to surpass conventional levels of statistical significance ($t = -1.72$, $df = 118$). Furthermore, if θ_1 were taken to be -.80, $\hat{\delta}$ would have equalled +6.59 with the associated t-statistic being 0.434!

Testing an Intervention Effect for an
ARIMA (0, 1, 2) Process

The ARIMA (0, 1, 2) process is such that the first differences of the observed variable follow a second-order moving averages model:

$$z_t - z_{t-1} = a_t - \theta_1 a_{t-1} - \theta_2 a_{t-2}. \tag{6.38}$$

It follows from the assumption that errors at times $t < 1$ are zero that

$$z_1 = L + a_1,$$

$$z_2 = L + (1-\theta_1)a_1 + a_2,$$

$$z_3 = L + (1-\theta_1-\theta_2)a_1 + (1-\theta_1)a_2 + a_3,$$

$$\vdots$$

$$z_t = L + (1-\theta_1-\theta_2)(a_1 + \ldots + a_{t-2}) + (1-\theta_1)a_{t-1} + a_t, \tag{6.39}$$

where

$\underline{L}$ is the level of the series at $\underline{t} = 0$,

and

$$\underline{a}_i \sim NID\ (0,\ \sigma^2).$$

If the first differences of an ARIMA (0, 1, 2) process are to conform to a stationary process, then θ_1 and θ_2 must satisfy the following restrictions:

$$-1 < \theta_2 < 1; \qquad \theta_2 + \theta_1 < 1; \qquad \theta_2 - \theta_1 < 1. \qquad (6.40)$$

As was indicated in Chapter Five, the values of θ_1 and θ_2 satisfying the restrictions in (6.40) lie in a triangle in the two-dimensional space (θ_1, θ_2) whose vertices lie at $(0, 1)$, $(+2, -1)$ and $(-2, -1)$. The ARIMA (0, 1, 2) can be recognized for the following properties of its correlogram: 1) the autocorrelations for the data $\underline{z}$ fail to die out rapidly; 2) the autocorrelations for the first differences $\underline{z_t - z_{t-1}}$ are nonzero for large lags 1 and 2 and are zero for lags greater than 2.

It is assumed that the intervention $\underline{I}$ produces an immediate and constant effect δ beginning at time $\underline{t} = \underline{n_1} + 1$.

The following transformation carries $\underline{z}$ into $\underline{y}$ which is in the form of the general linear model (i.e., $\underline{y_t}$ is a function of the first powers of fixed parameters and only the random error $\underline{a_t}$ introduced into the system at the $\underline{t}$th point in time):

$$y_1 = z_1 = L + a_1,$$

$$y_2 = z_2 - z_1 + \theta_1 z_1 = \theta_1 L + a_2,$$

$$\vdots$$

$$y_t = (z_t - z_{t-1}) + \theta_1 y_{t-1} + \theta_2 y_{t-2}. \qquad (6.41)$$

By examination of the weights for $\underline{L}$ and δ produced by the above transformation, the following specification of the general linear model for the ARIMA (0, 1, 2) model can be written in the form $\underline{y} = \underline{X}\beta + \underline{a}$.

$$
\begin{bmatrix}
y_1 \\
y_2 \\
\vdots \\
y_{n_1} \\
\hline
y_{n_1+1} \\
y_{n_1+2} \\
\vdots \\
y_N
\end{bmatrix}
=
\begin{bmatrix}
f_1(L) = 1 & 0 \\
f_2(L) = \theta_1 & 0 \\
\vdots & \vdots \\
f_{n_1}(L) = \theta_1 f_{n_1-1}(L) + \theta_2 f_{n_1-2}(L) & 0 \\
\hline
 & f_{n_1+1}(\delta) = 1 \\
 & f_{n_1+2}(\delta) = \theta_1 \\
 & \vdots \\
 & f_N(\delta) = \theta_1 f_{N-1}(\delta) + \theta_2 f_{N-2}(\delta)
\end{bmatrix}
\begin{bmatrix}
L \\
\delta
\end{bmatrix}
+
\begin{bmatrix}
a_1 \\
a_2 \\
\vdots \\
a_N
\end{bmatrix}
$$

Least-squares estimates of $\underline{L}$ and δ are obtained and tested for statistical significance in the usual manner.

Testing an Intervention Effect for an ARIMA $(0, 2, 2)$ Process

We need not deal specifically with the ARIMA $(0, 2, 1)$ case in Figure 33 since it is subsumed by the more general case examined here, namely, the ARIMA $(0, 2, 2)$ in which the second differences of the data follow a second-order moving averages model. The second differences of $\underline{z}$ are

$$(1-B)^2 z = (1-2B+B^2) z_t = z_t - 2z_{t-1} + z_{t-2}.$$

If these differences follow a second-order moving averages process—specified in ARIMA $(0, 2, 2)$—then

$$z_t - 2z_{t-1} + z_{t-2} = a_t - \theta_1 a_{t-1} - \theta_2 a_{t-2}. \qquad (6.42)$$

If we assume that $\underline{a}_0, \underline{a}_{-1}, \ldots$ are zero, then algebraic manipulation of (6.42) leads to

$$z_t = L + (1+\theta_2) \sum_{i=1}^{t-1} a_i + (1-\theta_1-\theta_2) \sum_{i=1}^{t-1} (t-i)a_i + a_t, \qquad (6.43)$$

where

> $\underline{L}$ is the level of the series at $\underline{t}=0$,
>
> $\underline{a}_i \sim \text{NID}\,(0,\sigma^2)$,

and

> θ_1 and θ_2 conform to the stationarity-invertibility conditions
>
> $$-1 < \theta_2 < 1,$$
>
> $$\theta_2 - \theta_1 < 1,$$
>
> $$\theta_2 + \theta_1 < 1.$$

The model in (6.43) is assumed to hold for the n_1 observations prior to intervention. For the n_2 observations after intervention, the model is augmented by the intervention effect δ:

$$z_t = L + (1+\theta_2) \sum_{i=1}^{t-1} a_i + (1-\theta_1-\theta_2) \sum_{i=1}^{t-1} (t-i)a_i + a_t + \delta. \qquad (6.44)$$

Again we seek a transformation which eliminates from z_t all of the random variables a_i except a_t, and which involves only first powers of L and δ, i.e., we wish to transform z into the form of the general linear model.

Since $z_1 = L + a_1$, we can associate the first transformed variable y_1 with z_1, i.e.,

$$y_1 = z_1 = L + a_1.$$

Now z_2 is of the form,

$$z_2 = L + (1+\theta_2)a_1 + (1-\theta_1-\theta_2)a_1 + a_2 = L + (2-\theta_1)a_1 + a_2.$$

Since a_1 is available from y_1, the appropriate form of y_2 is suggested:

$$y_2 = z_2 - (2-\theta_1)y_1 = z_2 - 2z_1 + \theta_1 y_1 = (\theta_1-1)L + a_2.$$

It is clear from (6.42) that

$$z_3 = 2z_2 - z_1 + a_3 - \theta_1 a_2 - \theta_2 a_1. \qquad (6.45)$$

Since y_1 and y_2 provide a_1 and a_2 respectively, z_3 can be transformed into a y_3 which will involve only the random variable a_3 as follows:

$$y_3 = z_3 - 2z_2 + z_1 + \theta_1 y_2 + \theta_2 y_1 = [\theta_1(\theta_1-1)+\theta_2]L + a_3.$$

Equation (6.45) suggests the general form of the transformation

$$y_t = z_t - 2z_{t-1} + z_{t-2} + \theta_1 y_{t-1} + \theta_2 y_{t-2}. \tag{6.46}$$

The recursive equation (6.46) will transform an ARIMA (0, 2, 2) process into the form of the general linear model. The coefficients of $\underline{L}$ in $\underline{y_t}$ (i.e., the values of $\underline{f_t}$ in $\underline{y_t} = \underline{f_t}\underline{L} + \underline{a_t}$ have the following form:

$$f_1 = 1, \quad f_2 = \theta_1 - 1, \ldots, \quad f_t = \theta_1 f_{t-1} + \theta_2 f_{t-2}. \tag{6.47}$$

The transformation (6.46) applied to the post-intervention observations (6.44) converts $\underline{z}$ into a function of $\underline{L}$, δ and $\underline{a_t}$ of the following form:

$$y_t = f_t L + g_t \delta + a_t, \tag{6.48}$$

where

f_t is given in (6.47),

and

g_t has the form:

$$g_t = 0, \qquad\qquad t = 1, \ldots, n_1,$$

$$g_{n_1+1} = 1,$$

$$g_{n_1+2} = \theta_1 - 1,$$

$$g_t = \theta_1 g_{t-1} + \theta_2 g_{t-2}, \quad t = n_1 + 3, \ldots, N.$$

The transformed $\underline{y}$ in (6.48) is in the form of the general linear model $\underline{y} = X\beta + \underline{a}$ and we may write

$$
\begin{bmatrix} y_1 \\ y_2 \\ \cdot \\ \cdot \\ \cdot \\ y_{n_1} \\ \text{---} \\ y_{n_1+1} \\ \cdot \\ \cdot \\ \cdot \\ y_N \end{bmatrix} = \begin{bmatrix} f_1 & 0 \\ f_2 & 0 \\ \cdot & \cdot \\ \cdot & \cdot \\ \cdot & \cdot \\ f_{n_1} & 0 \\ \text{---} & \text{---} \\ f_{n_1+1} & g_{n_1+1} \\ \cdot & \cdot \\ \cdot & \cdot \\ \cdot & \cdot \\ f_N & g_N \end{bmatrix} \begin{bmatrix} L \\ \delta \end{bmatrix} + \begin{bmatrix} a_1 \\ a_2 \\ \cdot \\ \cdot \\ \cdot \\ \cdot \\ \cdot \\ \cdot \\ \cdot \\ a_N \end{bmatrix} \qquad (6.49)
$$

For fixed values of θ_1 and θ_2, all of the entries in $\underline{y}$ and $\underline{X}$ can be calculated from θ_1, θ_2 and $\underline{z}$, and the least-squares estimates of $\underline{L}$ and δ can be obtained from

$$
\begin{bmatrix} \hat{L} \\ \hat{\delta} \end{bmatrix} = (X^T X)^{-1} X^T y. \qquad (6.50)
$$

Tests of $\hat{L}$ and $\hat{\delta}$ against any hypothesized values L and δ are made, under normal distribution assumptions on $\underline{a}_i$, using the following distributional statements:

$$
\frac{\hat{L} - L}{s_a \sqrt{c^{11}}} \sim t_{N-2} , \qquad (6.51)
$$

$$
\frac{\hat{\delta} - \delta}{s_a \sqrt{c^{22}}} \sim t_{N-2} , \qquad (6.52)
$$

where

$$
s_a^2 = \frac{(y - X\hat{\beta})^T (y - X\hat{\beta})}{N - 2} \qquad (6.53)
$$

$\underline{c}^{jj}$ is the jth diagonal element in $(\underline{X}^T \underline{X})^{-1}$,

and

$$\underline{t}_{N-2} \quad \text{is Student's } \underline{t}\text{-distribution with } \underline{N}\text{-2 degrees of freedom.}$$

Since θ_1 and θ_2 are unknown, their maximum likelihood estimates may be obtained by minimization of $\underline{s}_a^2$ in (6.53). The values of (θ_1, θ_2) are allowed to range over the invertibility-stationarity region defined by the triangle with vertices at $(0, 1)$, $(2, -1)$ and $(-2, -1)$; at each point, the least-squares solution for $\hat{L}$ and $\hat{\delta}$ is obtained and the residual variance, $\underline{s}_a^2$, is calculated. Those values for which the residual variance is minimized are the maximum likelihood estimates of θ_1 and θ_2. The values of $\hat{L}$ and $\hat{\delta}$ are then tested for significance or interval estimates of L and δ are obtained for the maximum likelihood values of θ_1 and θ_2.

Illustrative Analysis for ARIMA (0, 2, 2) Model

Thirty observations $(\underline{n}_1 = 15, \underline{n}_2 = 15)$ of an ARIMA $(0, 2, 2)$ process were generated with $\theta_1 = 1.3$, $\theta_2 = -.70$, $\underline{L} = 50$, $\delta = 7$, and $\sigma^2 = 1$. A graph of the data appears as Figure 36.

Since θ_1 and θ_2 for the data in Figure 36 will be assumed to be unknown, the first task of the analysis is to determine the values of $\underline{s}_a^2$ for values of θ_1 and θ_2 in the invertibility-stationarity region. A portion of the matrix of estimated error variances appears as Table 8.

From inspection of Table 8 it can be seen that the residual error variance is minimized in the vicinity of θ_2 approximately $-.70$ and $-.80$ and θ_1 approximately 1.60 or 1.70. The maximum likelihood estimates of θ_1 and θ_2 are taken to be $\theta_1 = 1.60$ and $\theta_2 = -.70$. These estimates are quite close to the actual values $(\theta_1 = 1.30; \theta_2 = -.70)$ used in the simulation by which the data in Figure 36 were produced. In addition, the associated estimated error variance, $\underline{s}_a^2 = 0.93$, is reasonably close to the true value of unity.

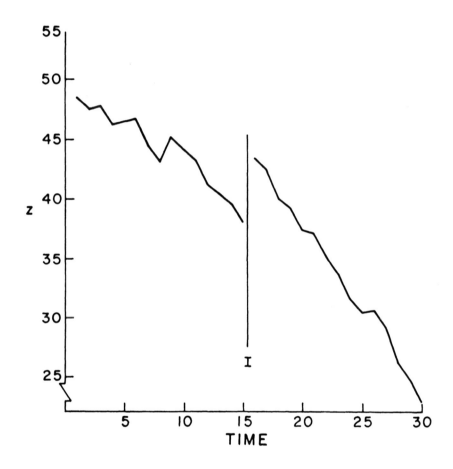

Figure 36. Thirty observations of an ARIMA $(0, 2, 2)$ process for which $\underline{L} = 50$, $\theta_1 = 1.30$, $\theta_2 = -.70$, $\delta = 7$, $\sigma^2 = 1$, $\underline{n}_1 = 15$ and $\underline{n}_2 = 15$.

TABLE 8

Estimated Error Variances, Formula (6.53), for
Various Values of θ_1 and θ_2*

θ_2	...	1.20	1.30	1.40	1.50	1.60	1.70	1.80	1.90
.									
.									
.									
-.20									
-.30	...	1.36							
-.40	...	1.38	1.25						
-.50	...	1.42	1.27	1.14					
-.60	...	1.50	1.32	1.15	1.02				
-.70	...	1.63	1.38	1.16	1.01	0.93			
-.80	...	1.80	1.42	1.15	1.01	0.97	0.93		
-.90	...	1.89	1.41	1.13	1.05	1.15	1.08	0.94	
-1.00	...	1.69	1.48	1.21	1.23	2.01	1.36	1.14	1.00

The top of the table is labeled θ_1.

*Values of θ_1 and θ_2 with no entries lie outside the stationarity-invertibility region. Ellipsis marks indicate that the region continued in that direction but that the error variances are large and need not be shown.

As the final steps in the analysis, confidence intervals on $\underline{L}$ and δ may be constructed using the maximum likelihood values of θ_1 and θ_2. For $\theta_1 = 1.60$ and $\theta_2 = -.70$, the following estimates of $\underline{L}$ and δ and their standard errors (the denominators of (6.51) and (6.52)) are obtained:

$$\hat{L} = 48.9689, \qquad s_{\hat{L}} = 0.6463,$$

$$\hat{\delta} = 6.9292, \qquad s_{\hat{\delta}} = 0.6475.$$

The 95-percent confidence interval on δ is given by

$$\hat{\delta} \pm {}_{.975}t_{N-2}s_{\hat{\delta}} .$$ (6.54)

For the data in Figure 36, the 95-percent confidence interval on δ is

$$6.9292 \pm (2.048)0.6475 = (5.603, 8.255).$$

The confidence interval on δ does not span zero; it does, however, capture the true value of the parameter, 7. From the hypothesis testing point of view, one concludes that the estimated change in level of the series between the fifteenth and sixteenth points in time is significantly different from zero at the .05 level. An interval estimate of L can be similarly obtained.

CHAPTER SEVEN

ESTIMATING AND TESTING INTERVENTION EFFECTS

IN THE GENERAL ARIMA (p, d, q) MODEL

In the previous chapter, the problem of transforming an ARIMA process into the form of the linear model and then estimating and testing intervention effects was dealt with in piecemeal fashion. In this chapter, a general approach is presented for transforming any ARIMA $(\underline{p}, \underline{d}, \underline{q})$ process into the form of the general linear model and testing any type of intervention effect. We take a somewhat different approach but arrive at solutions nearly equivalent to those obtained by Kepka (1972) in his doctoral thesis.

Formulation of ARIMA in Terms of Psi-Weights

The necessary transformations are most conveniently approached, perhaps, via the psi-weights reformulation of an ARIMA $(\underline{p}, \underline{d}, \underline{q})$ process (see Box and Jenkins, 1970, pp. 95-97). As before, the ARIMA $(\underline{p}, \underline{d}, \underline{q})$ process is of the form

$$\phi(B)(1-B)^d z_t = \theta(B)a_t, \qquad (7.1)$$

where

$$\phi(B) = (1 - \phi_1 B - \ldots - \phi_p B^p),$$

and

$$\theta(B) = (1 - \theta_1 B - \ldots - \theta_q B^q).$$

We desire a formulation of $\underline{z}_t$ in terms merely of a weighted function of the random variables $\underline{a}$, i.e.,

$$z_t = \sum_{j=0}^{\infty} \psi_j a_{t-j}. \tag{7.2}$$

Equation (7.2) can be formulated in terms of the backward shift operator, $\underline{B}$, as follows:

$$z_t = \psi(B) a_t, \tag{7.3}$$

where

$$\psi(B) = \psi_0 - \psi_1 B - \psi_2 B^2 - \ldots.$$

One may operate on both sides of (7.3) with the auto-regressive and differencing functions of (7.1):

$$\phi(B)(1 - B)^d z_t = \phi(B)(1 - B)^d \psi(B) a_t.$$

Noting that $\phi(\underline{B})(1 - \underline{B})^d \underline{z}_t = \theta(\underline{B}) a_t$, we can write

$$\theta(B) a_t = \phi(B)(1 - B)^d \psi(B) a_t. \tag{7.4}$$

$\theta(\underline{B})$ is a polynomial in $\underline{B}$ of degree $\underline{q}$; $\phi(\underline{B})(1 - \underline{B})^d$ is a polynomial in $\underline{B}$ of degree $\underline{p} + \underline{d}$. Thus, the ψ-weights can be evaluated by equating the coefficients of $\underline{B}$ on the right-hand side of (7.4) to the coefficients of $\underline{B}$ on the left-hand side. There are, of course, an infinite number of ψ-weights; however, one need only evaluate $\underline{N}$ of them (where $\underline{N}$ is the length of the observed series). By setting all errors $\underline{a}_0, \underline{a}_{-1}, \underline{a}_{-2}, \ldots$, equal to zero (see Aigner, 1971, p. 357, where this assumption is defended) and denoting the true level of the series at $\underline{t} = 0$ by $\underline{L}$, only the psi-weights $\psi_1, \ldots, \psi_N$ are required.

The equating of coefficients of $\underline{B}$ in (7.4) and subsequent solution for ψ_j is straightforward, but quite tedious. We shall skip the steps and state the result.

Let

$$a_k = \sum_{r=0}^{k} \binom{d}{r} (-1)^r (-\phi_{k-r}),$$ (7.5)

where

$\quad$ d is the index of the ARIMA (p, d, q) process,

$\quad \phi_1, \phi_2, \ldots \phi_p$ are the autoregressive parameters of the ARIMA process.

A few conventions must be adopted in dealing with $\underline{a_k}$:

a) If $\underline{r} > \underline{d}$, $\binom{d}{r} = 0$;

b) $-\phi_0$ is set equal to +1.

c) $\phi_{\underline{k-r}} = 0$ $\quad$ if $\quad \underline{k} - \underline{r} > \underline{p}$.

The coefficients $\underline{a_k}$ are used to establish a set of recursive relationships for obtaining ψ_j:

$$\psi_0 = 1$$

$$\psi_1 a_0 + \psi_0 a_1 = -\theta_1$$

$$\psi_2 a_0 + \psi_1 a_1 + \psi_0 a_2 = -\theta_2$$ (7.6)

$$\cdot$$
$$\cdot$$
$$\cdot$$

$$\psi_h a_0 + \psi_{h-1} a_1 + \cdots + \psi_1 a_{h-1} + \psi_0 a_h = -\theta_h,$$

where

$$\theta_{\underline{h}} = 0 \quad \text{if} \quad \underline{h} > \underline{q}.$$

In this manner, may all of the ψ's be evaluated. Consider an illustration previously developed in Chapter Five. There it was shown that the ARIMA (1, 0, 0) process could be written

$$z_t = L + \phi_1^{t-1} a_1 + \phi_1^{t-2} a_2 + \ldots + \phi_1 a_{t-1} + a_t. \qquad (7.7)$$

Equation (7.7) is already in psi-weight form with $\psi_0 = 1$ and $\psi_j = \phi_1^j$ for $j = 1, \ldots, \underline{N}$. We shall confirm that solution of (7.6) yields the same psi-weights in this case.

Noting that $\underline{p} = 1$, $\underline{d} = 0$, $\underline{q} = 0$ and that all parameters except ϕ_1 are zero, the coefficients $\underline{a_k}$ are obtained from (7.5):

$$a_0 = 1$$

$$a_1 = -\phi_1$$

$$a_2 = 0$$

$$\cdot \quad \cdot$$
$$\cdot \quad \cdot$$
$$\cdot \quad \cdot$$

$$a_N = 0.$$

Hence

$$\psi_0 = 1$$

$$\psi_1 + \psi_0(-\phi_1) = 0$$

$$\psi_2 + \psi_1(-\phi_1) + \psi_0(0) = 0$$

$$\cdot$$
$$\cdot$$
$$\cdot$$

from which it follows readily that $\psi_0 = 1$, $\psi_1 = \phi_1$, $\psi_2 = \phi_1^2$, $\ldots$, $\psi_j = \phi_1^j$.

Transformation into General
Linear Model

With the ARIMA $(\underline{p}, \underline{d}, \underline{q})$ model in psi-weights form, it is relatively simple to transform it into the form of the general linear model. First, disregarding the intervention effects which will be added in later, note that

$$z_t = L + \sum_{j=0}^{t-1} \psi_j a_{t-j} = L + \psi_{t-1} a_1 + \psi_{t-2} a_2 + \ldots + \psi_0 a_t. \quad (7.8)$$

Of course, the ψ_j can be calculated from the values of $\phi_1, \ldots, \phi_p, \theta_1, \ldots, \theta_q$, and $\underline{d}$. The objective is to transform z_t so that all random errors except $\underline{a}_t$ have been removed. How this can be done is most easily seen, perhaps, by inspecting the first few terms of (7.8):

$$z_1 = L + \psi_0 a_1,$$

$$z_2 = L + \psi_1 a_1 + \psi_0 a_2,$$

$$z_3 = L + \psi_2 a_1 + \psi_1 a_2 + \psi_0 a_3.$$

The transformed variable which is to satisfy the requirements of the general linear model will be denoted by $\underline{y}$. The observation $\underline{z}_1$ already satisfies the general linear model requirement; hence, we can associate $\underline{y}_1$ with $\underline{z}_1$: $\underline{y}_1 = \underline{z}_1$. Since it was established earlier that $\psi_0 = 1$, $\underline{y}_1 = \underline{L} + \underline{a}_1$.

The observation $\underline{z}_2$ would be in the form of the general linear model, if it were not for the term $\psi_1 a_1$. However, such a term is available to be subtracted from $\underline{z}_2$ if $\underline{y}_1$ is multiplied by the known coefficient ψ_1:

$$y_2 = z_2 - \psi_1 y_1 = L + \psi_1 a_1 + a_2 - \psi_1 (L + a) = (1 - \psi_1) L + a_2.$$

$$(7.9)$$

This expression for $\underline{y}_2$ provides the $\underline{a}_2$ by which $\underline{y}_3$ can be obtained:

$$y_3 = z_3 - \psi_1 y_2 - \psi_2 y_1 =$$

$$
\begin{array}{ll}
L + \psi_2 a_1 + \psi_1 a_2 + a_3 \\
-\psi_1(1-\psi_1)L \qquad -\psi_1 a_2 \\
\qquad\qquad -\psi_2 L - \psi_2 a_1 \\
\hline
[1 - \psi_1(1-\psi_1) - \psi_2]L \qquad\qquad + a_3.
\end{array}
$$

$$(7.10)$$

Thus does each y_t in succession yield the isolated variable a_t which can be used in subsequent transformations of z. In general, z can be transformed into the form of the linear model via the recursive relationship

$$y_t = z_t - \sum_{j=1}^{t-1} \psi_j y_{t-j}. \qquad (7.11)$$

The transformed y_t comprises only a_t plus a linear function of L, which will be elaborated on later.

The procedure must be expanded to include the effects of intervention into the process. Suppose that any effects of intervention can be represented by a linear function, f, of any number of intervention parameters $(\delta_1, \delta_2, \ldots)$. The function f will be specified by the investigator to describe the kind of intervention effects he wishes to estimate. For convenience we shall include L, the level of the series at time $t=0$, among the intervention parameters. Thus f will be of the form

$$f_t(L, \delta_1, \delta_2, \ldots) = x_{t1}L + x_{t2}\delta_1 + x_{t3}\delta_2 + \ldots .$$

$$(7.12)$$

One well-known formulation of f would be $f_t(L, \delta) = x_{t1}L + x_{t2}\delta$, where $x_{t1} = 1$ and $x_{t2} = 0$ for $t \leq n_1$ and 1 for $t > n_1$. This formulation describes a constant intervention effect δ which changes the level of the series from L to $L + \delta$ at $t = n_1 + 1$ and beyond.

The ARIMA (p, d, q) process with intervention can now be formulated as follows:

$$z_t = f_t(L, \delta_1, \delta_2, \ldots) + \sum_{j=0}^{t-1} \psi_j a_{t-j}. \qquad (7.13)$$

When z_t in (7.13) is transformed into y by means of the recursive relationship (7.11), all a_j's will be removed except a_t, as was noted before. It remains to examine the effect on f of transforming z into y. This effect can be evaluated most easily by means of a recursive relationship. Consider the first and second observations of a process in ψ-weights form with intervention effects added:

$$z_1 = x_{11}L + x_{12}\delta_1 + x_{13}\delta_2 + \ldots + a_1,$$

$$z_2 = x_{21}L + x_{22}\delta_1 + x_{23}\delta_2 + \ldots + \psi_1 a_1 + a_2.$$

Let x_{tk}^* ($t = 1, \ldots, N$; $k = 1, \ldots, m$) denote the weights of the intervention effects in the transformed variable y. As before, we associate y_1 with z_1, hence $x_{1k}^* = x_{1k}$ for $k = 1, \ldots, m$, where m is the number of intervention parameters. The value y_2 is obtained from the recursive relationship (7.11):

$$y_2 = z_2 - \psi_1 y_1 = \frac{\begin{array}{l} x_{21}L + x_{22}\delta_1 + \ldots + \psi_1 a_1 + a_2 \\ - \psi_1 x_{11}^* L - \psi_1 x_{12}^* \delta_1 - \ldots - \psi_1 a_1 \end{array}}{(x_{21} - \psi_1 x_{11}^*)L + (x_{22} - \psi_1 x_{12}^*)\delta_1 + \ldots + a_2.} \qquad (7.14)$$

Hence, $x_{21}^* = x_{21} - \psi_1 x_{11}^*$; $x_{22}^* = x_{22} - \psi_1 x_{12}^*$; etc.

In general,

$$x_{tk}^* = x_{tk} - \sum_{j=1}^{t-1} \psi_j x_{t-j,k}^*. \qquad (7.15)$$

Thus, y_t can be expressed as

$$y_t = x_{t1}^* L + x_{t2}^* \delta_1 + x_{t3}^* \delta_2 + \ldots + a_t. \qquad (7.16)$$

The expression in (7.16) is readily recognizable as of the form of the linear model. We can write

$$y = X^* \beta + a,$$

$$
\begin{bmatrix} y_1 \\ y_2 \\ \cdot \\ \cdot \\ \cdot \\ y_N \end{bmatrix}
=
\begin{bmatrix} x_{11}^* & x_{12}^* & \cdot & \cdot & \cdot \\ x_{21}^* & x_{22}^* & \cdot & \cdot & \cdot \\ \cdot & \cdot & & & \\ \cdot & \cdot & & & \\ \cdot & \cdot & & & \\ x_{N1}^* & x_{N2}^* & \cdot & \cdot & \cdot \end{bmatrix}
\begin{bmatrix} L \\ \delta_1 \\ \delta_2 \\ \vdots \end{bmatrix}
+
\begin{bmatrix} a_1 \\ a_2 \\ \cdot \\ \cdot \\ \cdot \\ a_N \end{bmatrix}
. (7.17)
$$

From this point on, least-squares estimation and significance testing or interval estimation of β proceeds as is typical in the case of normal theory linear models. The design matrix $\underline{X}^*$ and the vector of observations $\underline{y}$ in (7.17) can be established once $\underline{X}$ is specified and values of $\phi_1, \ldots, \phi_p$ and $\theta_1, \ldots, \theta_q$ are fixed. Of course, the true values of the ϕ and θ parameters are not known; therefore, each set of possible values of the ϕ and θ parameters which lie in the invertibility-stationarity region are specified and a solution of (7.17) is performed. That solution is accepted for which the residual error variance, $\underline{s_a^2}$, is minimal.

Illustration

The above general techniques will be applied to a familiar model by way of illustration. Consider ARIMA $(0, 1, 1)$ with a constant intervention effect appearing at $\underline{t} = \underline{n}_1 + 1$—see Chapter Six:

$$z_t = L + (1 - \theta_1)(a_1 + \ldots + a_{t-1}) + a_t \qquad (t \leq n_1),$$

$$z_t = L + \delta + (1 - \theta_1)(a_1 + \ldots + a_{t-1}) + a_t \qquad (t > n_1).$$

Notice that this model is already in the form of psi-weights: $\psi_0 = 1$, $\psi_j = 1 - \theta_1$. The transformation to $\underline{y}$ would be as follows:

$$y_1 = z_1,$$

$$y_2 = z_2 - \psi_1 y_1 = z_2 - (1 - \theta_1)y_1 = z_2 - z_1 + \theta y_1,$$

which agrees with the transformation developed in Chapter Six. In general for the $(0, 1, 1)$ model,

$$y_t = z_t - \sum_{j=1}^{t-1} \psi_j y_{t-j} = z_t - (1 - \theta_1) \sum_{j=1}^{t-1} y_{t-j},$$

which yields

$$y_t = z_t - y_{t-1} + \theta_1 y_{t-1} - \sum_{j=1}^{t-2} y_{t-j} + \theta_1 \sum_{j=1}^{t-2} y_{t-j},$$

which upon substituting

$$y_{t-1} = z_{t-1} - (1 - \theta_1) \sum_{j=1}^{t-2} y_{t-j}$$

immediately reduces to

$$y_t = z_t - z_{t-1} + \theta_1 y_{t-1}. \tag{7.18}$$

Equation (7.18) agrees with the transformation derived in the special case of the ARIMA $(0, 1, 1)$ process.

The linear equation of $\underline{L}$ and δ is

$$f_t(L, \delta) = x_{t1} L + x_{t2} \delta,$$

where

$$x_{t1} = 1, \qquad\qquad t = 1, \ldots, N,$$

and

$$x_{t2} = \begin{cases} 0 & t \le n_1 \\ 1 & t > n_1 \end{cases}.$$

In the transformed design matrix $\underline{X}^*$ corresponding to $\underline{y}$,

$$x_{tk}^* = x_{tk} - (1 - \theta_1) \sum_{j=1}^{t-1} x_{jk}^*.$$

Thus,

$$x_{11}^* = x_{11} = 1,$$

$$x_{21}^* = x_{21} - (1 - \theta_1)x_{11}^* = 1 - (1 - \theta_1) = \theta_1,$$

$$x_{31}^* = x_{31} - (1 - \theta_1)(x_{21}^* + x_{11}^*) = 1 - (1 - \theta_1)(1 + \theta_1) = \theta_1^2.$$

It is relatively easy to verify that $\underline{x}_{t1}^* = \theta_1^{t-1}$. The coefficients $\underline{x}_{t2}^*$ can similarly be shown to equal

$$\theta_1^{t-(n_1+1)} \quad \text{for} \quad \underline{t} > \underline{n}_1,$$

which agrees with the design matrix for $\underline{y}$ transformed from an ARIMA $(0, 1, 1)$ process, as shown in Chapter Six.

General Formulation of Intervention Effects

The intervention effects and their nature across time are specified by the investigator as he formulates $\underline{f}(\underline{L}, \delta_1, \delta_2, \ldots)$. Since $\underline{f}$ is a linear function of $\underline{L}, \delta_1, \delta_2, \ldots$, it can be written in matrix form

$$f(L, \delta_1, \delta_2, \ldots) = X\beta,$$

where

$$
\underline{X} = \begin{bmatrix} x_{11} & x_{12} & \cdots \\ x_{21} & x_{22} & \cdots \\ \cdot & \cdot \\ \cdot & \cdot \\ \cdot & \cdot \\ x_{N1} & x_{N2} & \cdots \end{bmatrix}
\quad \text{and} \quad
\beta = \begin{bmatrix} L \\ \delta_1 \\ \delta_2 \\ \cdot \\ \cdot \\ \cdot \end{bmatrix}
\qquad (7.19)
$$

Example 1. The $\underline{N} \times \underline{m}$ matrix $\underline{X}$ is essentially a "design matrix." It is formulated to reflect the desired behavior of intervention effects. For example, suppose that an investigator designs a time-series experiment with two interventions ($\underline{I}_1$ and $\underline{I}_2$) on a single unit; $\underline{I}_1$ occurs at $\underline{t} = 5$, and $\underline{I}_2$ at $\underline{t} = 7$. Further, he assumes that each intervention will work an immediate and constant effect, δ_1 for $\underline{I}_1$ and δ_2 for $\underline{I}_2$. Hence, the function of intervention effects would be formulated as follows:

$$
X\beta = \begin{bmatrix} 1 & 0 & 0 \\ 1 & 0 & 0 \\ 1 & 0 & 0 \\ 1 & 0 & 0 \\ 1 & 1 & 0 \\ 1 & 1 & 0 \\ 1 & 1 & 1 \\ 1 & 1 & 1 \\ 1 & 1 & 1 \\ 1 & 1 & 1 \end{bmatrix} \begin{bmatrix} L \\ \delta_1 \\ \delta_2 \end{bmatrix} .
\qquad (7.20)
$$

All three parameters may be estimated and tested by means of normal theory least-squares analysis after $\underline{z}$ has been transformed into $\underline{y}$ and $\underline{X}$ into $\underline{X}^*$ by means of the transformations (7.11) and (7.15).

Example 2. An investigator believes that an intervention will be felt at full force δ immediately at $t = 7$ but that its effect will diminish geometrically across time thereafter. Thus, the intervention effect could be formulated as follows:

$$X\beta = \begin{bmatrix} 1 & 0 \\ 1 & 0 \\ 1 & 0 \\ 1 & 0 \\ 1 & 0 \\ 1 & 0 \\ 1 & 1 \\ 1 & 1/2 \\ 1 & 1/4 \\ 1 & 1/16 \\ 1 & 1/32 \\ 1 & 1/64 \end{bmatrix} \begin{bmatrix} L \\ \delta \end{bmatrix} . \qquad (7.21)$$

The rate at which the intervention effect decays can be controlled by choice of the coefficient which is powered in the geometric series. In the above illustration, the coefficient was taken to be 1/2; a value of .9—i.e., the effect was at 90 percent strength two time units after intervention—would give a more gradual decay of the effect (1, .9, .81, .66, etc.).

It should be obvious that the design matrix can be formulated to accommodate an endless variety of intervention effects.

Computer Program

A computer program, TSX (for Time-Series Experiment), based on the methods derived above is now being developed. The basic input to this program is the data, z_t, the values of n_1 and n_2 and the indices p, d and q of the ARIMA which the data have been identified as following. The program transforms the observations by means of the psi-weights formulation into $\underline{y}$, which is in linear model form; a least-squares analysis is then performed. Output from the program comprises error variances from the least-squares analysis and the point estimates and $\underline{t}$-tests (for significance of difference from zero) for $\underline{L}$ and δ. Since $\phi_1, \ldots, \phi_p$ and $\theta_1, \ldots, \theta_q$ are unknown, the transformation and least-squares analysis is performed for all combinations of values of these parameters which lie in the invertibility-stationarity regions. Upper limits on the indices $\underline{p}$, $\underline{d}$ and $\underline{q}$ are 3, 4 and 3, respectively; nearly every process encountered in practice can be accommodated within these limits.

Unless otherwise specified, it is assumed in the program that the intervention effect is an abrupt and constant change, δ, in level of the series. This option can be overridden by entering a design matrix $\underline{X}$ which specifies the number and nature of the intervention effects across time.

A users' manual and source deck for programs CORREL and TSX are available from the first author upon request.

CHAPTER EIGHT

CONCOMITANT VARIATION IN

TIME-SERIES EXPERIMENTS

Related time-series may be observed in most systems. In economics, wholesale and retail prices are seen to vary in the same way, usually with several weeks or months separating the series. In sociology, marriage and birth rates tend to increase and decrease together. The co-variation of sunspot activity and thunderstorms was noted in Chapter One. Such series exhibit concomitant variation, which may be useful for estimating an intervention effect in one of the series. When one series is affected and others are not, a model which includes the unaffected or "concomitant" series as covariates in the mathematical expression of the affected variable may be statistically and conceptually useful. The expression of one series as a function of another will in general increase the precision of estimates of all parameters. The estimates themselves may be changed, and the logical inference of causation may be altered.

The procedure used when two or more time-series are expressed in one equation has three stages: model identification is used to determine the complexity and interrelationships across time of the time-series; parameter estimation is made

165

after suitable transformation of the statistical model into general linear form; <u>tests of hypothesis</u> about parameter values are finally made.

Design Considerations

When two series are causally linked, the alternative explanation for an intervention effect of <u>history</u> may be eliminated by using as covariate a variable not affected by the intervention. Presumably, an historical effect occurring at the time of intervention will be estimated through the regression on the covariate unless the history effect is entirely independent of the covariate.

Campbell and Ross (1968) discussed the time-series analysis of data on traffic fatalities in Connecticut between 1951 and 1960. An intervention effect was hypothesized to have occurred on January 1, 1956, based upon a "crackdown" on speeding offenders ordered by Governor Ribicoff. Inspection of the traffic fatality rate per 100,000,000 driver miles shows a large drop in the rate between December 1955 and January 1956 figures. Analysis of the Connecticut data in which seasonal variations were removed showed a statistically significant intervention effect. Similar data for nearby states—Mass. Rhode Island, N.Y., and N.J.—were examined, and similar drops in level were noted in three of the states. This evidence was presented as disconfirmation of the hypothesis that the crackdown produced the drop in the level of Connecticut fatalities (see Glass, 1968). Thus, an apparent intervention effect may be explained by an historical effect found to occur in the region at the time of intervention. Similarly, the introduction of a covariate may provide support for the intervention hypothesis by militating against rival historical explanations.

When used to control for an historical rival explanation, the covariate must be independent of the intervention. For example, the speeding crackdown in Connecticut as an intervention is unlikely to have had any effect in New Jersey. When there is a connection, the true intervention effect may be masked by the causal linkage between intervention, covariate, and dependent variable.

Inclusion of covariates may help to reduce biases due to instrumentation changes. Concomitant changes in the method of measuring both dependent variable and covariate would be expected to show changes of the same relative magnitude and direction, although this will certainly not always be true if different measurement procedures are used. Maturation effects may be similarly ameliorated when the same processes operate in both covariate and dependent variable.

In many time-series analyses seasonal components occur which may be explained by a multiplicative model, as given by Box and Jenkins (1970). An alternative is possible when covariate data are available which are of the same seasonal form as the dependent series. The regression form of the covariate in an analysis may account quite nicely for the seasonal variation. Willson (1972) examined inclusion of seasonal components which function in a manner similar to covariates.

Simple Model with One Covariate

A conceptually simple model for one time-series which includes a second time-series as a covariate or regressor was discussed by Hibbs (1974). For a dependent variable series z and covariate series g, with intervention after n_1 observations,

$$z_t = L + \gamma \tilde{g}_{t-v} + u_t, \qquad t \leqq n_1, \qquad (8.1)$$

$$z_t = L + \gamma \tilde{g}_{t-v} + \delta + u_t, \qquad n_1 < t \leqq N, \qquad (8.2)$$

where

$$\tilde{g}_t = g_t - \bar{g}.$$

The parameters are already familiar except for γ, u, and v. The term γ is the regression coefficient of g upon z. The term u is included to account for autocorrelation in z not due to g. This may take either autoregressive or moving-average form:

$$u_t = \phi u_{t-1} + a_t \qquad \text{(autoregressive)}, \qquad (8.3)$$

$$u_t = a_t - \theta a_{t-1} \qquad \text{(moving average)}. \qquad (8.4)$$

The $\underline{a}$ are independent, identically-distributed random shocks, $\underline{a} \sim \text{NID}\ (0, \sigma^2)$. The term v is the lead of $\underline{g}$ upon $\underline{z}$ or lag of $\underline{z}$ on $\underline{g}$. The value of v may be determined empirically or may be specified a priori. The estimation of v is part of the model identification procedure.

Model Identification for z and g

Model identification for the two series $\underline{z}$ and $\underline{g}$ is made in the manner described earlier for individual series. Inspection of the correlograms of $\underline{z}$ and $\underline{g}$ will yield estimates of the complexity of the ARIMA models underlying the two.

For the Hibbs model under consideration, $\underline{g}$ is a stationary first-order autoregressive process:

$$g_t = \phi_g g_{t-1} + \epsilon_t, \qquad \text{where} \qquad \epsilon_i \sim \text{NID}\ (0, \sigma_\epsilon^2). \qquad (8.5)$$

A similar inspection of the correlogram of original observations of $\underline{z}$ may yield the same result for the Hibbs model, but this is not guaranteed because of the regression of $\underline{z}$ on $\underline{g}$. Thus, the residuals of the regression provide the clue to the nature of $\underline{z}$. It can be shown (Hibbs, 1974) that when $\underline{g}$ is first-order autoregressive and the residual in $\underline{z}$ is first-order autoregressive or moving averages, the estimated residuals under ordinary least-squares regression will exhibit the autoregressive or moving averages property, respectively, although a warning is given about the noisy interference involved (Box and Jenkins, 1970). The residual estimates are given by

$$\hat{u}_t = z_t - \hat{\gamma}\tilde{g}_{t-v} - \hat{L}, \qquad (8.6)$$

where $\hat{\gamma}$ and $\hat{L}$ are least-squares estimates.

Identification of v

The estimation of the integer value for v in the Hibbs model (8.1) is based upon inspection of the cross-correlogram, the correlogram between various lags of $\underline{z}$ and $\underline{g}$. The sample cross-correlation is given by

$$r_{g_t z_t} = \left(\sum_{i=1}^{N} \frac{(g_i - \overline{g}.)(z_i - \overline{z}.)}{N} \right) \Big/ s_g s_z \qquad (8.7)$$

Note that the correlation coefficient is based on <u>contempora-neous</u> observations. The cross-correlation of <u>z</u> <u>lagged</u> on <u>g</u> by <u>k</u> units is estimated by

$$r_{z_t g_{t-k}} = \left(\sum_{i=1}^{N} \frac{(z_i - \overline{z}.)(g_{i-k} - \overline{g}.)}{N} \right) \Big/ s_g s_z . \qquad (8.8)$$

This relationship is non-symmetric, i.e., $r_{\underline{g_t z_{t+k}}} \neq r_{\underline{g_{t+k} z_t}}$, in general. When the two series $\underline{z}$ and $\underline{g}$ are related by a lag ν, then one would expect only the cross-correlation $r_{\underline{z_t g_{t-\nu}}}$ to be non-zero. By considering the observed series $\underline{z}$ and $\underline{g}$ to be realizations of a universe of realizations, parameter values may be postulated for the cross-correlations between $\underline{g}$ and $\underline{z}$ lagged $\underline{k}$ units:

$$\rho_{z_t g_{t-k}} = \frac{E(z_t - \overline{z}.)(g_{t-k} - \overline{g}.)}{\sigma_z \sigma_g} . \qquad (8.9)$$

When only $\rho_{\underline{z_t g_{t-\nu}}}$ is non-zero, its expected value is

$$\rho_{z_t g_{t-\nu}} = \frac{\gamma \sigma_g}{\sigma_g^2 + \sigma_u^2} . \qquad (8.10)$$

When only $\rho_{\underline{z_t g_{t-\nu}}}$ is non-zero, the variance error of estimate for each sample cross-correlation $r_{\underline{z_t g_{t-k}}}$, for $\underline{k} = \nu$, may be approximated by the formula due to Bartlett (1946):

$$VAR(r_{z_t g_{t-k}}) \cong (N-k)^{-1} \sum_{i=-\infty}^{\infty} \rho_{g_t g_{t+i}} \cdot \rho_{z_t z_{t+i}} .$$

Thus, the variance of estimate for sample cross-correlations depends only upon the complexity of $\underline{z}$ and $\underline{g}$. When both $\underline{z}$ and $\underline{g}$ are first-order moving-averages series, the variance becomes

$$\text{VAR}(r_{z_t g_{t-k}}) \cong (N-k)^{-1} \rho_{z_t z_{t+1}} \rho_{g_t g_{t+1}}.$$

The observed lagged cross-correlation coefficients are normally distributed about zero under the null hypothesis. The variance of $\underline{r_{z_t g_{t-k}}}$ is estimated by

$$\text{VAR}(r_{z_t g_{t-k}}) \cong (N-k)^{-1} r_{z_t z_{t+1}} r_{g_t g_{t+1}}. \tag{8.11}$$

Estimation of Parameters for
  Autoregressive Residual

Once the lag time ν is known (or estimated) and the $\underline{z}$ series is identified as a simple first-order autoregressive process, the parameters in the model can be estimated. The model is given by substituting for $\underline{u_t}$ in the expression for $\underline{z}$ (see Equations (8.1) and (8.3)):

$$z_t = L + \gamma \tilde{g}_{t-\nu} + \phi u_{t-1} + a_t. \tag{8.12}$$

Equation (8.12) may be rewritten,

$$z_t = L + \gamma \tilde{g}_{t-\nu} + \sum_{i=1}^{t-1} \phi^{t-i} a_i + a_t. \tag{8.13}$$

The following transformation results in an uncorrelated residual:

$$y_1 = z_1 \quad \text{and} \quad y_t = z_t - \phi z_{t-1}. \tag{8.14}$$

In terms of parameters,

$$y_t = (1-\phi)L + \gamma(\tilde{g}_{t-\nu} - \phi \tilde{g}_{t-\nu-1}) + a_t, \qquad t \le n_1, \tag{8.15}$$

and

$$y_t = (1-\phi)L + \gamma(\tilde{g}_{t-\nu} - \phi \tilde{g}_{t-\nu-1}) + (1-\phi)\delta + a_t, \qquad n_1 < t \le N. \tag{8.16}$$

In matrix notation, $\underline{y}$ is represented in the form of the general linear model $\underline{y} = X\beta + \underline{a}$:

$$
\begin{bmatrix} y_1 \\ y_2 \\ \cdot \\ \cdot \\ \cdot \\ y_{n_1} \\ \hline y_{n_1+1} \\ \cdot \\ \cdot \\ \cdot \\ y_N \end{bmatrix}
=
\begin{bmatrix}
1 & \tilde{g}_{1-\nu} & 0 \\
1-\phi & \tilde{g}_{2-\nu} - \phi\tilde{g}_{1-\nu} & 0 \\
\cdot & \cdot & \cdot \\
\cdot & \cdot & \cdot \\
\cdot & \cdot & \cdot \\
1-\phi & \tilde{g}_{n_1-\nu} - \phi\tilde{g}_{n_1-\nu-1} & 0 \\
\hline
1-\phi & \tilde{g}_{n_1+1-\nu} - \phi\tilde{g}_{n_1-\nu} & 1 \\
\cdot & \cdot & \cdot \\
\cdot & \cdot & \cdot \\
\cdot & \cdot & \cdot \\
1-\phi & \tilde{g}_{N-\nu} - \phi\tilde{g}_{N-\nu-1} & 1-\phi
\end{bmatrix}
\cdot
\begin{bmatrix} L \\ \gamma \\ \delta \end{bmatrix}
+
\begin{bmatrix} a_1 \\ a_2 \\ \cdot \\ \cdot \\ \cdot \\ a_{n_1} \\ \hline a_{n_1+1} \\ \cdot \\ \cdot \\ \cdot \\ a_N \end{bmatrix}.
$$

The least-squares estimates of $\underline{L}$, γ, and δ are given by

$$
\begin{bmatrix} \hat{L} \\ \hat{\gamma} \\ \hat{\delta} \end{bmatrix} = (X^TX)^{-1}X^Ty.
$$

When ϕ is not known, the usual case, iterative solutions over the range $(-1, 1)$ may be examined to determine the value which minimizes $(\underline{y} - X\hat{\beta})^T(\underline{y} - X\hat{\beta})$, the residual sum of squares.

Estimation of Parameters for
Moving Average Residual

Consider the Hibbs model with a moving averages residual component:

$$
z_t = L + \gamma\tilde{g}_{t-\nu} - \theta a_{t-1} + a_t, \qquad t \le n_1,
$$

and $\hspace{8cm}$ (8.17)

$$
z_t = L + \gamma\tilde{g}_{t-\nu} + \delta - \theta a_{t-1} + a_t, \qquad n_1 < t \le N.
$$

The simple transformation given earlier is appropriate for yielding independent errors in the transformed variable:

$$y_1 = z_1, \qquad y_t = z_t + \theta y_{t-1}. \tag{8.18}$$

This results in $\underline{y}$ being of the general linear form $\underline{y} = \underline{X}\beta + \underline{a}$:

$$
\begin{bmatrix}
y_1 \\
y_2 \\
\vdots \\
\vdots \\
y_{n_1} \\
\hline
y_{n_1+1} \\
\vdots \\
\vdots \\
y_N
\end{bmatrix}
=
\left[
\begin{array}{cccc}
1 & \tilde{g}_{1-\nu} & & 0 \\
1+\theta & \tilde{g}_{2-\nu} - \theta\tilde{g}_{1-\nu} & & 0 \\
\vdots & \vdots & & \vdots \\
\vdots & \vdots & & \vdots \\
(1+\theta)^{n_1-1} & \left(\tilde{g}_{n_1-\nu} - \displaystyle\sum_{i=1}^{n_1-1}\theta^{t-1}\tilde{g}_{i-\nu}\right) & & 0 \\
\hline
(1+\theta)^{n_1} & \tilde{g}_{n_1+1-\nu} - \displaystyle\sum_{i=1}^{n_1}\theta^{t-i}\tilde{g}_{i-\nu} & & 1 \\
\vdots & \vdots & & \vdots \\
\vdots & \vdots & & \vdots \\
(1+\theta)^{N-1} & \tilde{g}_{N-\nu} - \displaystyle\sum_{i=1}^{N-1}\theta^{N-i}\tilde{g}_{i-\nu} & (1+\theta)^{N-n_1-1} & \\
\end{array}
\right]
\begin{bmatrix}
L \\
\\
\gamma \\
\\
\delta
\end{bmatrix}
+
\begin{bmatrix}
a_1 \\
a_2 \\
\vdots \\
\vdots \\
a_{n_1} \\
\hline
a_{n_1+1} \\
\vdots \\
\vdots \\
a_N
\end{bmatrix}
$$

The value of θ is unknown; thus solutions are computed interatively over the range $(-1, 1)$ and examined for the minimum sum of squared residuals. Least-squares estimates are calculated in the usual manner:

$$
\begin{bmatrix}
\hat{L} \\
\hat{\gamma} \\
\hat{\delta}
\end{bmatrix}
= (X^T X)^{-1} X^T y. \tag{8.19}
$$

A Non-Stationary Residual

The problem of parameter estimation is increased greatly when the residual $\underline{u}$ in (8.1) and (8.2) is non-stationary. Suppose $\underline{u}$ is an ARIMA $(0, 1, 1)$ process of the form

$$u_t = \lambda \sum_{i=1}^{t-1} a_i + a_t, \tag{8.20}$$

where $\underline{a}_i$ is defined as usual and λ replaces the $1 - \theta_1$ of previous chapters for convenience. The residual $\underline{u}$ is estimated from ordinary regression of $\underline{g}$ on $\underline{z}$:

$$\hat{u}_t = z_t - \hat{\gamma}\tilde{g}_{t-\nu} - \hat{L}, \tag{8.21}$$

and the correlogram for $\underline{u}$ is computed. If $\underline{u}$ is an ARIMA $(0, 1, 1)$ process, the correlograms of original estimates and of first differences will follow the ARIMA $(0, 1, 1)$ pattern. The transformation given for such a process is

$$y_1 = z_1 \qquad \text{and} \qquad y_t = z_t - z_{t-1} + (1-\lambda)y_{t-1}.$$

This transformation produces a variable y which is in the form of the general linear model $y = X\beta + a$, as shown in (8.22). Least-squares estimates for L, γ, and δ are computed from $\beta = (X^T X)^{-1} X^T y$ for known λ. When λ is not known, the sum of squared residuals is minimized for values of λ between 0 and 2. Confidence intervals about the estimates may be computed.

An Illustrative Example

Two series were simulated to provide an example of the model identification and parameter estimation procedures for a non-stationary residual. The first series, series $\underline{g}$, was generated as an ARIMA $(0, 1, 1)$ process. The observations on $\underline{g}$ were then combined with an ARIMA $(0, 1, 1)$ series independently generated to form the dependent variable $\underline{z}$, in a form given by

$$z_t = L + \gamma g_{t-1} + \lambda \sum_{i=1}^{t-1} a_i + a_t, \qquad 1 \leq t \leq N.$$

$$
\begin{bmatrix} y_1 \\ y_2 \\ \vdots \\ y_{n_1} \\ \hline y_{n_1+1} \\ \vdots \\ y_n \end{bmatrix}
=
\begin{bmatrix}
1 & \tilde{g}_{1-\nu} & 0 \\
1-\lambda & \tilde{g}_{2-\nu} - \lambda\tilde{g}_{1-\nu} & 0 \\
\vdots & \vdots & \vdots \\
(1-\lambda)^{n_1-1} & \tilde{g}_{n_1-\nu} - \lambda \displaystyle\sum_{i=1}^{n_1-1}(1-\lambda)^i\,\tilde{g}_{n_1-\nu-i} & 0 \\
\hline
(1-\lambda)^{n_1} & \tilde{g}_{n_1+1-\nu} - \lambda \displaystyle\sum_{i=1}^{n_1}(1-\lambda)^i\,\tilde{g}_{n_1-\nu-i} & 1 \\
\vdots & \vdots & \vdots \\
(1-\lambda)^{N-1} & \tilde{g}_{N-\nu} - \lambda \displaystyle\sum_{i=1}^{N-1}(1-\lambda)^i\,\tilde{g}_{N-\nu-i} & (1-\lambda)^{N-n_1-1}
\end{bmatrix}
\cdot
\begin{bmatrix} L \\ \gamma \\ \delta \end{bmatrix}
+
\begin{bmatrix} a_1 \\ a_2 \\ \vdots \\ a_{n_1} \\ \hline a_{n_1+1} \\ \vdots \\ a_N \end{bmatrix}
\qquad (8.22)
$$

The parameter values were chosen as follows: $L = 0$, $\gamma = 1.0$, $\lambda = .5$, $\delta = 0$, $\sigma^2 = 12.7$. The intervention was deliberately left at zero to illustrate the use of the covariate in reducing an apparently significant intervention effect to non-significance. Fifty observations were generated for each series, of which forty-nine are used in the analysis. The intervention is hypothesized to occur after the twenty-fifth observation. Both series are graphed in Figure 37.

For the example, both g and z are assumed to be ARIMA (0, 1, 1) and positively related. The cross-correlogram should exhibit the property that only the true lag $v-1$ for the example— is non-zero for both original data and successive differences. The cross-correlograms for z and g are given in Table 9. The observed pattern fits the expectation for the lag value 1 of z on g. A lag 4 relationship is potentially significant, but the values for lag 1 are consistently positive and non-zero, so that v is estimated to be 1.

TABLE 9

Pre-Intervention Cross-Correlograms for the
Simulated Series, z and g, in Figure 37.

Differencing of z and g	Lag						
	0	1	2	3	4	5	6
0	-.27	.42*	-.33	-.54*	.25	-.19	-.39
1	-.23	.72**	-.27	.45*	.51*	-.07	-.47*
2	-.28	.69**	-.32	-.36	.54*	-.07	-.46*

*$p < .05$.
**$p < .01$.

Using the model,

$$z_t = L + \gamma g_{t-1} + \lambda \sum_{i=1}^{t-1} a_i + a_t, \qquad t \le n_1,$$

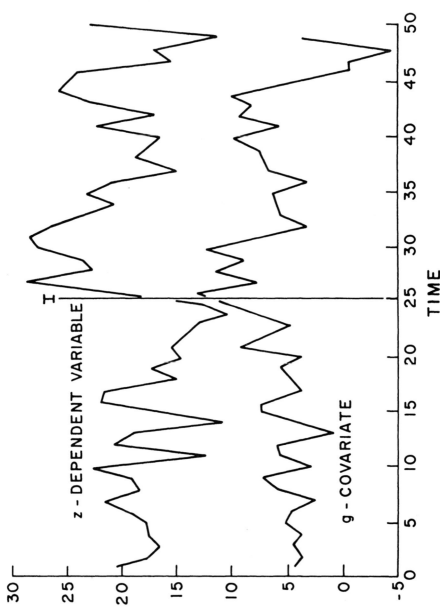

Figure 37. Graphs of two simulated time series with $L_z = 0$, $\lambda_z = .5$, $\nu = 1$, $\delta = 0$.

and

$$z_t = L + \gamma g_{t-1} + \delta + \lambda \sum_{i=1}^{t-1} a_i + a_t, \qquad n_1 < t \leq N,$$

the $\underline{z}$ series is transformed using

$$y_1 = z_1, \qquad y_t = z_t - z_{t-1} + (1-\lambda)y_{t-1}.$$

Least-squares estimates are obtained for values of λ between 0 and 2.0 for intervals of .1. The residual error is a minimum for $\lambda = .5$; least-squares estimates and their standard errors are given in Table 10.

TABLE 10

Least-Squares Estimates for Two Related Time-Series

Parameter	Estimate	Standard Error	95 Percent Confidence Interval
$\lambda_z = $ .5	.50	–	–
$L_z = 0$	4.72	2.97	(-1.28, 10.72)
$\delta = 0$	-.66	0.71	(-2.09, 0.77)
$\gamma = 1.0$	1.00	0.16	(0.68, 1.32)
$\sigma^2 = 12.7$	11.61	–	–

All estimates of parameters are close to the parameter values, and .95 confidence intervals capture the parameter values. The somewhat surprising result is shown that the estimated intervention is non-significant, even though analysis of the series without the covariate included would lead one to believe it to be large and positive.

A Combined Shock Model

The model discussed earlier is composed of separate components due to the covariate and to a random process. It was assumed that the two are statistically independent. Willson (1973) postulated a model in which this assumption is not made. He examined models which combined random shocks in the forms of moving averages or autoregressive terms. Only his work with the integrated moving averages model is presented here.

The ARIMA $(0, 1, 1)$ model was examined by Willson as a combined shock model with one covariate $\underline{g}$. The process $\underline{z}$ is given by

$$z_t - z_{t-1} = b_t - \theta_1 b_{t-1}, \tag{8.23}$$

where

$$b_t = \gamma \tilde{g}_{t-v} + a_t,$$

$$a_i \sim NID\,(0, \sigma^2), \text{ and}$$

$$COV(a_i, g_j) = 0 \text{ for all } i \text{ and } j.$$

The equation for $\underline{z}$, letting $\theta_1 = 1 - \lambda$, is given by

$$z_t = L + \gamma \tilde{g}_{t-v} + \lambda \sum_{i=1}^{t-1} (\gamma \tilde{g}_{t-v-i} + a_i) + a_t, \qquad \text{for} \quad t \leq n_1$$

and

$$z_t = L + \gamma \tilde{g}_{t-v} + \delta + \lambda \sum_{i=1}^{t-1} (\gamma \tilde{g}_{t-v-i} + a_i) + a_t, \qquad \text{for} \quad n_1 < 1 \leq N. \tag{8.24}$$

This model will be examined for identifying properties, and the form useful for the estimation of parameters will be derived.

Model Identification for a
Combined Shock Model

The examination of the correlograms for z and g and differences of them will provide evidence for the form of the processes. The series z in (8.23) will exhibit the ARIMA (0, 1, 1) pattern for successive differences. In the model presented above, the correlogram for the undifferenced data will appear to damp out only gradually. For the correlogram of first differences only the lag one autocorrelation will be significantly non-zero.

The form of g has not been specified. It seems likely, although not necessary, that processes observed to covary will have similar structures. Since one is estimating a latent residual in the z process, the nature of the z process may change by including the concomitant variable g in estimation. That is, z might be an ARIMA (0, 1, 1) process with $\theta_1 = .1$ when examined without including g, but might be estimated as an ARIMA (0, 1, 1) process with $\theta_1 = .6$ when g is included. The general theory of combining stochastic processes of this sort is unknown, but some empirical evidence provided in simulations examined by Willson (1973) suggests that for z and g both ARIMA (0, 1, 1), the θ_1 for z is approximately equal to the sum of the θ_1 for g and the θ_1 of the residual a process.

Once the forms of z and g have been identified, the lag value ν can be estimated. The forms of z and g must be known to estimate the variance error for the sample cross-correlation. The pattern of cross-correlations will be different in the combined shock model from that for the Hibbs model, since z contains a term for each g component $g_{t-\nu}, g_{t-\nu-1}, \ldots$:

$$\rho_{z_t g_i} = 0 \qquad \text{for all} \quad i > t - \nu,$$

and $\hspace{8cm}$ (8.25)

$$\rho_{z_t g_i} \neq 0 \qquad \text{for} \qquad i \leq t - \nu.$$

The actual lag value ν may be masked, since several correlations for values near ν may be large. Examination of the cross-correlations of first differences, however, will be useful. The proof is straightforward that

$$\rho_{\nabla z_t \nabla g_{t-k}} = \begin{bmatrix} 0 & k \neq \nu, \nu+1 \\ \theta\sigma_g^2/(\sigma_{\nabla z}\sigma_{\nabla g}) & k = \nu \\ -\theta\sigma_g^2/(\sigma_{\nabla z}\sigma_{\nabla g}) & k = \nu+1 \end{bmatrix} \qquad (8.26)$$

If $\underline{g}$ is an autocorrelated process, this result is complicated slightly, but the basic proof is identical. Thus, the cross-correlations of first differences will exhibit the property of non-zero correlations only at ν and $\nu-1$, which will be of opposite sign. Simulations which showed these results to hold were presented by Willson (1973). The simulations showed the cross-correlation for $\nu+1$ to be attenuated, so that in most instances only the lag ν cross-correlation of first differences is non-zero.

Estimation of Parameter in a
Combined Shock Model

The estimation of the parameters in the combined shock model in (8.24) proceeds directly after transformation of $\underline{z}$:

$$y_1 = z_1, \quad y_t = z_t - z_{t-1} + (1-\lambda)y_{t-1}. \qquad (8.27)$$

The transformed variable $\underline{y}$ is in the form of the general linear model, $\underline{y} = \underline{X}\beta + \underline{a}$, as shown in Equation (8.28).

The estimates $\hat{L}$, $\hat{\gamma}$, and $\hat{\delta}$ are computed from $\hat{\beta} = (\underline{X}^T\underline{X})^{-1}\underline{X}^T\underline{y}$ for known λ. When λ is not known the sums of squared residuals for different values of λ between 0 and 2 are examined to obtain the maximum likelihood estimate of λ; the estimates of $\underline{L}$, γ, and δ are then obtained and tested for this value of λ.

$$
\begin{bmatrix} y_1 \\ y_2 \\ \cdot \\ \cdot \\ \cdot \\ y_{n_1} \\ \hline y_{n_1+1} \\ \cdot \\ \cdot \\ \cdot \\ y_N \end{bmatrix} = \begin{bmatrix} 1 & \tilde{g}_{1-\nu} & 0 \\ (1-\lambda) & \tilde{g}_{2-\nu} & 0 \\ \cdot & \cdot & \cdot \\ \cdot & \cdot & \cdot \\ \cdot & \cdot & \cdot \\ (1-\lambda)^{n_1-1} & \tilde{g}_{n_1-\nu} & 0 \\ \hline (1-\lambda)^{n_1} & \tilde{g}_{n_1+1-\nu} & 1 \\ \cdot & \cdot & \cdot \\ \cdot & \cdot & \cdot \\ \cdot & \cdot & \cdot \\ (1-\lambda)^{N-1} & \tilde{g}_{N-\nu} & (1-\lambda)^{N-n_1-1} \end{bmatrix} \cdot \begin{bmatrix} L \\ \gamma \\ \delta \end{bmatrix} + \begin{bmatrix} a_1 \\ a_2 \\ \cdot \\ \cdot \\ \cdot \\ a_{n_1} \\ \hline a_{n_1+1} \\ \cdot \\ \cdot \\ \cdot \\ a_N \end{bmatrix}.
$$

$$(8.28)$$

Illustrative Example for a Combined Shock Model

To illustrate the procedure used in identifying and estimating parameters in the combined shock model, a simulation case due to Willson (1973) will be examined. Fifty observations of an ARIMA $(0, 1, 1)$ process were generated to represent the covariate. The series are shown in Figure 38. Parameters of the covariate are as follows: $\lambda_g = .5$, $L_g = 0$, $\sigma_g^2 = 9$. A dependent variable z was generated from the following combined shock model:

$$
z_t = 100 + g_{t-4} + .4 \sum_{i=1}^{t-1} a_i + a_t. \qquad (8.29)
$$

Thus, $L = 100$, $\gamma = 1.0$, $\lambda_z = .4$; the intervention effect δ was set at 20. The series are shown in Figure 38.

The correlograms of g and z for original observations and first differences are given in Table 11. Inspection of these suggests that both g and z are ARIMA $(0, 1, 1)$ processes. The cross-correlations of g and z, given in Table 12, follow the

182

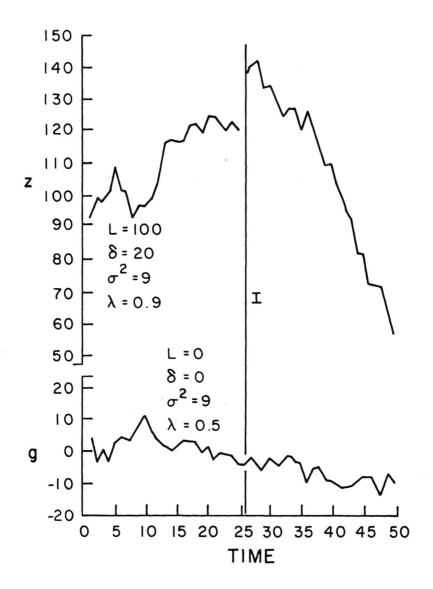

Figure 38. Fifty observations of two time series, each an ARIMA (0, 1, 1) process, related by a combined shock model. (Series $\underline{g}$ leads $\underline{z}$ by $\nu = 4$.)

TABLE 11

Autocorrelations of Two Simulation Time-Series in Figure 38,
Both Generated as ARIMA (0, 1, 1) Processes

| | Covariate | | | Dependent Variable | |
| | | Standard Error of | | | Standard Error of |
Lag	Autocorrelation	Autocorrelation	Lag	Autocorrelation	Autocorrelation
	Original Observations				
	g			z	
1	.487*	.248	1	.870*	.338
2	.318	.253	2	.787*	.346
3	-.081	.259	3	.674	.355
4	-.153	.265	4	.581	.364
5	-.203	.272	5	.504	.374
6	-.207	.279	6	.424	.385
7	-.131	.286	7	.451	.396
8	-.276	.295	8	.448	.409
	First Differences				
	$g_t - g_{t-1}$			$z_t - z_{t-1}$	
1	-.315	.228	1	-.225	.219
2	.198	.233	2	.038	.224
3	.256	.239	3	-.070	.229
4	-.029	.245	4	.104	.235
5	-.125	.251	5	-.302	.241
6	-.104	.258	6	-.323	.247
7	.115	.266	7	.036	.254
8	-.120	.274	8	.325	.262

*$p < .05$.

184

TABLE 12

Cross-Correlations of Two Simulation Time-Series,
Both ARIMA (0, 1, 1) Processes for
True Lead $v = 4$ of $\underline{g}$ on $\underline{z}$

Lag						
0	1	2	3	4	5	6
Original Observations—$\underline{z}$ and $\underline{g}$						
$-.54^*$	$-.48^*$	$-.32$	$-.18$	$.16$	$.20$	$.33$
First Differences—$z_t - z_{t-1}$ and $g_t - g_{t-1}$						
$-.20$	$-.20$	$.04$	$-.34$	$.66^*$	$-.25$	$.26$

$^*p < .05$, standard error = .20.

pattern of the combined shock model. The standard error of estimate, given with the cross-correlations, may be used to place confidence intervals about the statistics. Although several cross-correlations are significantly different from zero for the correlogram of original observations, only one cross-correlation, at $\underline{k} = 4$, is significant for the correlogram of first differences. Thus, v, the lead of $\underline{g}$ on $\underline{z}$, is taken to be 4.

The two series parameters were estimated by the least-squares procedure outlined above, utilizing the transformation (8.27). The estimates, given below, are close to the actual values:

Estimate	Standard Error	95 Percent Confidence Interval
$\hat{L}_z = 92.80$	3.66	(85.30, 100.10)
$\hat{\delta} = 16.20$	3.63	(8.90, 23.50)
$\hat{\gamma} = 0.87$	0.09	(.69, 1.05)

The 95-percent confidence intervals about each statistic capture the parameter values and none spans zero.

The maximum likelihood estimate for λ_z was $\hat{\lambda}_z = .6$; the true value was .4.

CHAPTER NINE

SPECIAL TOPICS IN THE ANALYSIS OF
TIME-SERIES EXPERIMENTS

Several topics which arise in analyzing time-series experiments deserve brief mention even though they either could not be integrated into the previous four chapters or are not at this time sufficiently developed in theory and practice to merit more extended treatment. In this chapter, a half dozen such topics will be examined.

Deterministic Drift

Occasionally, series are encountered which evidence a property not accounted for by the ARIMA $(\underline{p}, \underline{d}, \underline{q})$ formulation heretofore discussed. Processes of the basic ARIMA $(\underline{p}, \underline{d}, \underline{q})$ type may show phases of stochastic drift in level $(\underline{d} = 1)$ or slope $(\underline{d} = 2)$, but such drift by merit of being probabilistic must not persist indefinitely. However, some series appear to drift persistently in one direction in a manner that is suspiciously non-probabilistic. External considerations may sometimes suggest that this is so, e.g., when a frequency count (number of births, cases of chicken pox, etc.) is recorded on an ever-expanding population. Often, such non-stochastic, or

185

deterministic, drift can be taken care of by redefining the variable so that rate instead of frequency is observed (birth rate, chicken pox per 100,000 population, etc.). However, when the situation cannot be corrected by establishing a rate measure (e.g., a basal series for forming rates may not exist), an alteration in the basic ARIMA (p, d, q) model may be indicated. We illustrate such an alteration below in the case of the widely applicable ARIMA (0, 1, 1) model.

ARIMA (0, 1, 1) with
Deterministic Drift

Essentially the simple ARIMA (0, 1, 1) model implies that the system is subjected to periodic random shocks, a_t (with zero mean), a proportion, $1-\theta_1$, of which is absorbed into the level of the series. Data which conform to the model are such that the graph of the time-series follows an erratic, somewhat random path with slight, but no systematic, non-stochastic trends, or cycles. Data which show a systematic, persistent increase or decrease over time may indicate that the assumption of zero mean for the random variable a has been violated. For generality, the random variable portion of the model can be allowed to assume an expected value other than zero; thus, constantly "drifting" time-series—those showing a constant rise or fall over time—can be accommodated. The integrated moving averages model, ARIMA (0, 1, 1), with deterministic drift takes the following form:

$$z_1 = L + b_1 \quad \text{and} \quad z_t = L + (1-\theta_1) \sum_{i=1}^{t-1} b_i + b_t, \tag{9.1}$$

for the n_1 observations prior to the intervention, and

$$z_t = L + (1-\theta_1) \sum_{i=1}^{t-1} b_i + b_t + \delta, \tag{9.2}$$

for the n_2 observations following I, where L, θ_1 and δ are interpreted as in the basic ARIMA (0, 1, 1) model, but now b is a normal variable with variance σ_b^2 and mean equal to μ.

The parameter μ is related to the rate of ascent or descent of the time-series. It is illuminating to express $\underline{b}$ as $\mu + \underline{a}$ and manipulate (9.2) into the following form:

$$z_t = L + \mu(1-\theta_1)(t-1) + \mu + (1-\theta_1)\sum_{i=1}^{t-1} a_i + a_t. \qquad (9.3)$$

One sees by inspection of (9.3) that the time-series in (9.1) will be expected to have "drifted" nearly $\mu(1-\theta_1)\underline{t}$ units by time $\underline{t}$.

Interest centers on estimating δ in (9.2) and testing its significance. The following steps lead to the least-squares estimate of δ and the distribution of the estimate.

By setting $\underline{y}_1 = \underline{z}_1$, and $\underline{y}_t = \underline{z}_t - \underline{z}_{t-1} + \theta_1 \underline{y}_{t-1}$, the model can be written as $\underline{y} = \underline{X}\beta + \underline{a}$ where $\underline{X}$ is defined as an $\underline{N} \times 3$ matrix of weights as follows:

$$\underline{X}^T = \begin{bmatrix} 1 & 1 & \cdots & 1 & \vdots & 1 & \cdots & 1 \\ 1 & \theta_1 & \cdots & \theta_1^{n_1-1} & \vdots & \theta_1^{n_1} & \cdots & \theta_1^{N-1} \\ 0 & 0 & \cdots & 0 & \vdots & 1 & \cdots & \theta_1^{n_2-1} \end{bmatrix}.$$

β is a 3×1 vector such that $\beta^T = (\mu, L, \delta)$; and $\underline{a}$ is an $\underline{N} \times 1$ vector of random normal variables, $\underline{a}^T = (a_1, \ldots, a_N)$, the elements of which have mean μ and variance σ^2.

If θ_1 were known, simple least-squares estimates of μ, $\underline{L}$ and δ could be found from the familiar solution to the least-squares normal equations:

$$\hat{\beta} = \begin{bmatrix} \hat{\mu} \\ \hat{L} \\ \hat{\delta} \end{bmatrix} = (X^T X)^{-1} X^T y. \qquad (9.4)$$

The least-squares estimates in (9.4) each have a $\underline{t}$-distribution with $(\underline{N} - 3)\underline{df}$ when divided by appropriate estimates of their standard error. In particular,

$$\frac{\hat{\mu} - \mu}{s_a \sqrt{c^{11}}} \sim t_{N-3}, \tag{9.5}$$

$$\frac{\hat{L} - L}{s_a \sqrt{c^{22}}} \sim t_{N-3}, \tag{9.6}$$

and

$$\frac{\hat{\delta} - \delta}{s_a \sqrt{c^{33}}} \sim t_{N-3}, \tag{9.7}$$

where

$$s_a^2 = \frac{y^T y - \hat{\beta}^T X^T X \hat{\beta}}{N - 3}, \text{ and}$$

c^{jj} is the jth diagonal element of $(X^T X)^{-1}$.

All of the above operations on the linear model are made for a given value of θ_1. When θ_1 is unknown (as will generally be true), the value of s_a^2 is found for each value of θ_1 on the interval -1 to $+1$ and θ_1 is taken to be the value for which s_a^2 is minimized.

Illustrative Analysis

On January 1, 1900, the new Civil Code of the German Empire replaced the various legal statutes then in effect. The Civil Code brought about a general "tightening up" of divorce laws. The Civil Code divorce laws had been drafted in a spirit of hostility toward increasing divorce rate. (Divorce per 100,000 inhabitants in Germany rose from 8.7 in 1881 to 17.0 in 1899.) Under the new law, divorce was to be granted only in the case of guilty misconduct; divorce was not to be allowed in cases where there was mutual agreement that the marriage should be dissolved or where circumstances had thoroughly disrupted the marriage.

The divorce rate (divorce per 100,000 inhabitants) in Germany from 1881 to 1914 is graphed in Figure 39. (The data are due to Wolf, Lüke, and Hax, 1959). The data were analyzed by means of the methods developed above for the ARIMA (0, 1, 1) model with deterministic drift. The results appear in Figure 40.

189

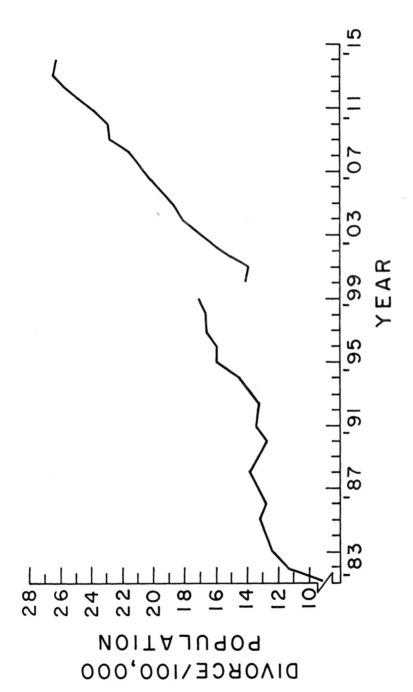

Figure 39. Divorce rate for German Empire (1881-1914).

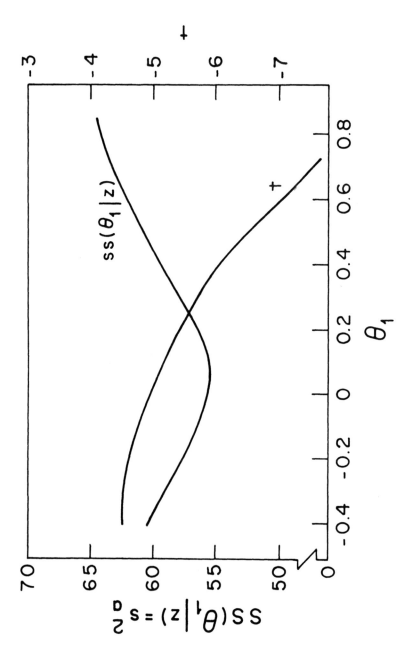

Figure 40. Results of analysis for change in level for the German divorce data.

The value of θ_1 for which $\underline{SS}(\theta_1 | \underline{z})$ is minimized is approximately .05. The value of the $\underline{t}$-statistic, $\underline{t} = \hat{\delta}/s_{\hat{\delta}}$, for $\theta_1 = .05$ is less than -4.00, indicating that the downward shift in the time-series at the year 1900 is highly statistically significant.

For a more detailed analysis of this example, see Glass, Tiao, and Maguire (1971).

Change in Deterministic Drift

The ARIMA (0, 1, 1) model with deterministic drift can be modified so that a parameter descriptive of a change in μ, the drift of the series, is incorporated. We shall see how it is then possible to estimate all of the parameters in the model for a given value of θ_1 and test hypotheses about each. Finally, the likelihood distribution of θ_1 can be found for a set of $\underline{n}$ observations for use in inferential analyses of δ, μ, and the change in μ.

Let $\underline{z}_t$ denote the observation of a series at time $\underline{t}$. The following model is proposed for the $\underline{n}_1$ observations prior to the intervention $\underline{I}$ (cf. Equation (9.3)):

$$z_t = L + (1-\theta_1) \sum_{i=1}^{t-1} b_i + b_t, \qquad (9.8)$$

where $\underline{b}_i \sim NID(\mu, \sigma_b^2)$. This is identical to the model in (9.1). We want the post-$\underline{I}$ model to reflect the impact of the intervention in two ways: 1) a change in level of δ; 2) a change in μ of Δ. Thus, the following model is put forward as descriptive of the behavior of the series for the $\underline{n}_2$ observations following $\underline{I}$:

$$z_t = L + (1-\theta_1) \sum_{i=1}^{t-1} (b_i+\Delta) + (b_t+\Delta) + \delta, \qquad (9.9)$$

where δ is the change of level of the series between times $\underline{n}_1$ and $\underline{n}_1 + 1$ and Δ is the change in the mean of the random errors between these two times. Prior to $\underline{I}$, the series drifts (on the average) at a rate of $(1-\theta_1)\mu$ units (up or down depending on the sign of μ) for each unit of time; after $\underline{I}$, the series drifts $(1-\theta_1)(\mu+\Delta)$ units on the average for each unit of time.

As before, a series of $\underline{n}_1 + \underline{n}_2$ observations of $\underline{z}$ is made; these values of $\underline{z}_t$ are then transformed for a given value of θ_1 by the usual ARIMA $(0, 1, 1)$ transformation:

$$y_1 = z_1;$$

$$y_t = z_t - z_{t-1} + \theta_1 y_{t-1}, \quad \text{for} \quad t = 2, \ldots, N. \qquad (9.10)$$

The $\underline{N}$ by 1 vector of $\underline{y}$'s can be expressed as a linear model in terms of the design matrix $\underline{X}$, the vector of parameters $\beta^T = (\mu, \Delta, L, \delta)$ and the vector, $\underline{a}$, of observations of a random normal variable with mean 0 and variance σ^2:

$$y = X\beta + a$$

$$
\begin{bmatrix} y_1 \\ y_2 \\ \cdot \\ \cdot \\ \cdot \\ y_{n_1} \\ \hline y_{n_1+1} \\ \cdot \\ \cdot \\ \cdot \\ y_N \end{bmatrix}
=
\begin{bmatrix}
1 & 0 & 1 & 0 \\
1 & 0 & \theta_1 & 0 \\
\cdot & \cdot & \cdot & \cdot \\
\cdot & \cdot & \cdot & \cdot \\
\cdot & \cdot & \cdot & \cdot \\
1 & 0 & \theta_1^{n_1-1} & 0 \\
\hline
1 & 1 & \theta_1^{n_1} & 1 \\
\cdot & \cdot & \cdot & \cdot \\
\cdot & \cdot & \cdot & \cdot \\
\cdot & \cdot & \cdot & \cdot \\
1 & 1 & \theta_1^{N-1} & \theta_1^{n_2-1}
\end{bmatrix}
\begin{bmatrix} \mu \\ \Delta \\ L \\ \delta \end{bmatrix}
+
\begin{bmatrix} a_1 \\ a_2 \\ \cdot \\ \cdot \\ \cdot \\ \hline \cdot \\ \cdot \\ \cdot \\ \cdot \\ a_N \end{bmatrix}
$$

For a single value of θ_1, the least-squares estimates of the parameters in β are obtained from the equation

$$\hat{\beta} = \begin{bmatrix} \hat{\mu} \\ \hat{\Delta} \\ \hat{L} \\ \hat{\delta} \end{bmatrix} = (X^TX)^{-1}X^Ty. \qquad (9.11)$$

The "residual variance" in fitting the model to the observations $\underline{z}_t$ is given by

$$s_a^2 = \frac{(y-X\hat{\beta})^T(y-X\hat{\beta})}{N-4} . \tag{9.12}$$

The following distribution statements about the estimates of the parameters follow from the assumption of normality of $\underline{a}_t$ and traditional inferential theory:

$$\frac{\hat{\mu} - \mu}{s_a \sqrt{c^{11}}} \sim t_{N-4} , \qquad \frac{\hat{\Delta} - \Delta}{s_a \sqrt{c^{22}}} \sim t_{N-4} ,$$

$$\tag{9.13}$$

$$\frac{\hat{L} - L}{s_a \sqrt{c^{33}}} \sim t_{N-4} , \qquad \frac{\hat{\delta} - \delta}{s_a \sqrt{c^{44}}} \sim t_{N-4} ,$$

where

$$\underline{c}^{jj} \text{ is the jth diagonal element of } (\underline{X}^T\underline{X})^{-1}.$$

The above calculations are performed for a single value of θ_1 which is restricted to the open interval $(-1, +1)$. Since θ_1 is generally unknown, information regarding its likely values must be found from the data themselves by determining the minimum value of $\underline{s}_a^2$ as a function of θ_1.

Illustrative Analysis

The data which comprise the total percentage of students by year in Ireland who passed intermediate and senior level examinations between 1879 and 1971 provide a time series for illustration of the change in deterministic drift analysis. In a paper by Airasian, Kellaghan, Madaus, and Ryan (1972) it is noted that from 1879 until 1924 payment of monies to the Intermediate Board of Education for Ireland was dependent upon the number of students attempting and passing the Results Examinations, essentially a performance contract program. After 1925 the Department of Education of the Republic of Ireland administered the Leaving Certificate Examination, the performance contracting having been abandoned. The break between 1924 and 1925 provides the point of intervention, allowing an analysis of percentage of pupils passing their examinations under performance contracting and under a standardized program.

Inspection of the correlogram of pre-intervention differences indicated that the ARIMA (0, 1, 1) model was appropriate. The data are presented graphically in Figure 41, with the point of intervention noted. The likelihood distribution was plotted against all possible values of θ_1 (Figure 42, part $\underline{A}$); the maximum likelihood estimate of θ_1 is about .40. Graphs of the distribution of $\hat{\delta}$, the estimator for change of level due to intervention, and of the $\underline{t}$-statistic (df = 89) for $\hat{\delta}$, are given for some values of θ_1 in Figure 42, part $\underline{B}$. Note that for the maximum likelihood estimate of θ_1, $\hat{\delta}$ is not statistically different from zero ($\underline{p}$ > .35), implying no change in level of percentage of students passing the examinations due to termination of performance contracting in 1925.

The drift parameter estimator, $\hat{\mu}$, and the $\underline{t}$-statistic for $\hat{\mu}$ are given in Figure 42, part $\underline{C}$. Recall that μ is the drift in the series which exists before intervention. For maximum likelihood estimate $\theta_1 = .4$, $\hat{\mu}$ is not statistically different from zero ($\underline{p}$ > .5), implying no deterministic drift existed for percentage of students passing under performance contracting.

The change in drift after intervention estimated by $\hat{\Delta}$, is given, along with the $\underline{t}$-statistic for $\hat{\Delta}$, in Figure 42, part $\underline{D}$. In the ARIMA (0, 1, 1) model with drift, drift after intervention is given by a parameter $\mu + \Delta$. Note that for $\theta_1 = .4$ the $\underline{t}$-statistic for $\hat{\Delta}$ is $\underline{t} = 1.3$ ($\underline{p}$ < .10, one-tailed), indicating a marginally significant change in drift (from none before $\underline{I}$ to small positive drift after).

Interpretation of the results, given by Airasian et al., suggests that the percentage of students passing, controlled by the Intermediate Board of Education for Ireland prior to 1925, was kept constant, probably by manipulating standards, so as to maintain a quota necessary to economize fees and maintain efficiency of operation. The change in level noted after 1925 reflects the standardization of examinations implemented by the Irish Board of Education. No financial management limitations dictated controls over the percentage of students passing after 1925, suggested by the drift in the series after 1925.

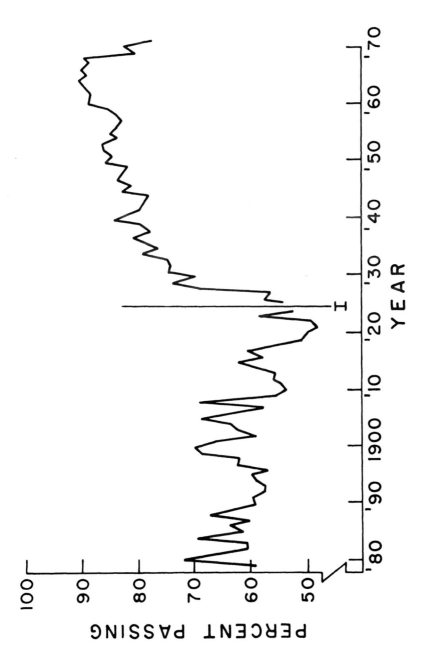

Figure 41. Percent of students passing intermediate and senior level examinations in Ireland (1879–1971). ($n_1 = 45$; $n_2 = 47$.)

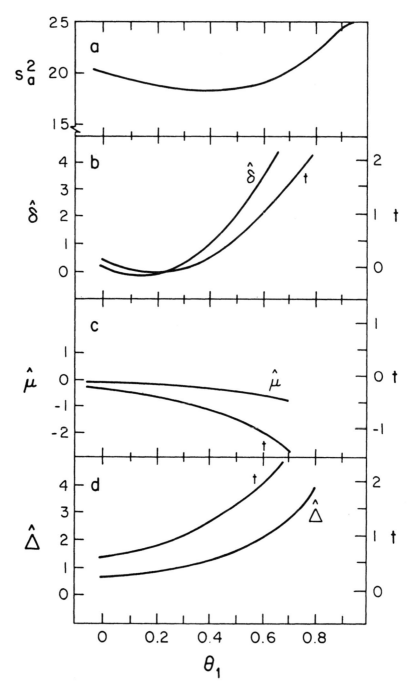

Figure 42. Results of analysis for change in level, drift, and change in drift for the Ireland examination data.

Testing Change in Variance

An intervention could affect a series by altering its variance independently of changes produced in level and direction of drift. Consider, for example, the data which appear in Figure 18 of Chapter Three. The "word-association relatedness" scores on the schizophrenic patient appear to have been uninfluenced in any respect by the administration of a tranquilizer from the 61st to the 120th days. However, introduction of electroshock on the 121st day worked simultaneous effects on level and variability of the series. Our purpose in this section is to indicate how error variances may be estimated individually for the pre-I and post-I series, and how the difference between the estimates may be tested for statistical significance.

Assume that a time-series prior to intervention, I, is of the general form

$$z_t = f(a_1, \ldots, a_{t-1}) + a_t, \qquad t = 1, \ldots, n_1, \qquad (9.14)$$

where f is some function of a_i involving m parameters—f could be ARIMA (p, d, q) in the most general case—and $a_i \sim NID\,(0, \sigma_1^2)$.

Further assume that following I,

$$z_t = f(a_1, \ldots, a_{t-1}) + a_t, \qquad t = n_1 + 1, \ldots, N, \qquad (9.15)$$

where

$$a_i \sim NID\,(0, \sigma_2^2).$$

Assumptions (9.14) and (9.15) typify the general case of I altering the variance of a but not the basic model f. The question of the existence of a δ or μ is beside the point of this discussion and can be dealt with independently of the problem of testing $\sigma_1^2 = \sigma_2^2$.

By the usual procedures one fits a model to the series, i.e., he determines f. By the application of this model to the observed data, "fitted" or estimated values, $\hat{z} = X\hat{\beta}$, of the series (or some transformation of it) are obtained; the estimated errors, $\hat{\underline{a}}$, can then be determined <u>via</u> $\hat{\underline{a}} = \underline{z} - \hat{\underline{z}}$.[*] If this process is applied separately to the pre-$\underline{I}$ and post-$\underline{I}$ data, one obtains estimated errors with the following well-known properties:

$$s_1^2 = \left(\sum_{i=1}^{n_1} \hat{a}_i^2\right) \Big/ (n_1 - m) \quad \text{is distributed as} \quad \sigma_1^2 \frac{X_{(n_1-m)}^2}{(n_1-m)},$$

$$s_2^2 = \left(\sum_{i=n_1+1}^{N} \hat{a}_i^2\right) \Big/ (n_2 - m) \quad \text{is distributed as} \quad \sigma_2^2 \frac{X_{(n_2-m)}^2}{(n_2-m)}.$$

In general, $\underline{m}$ will equal $\underline{p} + \underline{q}$.

Under the null hypothesis that $\sigma_1^2 = \sigma_2^2$, $\underline{s}_1^2 / \underline{s}_2^2$ is distributed as a central $\underline{F}$ with $\underline{df} = \underline{n}_1 - \underline{m}$ and $\underline{n}_2 - \underline{m}$.

Testing Changes in the Model

An intervention could change the basic nature of a stochastic model (e.g., from ARIMA (0, 1, 1) to ARIMA (0, 2, 2) as well as merely change the level or direction of drift of a time-series. Such changes in the model are probably not of as great interest as level or direction changes, but they can be tested in those instances in which they may be meaningful. The methods of testing are indicated in the following paragraphs.

Assume that the model for the pre-$\underline{I}$ data has been correctly determined—this will generally require a relatively large number of time points (50 to 100 or more) before the model is identified with confidence. When the model has been correctly determined, the estimated errors, $\hat{\underline{a}}_i$, for the pre-$\underline{I}$ data, should show the properties of a set of observations of independent random normal variables with zero expectation: namely, they should average near zero—though not exactly zero—"nearness" being measured in units of the standard deviation of the estimated errors, and the correlogram of the $\hat{\underline{a}}$'s should show all lag

---

[*]The variance of estimated errors is obtained routinely in the least-squares solution for intervention effects.

correlations within sampling error of zero (standard error of all r_k is approximately equal to $1/\sqrt{n_1}$; see Box and Jenkins, 1970, p. 35).

The possible change in the model due to $\underline{I}$ is now investigated by applying the correctly fitted pre-$\underline{I}$ model to the post-$\underline{I}$ data and obtaining the corresponding estimated errors. If these estimated errors show significant departure from the assumption made about random errors (e.g., if their mean is significantly non-zero or if their correlogram shows some significant deviations[*] from zero lag correlations), the departures are attributed to a change in the model from pre-$\underline{I}$ to post-$\underline{I}$.

For example, suppose that a time-series process has been reliably determined to be ARIMA $(0, 1, 1)$ with parameter value $\theta_1 = 0.5$ prior to $\underline{I}$. The transformation $\underline{y}_t = \underline{z}_t - \underline{z}_{t-1} + 0.5\underline{y}_{t-1}$ is then applied to the post-$\underline{I}$ data. The resulting $\underline{y}_t$'s will be of the form $(0.5)^{t-1}\underline{L} + \underline{a}_t$ provided that the post-$\underline{I}$ model is also ARIMA $(0, 1, 1)$ with $\theta_1 = 0.5$. The parameter $\underline{L}$, and any intervention parameters are estimated via least-squares analysis using the pre-$\underline{I}$ model with $\theta_1 = 0.5$. This least-squares analysis will yield the estimated errors, $\hat{\underline{a}}_i$. The mean and correlogram of these estimated errors is then investigated to determine whether they are consistent with the assumption that $\underline{a}_i \sim \text{NID}(0, \sigma^2)$ which must hold if the pre-$\underline{I}$ and post-$\underline{I}$ model are identical. If, for example, the lag 1 autocorrelation of the estimated errors equals $-.80$ for the one hundred post-$\underline{I}$ observations, then strong evidence exists for concluding that $\underline{I}$ has altered the model since $\sigma_{\underline{r}_1} = 1/\sqrt{n_2} = .10$.

The above method will detect changes in the basic model or changes in the values of the parameters of the basic model (i.e., the ϕ's and θ's).

---

[*]For this purpose, a chi-square test on the entire set of autocorrelations is recommended (see Box and Jenkings, 1970, pp. 290-291).

When to Intervene

If the investigator is free to choose the point in time at which to intervene, is there any reason to prefer one point of intervention to another? There are several facts which indicate that this choice does affect the precision of estimates and the power to detect real differences from zero in the intervention effect. For the ARIMA $(0, 1, 1)$ case, a proof is possible which shows that the shortest confidence interval about δ, the change-in-level effect of intervention, occurs when n_1, the number of observations before intervention, equals n_2, the number of observations after intervention.

Proof:

$$\sigma_{\hat{\delta}}^2 = \frac{\sigma^2(1-\theta_1^2)(1-\theta_1^{2N})}{(1-\theta_1^{2n_1})(1-\theta_1^{2n_2})}$$

$$= \sigma^2 G^{-1},$$

(9.16)[*]

where

$$G = \frac{1}{(1-\theta_1^2)(1-\theta_1^{2N})}(1 - \theta_1^{2n_1})(1 - \theta_1^{2n_2}).$$

For $-1 < \theta_1 < 1$, $0 < G < 1$. Hence, G attains a maximum and G^{-1} attains a minimum on the interval.

Differentiating G with respect to n_1, one obtains

$$\frac{\partial}{\partial n_1} G = \frac{\partial}{\partial n_1} \frac{1}{K}(1 - \theta_1^{2n_1})(1 - \theta_1^{2n_2}),$$

where

$$K = \frac{1}{(1-\theta_1^2)(1-\theta_1^{2N})}.$$

---

[*]See Box and Tiao (1965, formula 3.5).

$$\frac{\partial G}{\partial n_1} = -2K^{2n_1} \lg \theta_1 \left[1 - \theta_1^{2(N-n_1)}\right] + K\left[1 - \theta_1^{2n_1}\right] \cdot \left[2\theta_1^{2(N-n_1)} \lg \theta_1\right],$$

$$= 2K\theta_1^{2n_1} \lg \theta_1 + 2K\theta_1^{2(N-n_1)} \lg \theta_1,$$

$$= 0 \quad \text{at the maximum.}$$

Hence, $\theta_1^{n_1} = \theta_1^{(N-n_1)}$ at the maximum point, which implies that $\underline{n}_1 = \underline{N} - \underline{n}_1$.

Thus, when $\underline{n}_1 = \underline{n}_2$, $\underline{G}$ is maximized which implies that $\sigma_{\hat{\delta}}^2$ is minimized. A further consequence of equal $\underline{n}$'s before and after intervention is the general robustness of the $\underline{t}$-test with respect to violations of homogeneous error variances of pre- and post-intervention samples.

Padia* showed that in the case of the ARIMA (1, 0, 0) process, the variance error of the estimated intervention effect δ is minimized when

$$n_1 - n_2 = \frac{-\phi_1^2}{(1-\phi_1)^2} . \tag{9.17}$$

Unlike the ARIMA (0, 1, 1) case, the optimal division of $\underline{N}$ into $\underline{n}_1$ and $\underline{n}_2$ in the first-order autoregressive model (ARIMA (1, 0, 0)) depends on the value of an unknown parameter. If $\phi_1 = 0$—in which case the analyses developed in this text reduce to the independent groups $\underline{t}$-test—the optimal choice is $\underline{n}_1 = \underline{n}_2$. As ϕ_1 departs from zero, $\underline{n}_2$ should be increased as $\underline{n}_1$ is decreased, according to (9.17). No comparably simple results have been obtained for other ARIMA models.

Since power increases with sample size, ordinarily, as many observations as possible are desired. In some cases, however, the expenditure involved in obtaining observations becomes unjustified. For ARIMA (0, 1, 1) it can be shown that $\sigma_{\hat{\delta}}^2 \rightarrow \sigma^2(1-\theta_1^2)$ as $\underline{N} \rightarrow \infty$, where $\underline{N}$ is the total number of observations. Note that the standard error of $\hat{\delta}$ does not converge to

---

*W. L. Padia, personal communication, 1974.

zero as $\underline{N}$ increases without bound, unlike the estimate of the population mean via independent random samples, for example. This is an important result, since it reveals that beyond a certain point, extending the number of observations of a time-series does not significantly improve the estimation of $\hat{\delta}$. (The point may be seen by examining the expression for $\hat{\delta}$ in Box and Tiao, 1965, p. 184, in which $\hat{\delta}$ is given as an exponentially weighted average of the observations $\underline{z}$.)

For values of θ_1 moderately above -1, the weight given to an observation a few points distant from the intervention in determining $\hat{\delta}$ is very small. In general, extending a time-series by a large number of observations will improve estimation of the nature of the process (e.g., whether it is ARIMA (0, 1, 1) or ARIMA (0, 2, 2)), but the extension will not greatly improve the estimate of the intervention effect. If reasonably credible a priori knowledge exists concerning the nature of the time-series process into which intervention will be made, the standard error of $\hat{\delta}$ may be calculated using $\sigma^2 (\underline{X}^T \underline{X})^{-1}$ for various values of $\underline{n}_1$ and $\underline{n}_2$ to determine an efficient sample size for cost limitations.

Cyclic ("Seasonal") Data

A variable observed over a period of several months or weeks is apt to show seasonal cycles (e.g., traffic flow, frequency of colds, absences from school). For example, the time-series of Siberian thunderstorms in Figure 1 of Chapter One shows a clear cyclic trend with an eleven-year cycle. None of the models examined in this text would account for regular seasonal cycles in a series.

A few "stop-gap" solutions to the problems presented by seasonality in time-series experiments have been tried. Suppose a series follows a twelve-month cycle and that data by month for several years are available. If the seasonality is of a particularly simple form, it might be removed by deviating each observation around the average score for like months, e.g., subtract from January 1961 the average for all Januaries observed in the series. Although serviceable (see Glass, 1968), this technique strikes us as being neither very elegant nor very safe. For instance, what manner of interdependence among the observations is introduced when only four years' data

are available? The answer is uncertain, but clearly the deviation scores for like months will possess a negative intercorre-
lation. A more sophisticated means of coping with seasonality
involves a concomitant variable. If a concomitant variable can
be found which has the same cycle length as the primary
dependent variable, then the application of covariance analysis
as indicated in Chapter Eight is likely to remove the seasonality, as well as increase power through reduction of error variance.

We suspect, however, that seasonal processes should be
dealt with by means of Box and Jenkins's multiplicative models
(1970, Chapter 9). We will consider briefly the simplest seasonal model which still shows the multiplicative feature.

Suppose that a seasonal series possesses a cycle of
known length $s = 12$. Assume that the difference between any
two points in the series lagged by twelve units is a first-order
moving averages process:

$$z_t - z_{t-12} = (1 - \theta_1^* B^{12}) e_t.$$

The error component e_t represents the random shock to the
system at time t. This random shock can be further decomposed
by assuming that it bears a first-order moving averages relationship to the preceding time point:

$$e_t = (1 - \theta_1 B) a_t.$$

The joint multiplicative model would take the following
form:

$$z_t - z_{t-12} = (1 - \theta_1^* B^{12})(1 - \theta_1 B) a_t. \tag{9.18}$$

Techniques of identification of multiplicative models have
been explicated by Box and Jenkins (1970, Chapter 9). The
estimation and testing of intervention effects could proceed
along the following lines. Models like that one in (9.18) could
be transformed into psi-weight form (see Chapter Seven). Then
the y-transformation of Chapter Seven could be applied to

transform the data into the form of the general linear model, from which estimates and tests of any intervention effects may be readily obtained. Our work is progressing along these lines, but is not sufficiently developed to report.

APPENDIX A

SPECTRAL ANALYSIS OF TIME-SERIES

This appendix on spectral analysis is intended as a brief introduction to orient the reader to spectral terminology (or the spectre of terminology) and appropriate source materials for further study.

The work of this book has emphasized the analysis of time-series experiments with few observations. Spectral analysis is particularly suited to those areas of research which involve continuous or nearly continuous monitoring of a variable or set of variables across time. Granger and Hatanaka (1964) suggest that the amount of data necessary before "it becomes sensible to attempt to estimate the spectrum would seem to be about 100. $N = 200$ can be thought of as a desirable minimum, in general, although crude spectra have occasionally been estimated with N as low as 80." (p. 61.)

The important distinction of spectral analysis is that it treats time-series data with another metaphor, namely, cyclic variation. Much has been learned in other sciences merely by describing the fluctuations of a series, its cycles and component parts. For example, an astronomer may look at the brightness of a variable star on six hundred successive days (Whittaker and Robinson, 1924) and find that the data are

205

essentially periodic. He may begin by assuming that all the fluctuations in the data can be explained by one simple sine curve of appropriate phase and amplitude. If this were true, the subtraction of such a curve would leave an independent random series ("white noise") as a remainder. However, if the remainder also appears periodic, the astronomer can repeat the process until the remainder does look like white noise. In fact, for the brightness problem Whittaker and Robinson found that their data could be described by two periodic terms with periods of twenty-four and twenty-nine days. Of course, it still remains to interpret these two components fluctuations by constructing a model for understanding the physical processes of brightness fluctuations.

There is an important distinction between continuous monitoring and periodic sampling even when the total number of data points is large. Cycles of major importance in the time series will depend upon the choice of time unit. Figure A-1 is an indication of this point.

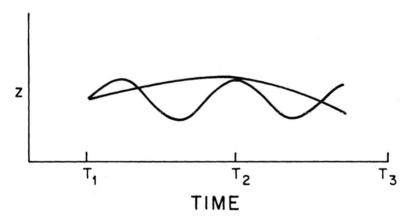

Figure A-1. Choice of time unit and its effect on the determination of major cycles in the series.

The series may have the continuous nature indicated by the solid line, but sampling at times T_1, T_2, T_3, etc., will lead to the conclusion that the series takes the form shown by the dotted line. In the interrupted time-series experimental design this choice of time unit may result in an ephemeral effect of an intervention going unnoticed.

It is well-known that any periodic series with period P can be approximated by a sum of sine curves with periods P, $P/2$, $P/3$, etc. However, the problem of describing time series is not as easily solved because series usually manifest a mixture of regularity and unpredictability. In fact, any series can be decomposed into two uncorrelated parts, a deterministic and non-deterministic component. The deterministic component corresponds to a linear cyclic process, i.e., a weighted sum of sine and cosine functions of different frequencies called a Fourier representation. The non-deterministic component contains moving average, autoregressive, and mixed processes. Spectral analysis is an extension of Fourier analysis to the non-deterministic component to determine the major frequency bands in the non-deterministic component. Although stationarity is usually assumed, non-stationarity can be dealt with either by removing trend or by considering it to be a long cycle extending twice the period of the data at hand (see Figure A-2).

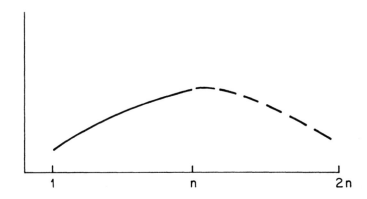

Figure A-2. Trend in the data can be considered as a long cycle extending twice the period of the observed data.

Whittaker and Robinson (1924) found the frequencies of the two basic fluctuations of star brightness data by using a method called the periodogram invented by Schuster in 1898. The periodogram was the first attempt at extending Fourier series to non-deterministic series. Tukey (1967, p. 25) has called it "one of the most misleading devices I know." The method consists of looking for peaks in a function called the "intensity" of the observations. Peaks in this function occur where the data contain a periodic term. Schuster calculated the sum of the squared coefficients in a Fourier expansion of the time series, $\underline{X_t}$,

$$I_n(\omega) = \frac{1}{n}\left[\left(\sum_{t=1}^{n} X_t \sin \omega t\right)^2 + \left(\sum_{t=1}^{n} X_t \cos \omega t\right)^2\right],$$

where $\underline{n}$ is the number of observations and $\omega = 2\pi/\underline{P}$, where $\underline{P}$ is the period of a fluctuation presumed to be in the series. $\underline{I_n}(\omega)$ will have a peak at $\omega = \omega_0$ if the data contain a periodic term of period $2\pi/\omega_0$, and subsidiary peaks at $\omega = \omega_0 + (2\pi\omega_0/\underline{n})$.

Despite the fact that the periodogram has proved useful for some data, its usefulness is severely limited. Hannan (1960) showed that $I_n(\omega)$ does not give a consistent estimate of the spectrum, nor is the estimate at all smooth.[*] Tukey (1967, p. 25) said of the periodogram,

> If we dealt with problems involving the superposition of a few simple periodic phenomena, as do astronomers inter-ested in binary stars and related problems, we can learn much from the periodogram. Sadly, however, almost no one else has this kind of data.

Tukey also pointed out that if the time series is noise-like, the stability of an individual periodogram value is distributed as chi square with two degrees of freedom and its standard deviation is equal to its average and is therefore "horribly unstable" (p. 26).

To find which band of frequencies contribute a major determining portion of the non-deterministic oscillation of a series, a measure is needed. For the deterministic component

---

[*] $E(\underline{I_n}(\omega)) = 2\pi\underline{f}(\omega)$ where $\underline{f}(\omega)$ is the power spectrum (defined later in the text) of the process. Also $\underline{\text{var}}[I_n(\omega)] \cong [2\underline{f}(\omega)]^2 + 0(\underline{n}^{-1})$ and so $\underline{\text{var}}[I_n(\omega)] \to 0$ as $\underline{n} \to \infty$. Also $\underline{\text{cov}}[I_n(\omega_1)I_n(\omega_2)] = 0(\underline{n}^{-1})$ at most for $\omega_1 \neq \omega_2$ and so the periodogram does not pro-vide a smooth estimate.

209

this measure is the amount contributed to the overall variance of
the frequency component being considered. In a series which is
assumed to contain a periodic component of frequency ω, this
term is the reduction of variance when the component is
removed. The reduction in variance due to removing frequency
component ω is called the <u>power spectral distribution</u> function,
denoted $\underline{F}(\omega)$. $\underline{F}(\omega)$ is then defined by $\underline{F}(\omega_2) - \underline{F}(\omega_1)$ = the amount
of total variance attributable to the <u>band</u> of frequencies between
ω_1 and ω_2. This function can be understood graphically by considering a purely deterministic series composed of only two frequencies, ω_1 and ω_2.

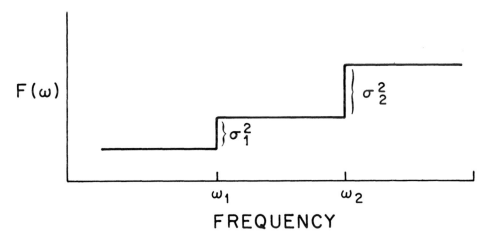

Figure A-3. The power spectral distribution function for a
process which is exactly the sum of two periodic functions of
frequencies ω_1 and ω_2.

A jump in $\underline{F}(\omega)$ corresponds to a sudden peak in its slope. The
slope of $\underline{F}(\omega)$ is called the <u>spectrum</u> and is written $\underline{f}(\omega)$. Note
that $\underline{f}(\omega)$ is analogous to the Schuster periodogram since it has
peaks at frequencies which contribute to the total variance. In
a small frequency band, $\underline{d\omega}$, $\underline{f}(\omega)\underline{d\omega}$ is the contribution to the
total variance by the frequency band ω to $\omega + \underline{d\omega}$.

Fourier Transforms

An important transformation for generalizing Fourier representations of discrete deterministic process is the Fourier

transform. For a continuous, aperiodic function, $\underline{s}(t)$, the Fourier transform $\underline{S}(f)$ is defined as

$$S(f) = \int_{-\infty}^{\infty} s(t)e^{-j2\pi ft}dt,$$

where

$$j = \sqrt{-1}.$$

Note that a real series, $\underline{s}(t)$, is transformed to a complex quantity.

It turns out that the spectrum, $\underline{f}(\omega)$ of a time series is the Fourier transform of the autocovariance function.

Smoothing and Window Carpentry

The problems with the periodogram turn out to be general problems with the stability of the average value of any quadratic form coming from a stationary process with power spectrum $\underline{F}(\omega)$. If $\underline{Q}$ is a quadratic form then it can be shown that

$$ave[Q] = \int q(\omega)dF(\omega)$$

where $\underline{q}(\omega)$ must be a polynomial in $\underline{cos}\ \omega$ of degree less than the number of data points. Tukey (1967) said that, "as a consequence, all but a finite number of frequencies must contribute to any quadratic function of the data. Though we may wish to concentrate on only frequencies of a certain band, nearly all other frequencies will leak in to some degree. The best that we can do is to make $\underline{q}(\omega)$ large where we wish to concentrate and small everywhere else." (p. 28.) A function with those properties is called a spectral window. The use of a window results in reducing the variance of the spectral estimate, and is therefore called smoothing. Several windows are in current use, the most common due to Bartlett and Parzen (see Tukey, 1967).

Spectral Estimates of Smoothed Data

All spectral estimates are of the form

$$f(\omega_j) = \frac{1}{2\pi}\left\{\lambda_0 C_0 + 2\Sigma\lambda_k C_k \cos \omega_j k\right\},$$

where $\omega_j = (\pi j/n)$, $j = 0, 1, 2, \ldots, n$, and C_k are estimated sample autocovariances. A common choice of the weights, λ_k, is the Tukey-Hanning estimate which uses the weights

$$\lambda_k = \frac{1}{2}\left[1 + \cos\frac{\pi k}{m}\right].$$

The integer m represents the number of frequency bands for which the spectrum is estimated. Computer programs are available for the IBM 650 (known as Statisan II and III), the IBM 707, 709, 7090, and the CDC 1604. The integer m is at the user's control, though in practice m should rarely be larger than $n/6$.

The $(100 - \alpha)$-percent confidence band for these spectral estimates is given for all j by

$$T_\alpha(m, n)\hat{f}(\omega_j), \quad T'_\alpha(m, n)\hat{f}(\omega_j)$$

The values $T_\alpha(m, n)$ and $T'_\alpha(m, n)$ for the Tukey-Hanning estimates follow chi-square distributions. $T_\alpha(m, n)$ is

$$\frac{\chi^2_{(100-\alpha)}(k)}{k},$$

and $T'_\alpha(m, n)$ is

$$\frac{\chi^2_\alpha(k)}{k},$$

where $\chi^2_\beta(s)$ is the β-percent value of χ^2 with s degrees of freedom, and $k = 2n/m$. See Granger and Hatanaka (1964, p. 62ff) for a more complete discussion with examples.

Cross Spectral Analysis

The generalization of spectral theory to the bivariate case is not difficult. However, estimators of sample cross spectra (Fourier transform of the cross covariance, $\mu_{xy}(K) = E[(X_t - m_x) \cdot (Y_{t-k} - m_y)]$) have the same undesirable properties as the sample spectrum. Their variances are dominated by a constant term which does not tend to zero as record length increases (see Jenkins and Watts, 1968, p. 370 ff). Cross spectral estimators must be smoothed by a spectral window just as it is necessary to smooth auto-spectral estimators.

If $X_1(t)$ and $X_2(t)$ are two time-series with Fourier transforms $X_1(f)$ and $X_2(f)$ respectively, then the Fourier transform gives the amplitude and phase distributions of the signals.

$$X_i(f) = A_i(f)e^{jF_i(f)}, \quad i = 1, 2, \quad j = \sqrt{-1},$$ where $A_i(f)$ is a positive even function and $F_i(f)$ is an odd function.* The sample cross spectrum is

$$C_{X_1 X_2}(f) = \frac{A_1(f)A_2(f)e^{j(F_2(f) - F_1(f))}}{T}$$

which can be written

$$C_{X_1 X_2}(f) = A_{12}(f)e^{jF_{12}(f)},$$

where the sample phase spectrum

$$F_{12}(f) = F_2(f) - F_1(f)$$

and the sample cross amplitude spectrum

$$A_{12}(f) = \frac{A_1(f)A_2(f)}{T}.$$

---

*A function, $g(X)$, is even if $g(-X) = g(X)$ and odd if $g(-X) = -g(X)$. The sine is an odd function and the cosine is an even function.

Note that since $\underline{C}_{X_1 X_2}(f)$ is a complex number it can be written

$$C_{12}(f) = L_{12}(f) + jQ_{12}(f).$$

This is common notation. $\underline{L}_{12}(f)$ is called the sample in phase or sample cospectrum. It is the covariance between two cosine components and two sine components, that is, the covariance between in-phase components for a particular frequency, $\underline{f}$. (See Jenkins and Watts, 1968, p. 343.) $\underline{Q}_{12}(f)$ is called the sample quadrative spectrum. It measures the covariance between sine and cosine components, that is, the covariance between out of phase components for a particular frequency, $\underline{f}$.

The sample cross spectrum, $\underline{C}_{12}(f)$, is the Fourier transform of the sample cross covariance function and can be written

$$C_{12}(u) = \int_{-\infty}^{\infty} L_{12}(f) \cos 2\pi f u \, df + \int_{-\infty}^{\infty} Q_{12}(f) \sin 2\pi f u \, df,$$

where $\underline{C}_{12}(u)$ is the sample cross covariance function of the lag $\underline{u}$ between series $\underline{X}_1(t)$ and $\underline{X}_2(t)$.

The smoothed cross spectral estimator is defined by

$$\overline{C_{12}}(f) = \int_{-\tau}^{\tau} w(u) C_{12}(u) e^{-j2\pi f u} du$$

$$= \overline{L}_{12}(f) + j\overline{Q}_{12}(f),$$

where $\overline{L}_{12}(f)$ and $\overline{Q}_{12}(f)$ are the smoothed co- and quadrative spectra and $\underline{w}(u)$ is a lag window with the usual properties.

The reader is referred to Jenkins and Watts (1968, p. 379), for a discussion of confidence intervals for smoothed spectral estimators, and to Granger and Hatanaka (1964, p. 101). We will summarize Granger and Hatanaka estimates here.

For the bivariate case a measure of the correlation between frequency components of a particular frequency is given by a function called the coherence which behaves like the square of a correlation coefficient and is interpreted in the same way. The coherence

$$C(f) = \frac{L_{12}^2(f) + Q_{12}^2(f)}{X_1(f)X_2(f)}$$

where, you will recall, $\underline{X}_1(f)$ and $\underline{X}_2(f)$ are the power spectra of $\underline{X}_1(t)$ and $\underline{X}_2(t)$, obtained by Fourier transforms of the auto-covariances. The __phase angle__ between two components of the same frequency is defined as $\phi(\underline{f}) = \arctan(Q_{12}(\underline{f})/L_{12}(\underline{f}))$. The phase angle gives lead-lag relationships for a given frequency component.

Estimates given by Granger and Hatanaka are of the form

$$\hat{L}_{12}(\omega_j) = \frac{1}{\pi}\left\{ \frac{a_0\lambda_0(\omega)}{2} + \sum_{k=1}^{m-1} \lambda_k(\omega)a_j \cos k\omega_j \right\}$$

$$\hat{Q}_{12}(\omega_j) = \frac{1}{\pi} \sum_{k=1}^{m-1} \lambda_k(\omega)b_k \sin k\omega_j ,$$

where

$$\omega_j = \frac{\pi j}{m}, \quad j = 0, 1, \ldots, m.$$

The $\underline{a}_k$'s and $\underline{b}_k$'s are given by

$$a_k = \left(\frac{1}{n-k}\right) \sum_{j=1}^{n-k} \left(X_j Y_{j-k} + Y_j X_{j-k} \right)$$

$$b_k = \left(\frac{1}{n-k}\right) \sum_{j=1}^{n-k} \left(X_j Y_{j-k} - Y_j X_{j-k} \right), \qquad k = 0, 1, \ldots, m.$$

It is assumed that $\overline{X}. = \overline{Y}. = 0$. The weights suggested by Parzen

$$\lambda_k = 1 - \frac{6k^2}{m^2}\left(1 - \frac{k}{m}\right), \qquad 0 \leqq k \leqq m/2$$

$$= 2\left(1 - \frac{k}{m}\right)^3, \qquad m/2 \leqq k \leqq m$$

have advantages over the Tukey estimates if used with the following estimates of the cross covariances

$$C_{yx}(k) = \frac{1}{n}\sum_{t=1}^{n-k}(X_t - \overline{X})(Y_{t+k} - \overline{Y}),$$

$$C_{xy}(k) = \frac{1}{n}\sum_{t=1}^{n-k}(Y_t - \overline{Y})(X_{t+k} - \overline{X}),$$

where

$$\overline{X} = \frac{1}{n}\sum_{t=1}^{n}X_t \quad\text{and}\quad \overline{Y} = \frac{1}{n}\sum_{t=1}^{n}Y_t.$$

From this estimate the coherence and phase angle are estimated for the m frequencies.

The Multivariate Case

For the p time-series $(z_{t1}, z_{t2}, \ldots, z_{tp})$, the matrix of auto- and cross-spectra, $\Sigma = (S_{tj}(\omega))$ estimates the covariance matrix of the time-series around frequency ω. In the matrix $S_{tt}(\omega)$ is the power spectrum of z_{tj} and $S_{tj}(\omega)$ is the power cross-spectrum of series X_{tj} and $X_{tj}*$.

If we denote the ω frequency component of the $j\underline{th}$ time-series by $z_j(\omega)$. We can compute the partial correlation esti-mates $p_{12}(\omega)$ of the ordered pair $(z_1(\omega), z_2(\omega))$ by partitioning Σ into submatrices

$$\Sigma = \begin{bmatrix} \Sigma_{11} & \Sigma_{12} \\ \\ \Sigma_{21} & \Sigma_{22} \end{bmatrix}$$

and forming the matrix $\Sigma_{12 \cdot k} = \Sigma_{11} - \Sigma_{12}\Sigma_{22}^{-1}\Sigma_{21}$. Then

$$\Sigma_{12 \cdot k}(\omega) = \begin{bmatrix} S_{11 \cdot k}(\omega) & S_{12 \cdot k}(\omega) \\ \\ S_{21 \cdot k}(\omega) & S_{22 \cdot k}(\omega) \end{bmatrix}$$

is the partial auto- and cross-spectral matrix for the series $\underline{z}_{t1}$ and $\underline{z}_{t2}$ with $\underline{k}$ denoting the set $3, 4, \ldots, \underline{p}$.

The partial coherence is given by

$$C_{12 \cdot k} = \frac{|S_{12 \cdot k}(\omega)|^2}{S_{11 \cdot k}(\omega)S_{22 \cdot k}(\omega)} .$$

Goodman (1957) studied the distribution properties of cross-spectral estimates for the bivariate case. Jenkins and Watts (1968, Chapter 9) derived general variances and covariances for smoothed co- and quadrative spectra and the smoothed spectrum.

APPENDIX B

DATA LISTS

Data used in illustrations in the text are listed below.
The order of data is from left to right within each row.

ARIMA (0, 0, 1) Data, Figure 24 ($\underline{n}$ = 40):

101.2	100.0	100.2	101.8	102.1	100.5	100.2	99.2
99.4	98.2	99.0	100.0	99.9	100.1	98.9	101.5
100.8	101.1	100.5	98.6	99.0	100.8	101.2	101.1
102.0	100.5	98.8	98.5	99.1	99.2	99.0	101.2
100.0	98.9	99.0	99.5	99.9	101.4	100.3	101.0

ARIMA (1, 0, 0) Data, Figure 25 ($\underline{n}$ = 40):

100.0	100.3	99.3	99.6	98.2	98.8	99.3	99.5
99.8	98.8	100.5	101.2	101.0	101.5	100.8	99.2
99.3	100.5	101.0	101.2	100.2	100.0	100.0	101.5
100.5	101.5	103.7	102.2	101.6	101.5	102.6	101.2
99.6	98.8	98.7	98.7	98.5	100.6	99.8	99.1

Ireland Data, Figures 29 and 41 (n_1 = 46, n_2 = 47):

59.0	72.0	67.2	60.5	60.7	69.7	61.2	63.3
60.0	67.5	63.0	59.2	59.6	57.7	57.3	58.9
59.8	57.0	62.4	62.1	68.3	69.8	65.7	58.9
62.1	63.3	68.9	63.0	57.5	69.2	55.3	53.7
54.3	55.7	55.6	59.4	62.4	57.7	60.1	55.7
50.8	49.5	47.6	49.4	58.9	53.4		

54.0	57.6	56.2	68.6	73.8	69.7	74.6	74.2
74.4	79.2	76.3	78.3	80.8	77.3	79.3	84.4
82.0	79.8	78.8	78.0	82.6	81.2	83.7	82.6
81.9	85.6	84.3	85.7	86.0	83.6	85.0	83.2
82.8	83.2	85.0	88.7	88.3	88.7	89.3	90.5
89.0	90.0	88.2	89.5	80.0	82.5	77.0	

New York Traffic Fatality Data, Figure 31 (n = 100):

1.52	2.32	1.61	2.48	2.38	2.03	2.33	2.82
1.22	2.73	1.93	2.72	3.32	1.84	2.12	1.62
2.39	2.89	2.98	2.39	2.62	2.77	2.19	1.89
2.26	2.40	2.14	2.50	2.03	2.06	2.07	1.93
3.27	2.42	3.50	0.95	2.80	2.78	3.15	2.37
3.23	2.98	4.11	2.66	2.71	2.68	3.65	3.62
3.10	3.36	3.70	3.68	3.11	2.84	2.77	2.78
3.05	2.53	2.82	3.25	2.92	3.05	3.21	3.76
3.50	3.63	3.17	3.50	3.13	3.07	3.34	2.43
4.09	3.57	3.15	3.65	3.70	3.72	2.95	3.51
3.13	3.17	3.09	3.52	2.65	4.31	3.82	3.78
3.29	2.47	3.46	4.06	4.21	3.72	3.40	4.67
4.31	3.34	4.07	3.13				

"Talking Out" Data, Figure 34 (n_1 = 20, n_2 = 20):

20	18	20	18	21	20	19	22	23	20
22	18	21	19	20	18	20	16	14	18

12	9	6	6	4	6	6	4	2	3
4	4	5	4	2	4	6	4	4	2

Burglaries Data, Figure 35 ($n_1 = 41$, $n_2 = 17$):

60	44	37	54	59	69	108	89
82	61	47	72	87	60	64	50
79	78	62	72	57	57	61	55
56	62	40	44	38	37	52	59
58	69	73	92	77	75	71	68
102							

88	44	60	56	70	91	54	60
48	35	49	44	61	68	82	71
50							

Perceptual Speed Data, Figure 8 ($n_1 = 60$, $n_2 = 60$):

55	56	48	46	56	46	59	60	53	58
73	69	72	51	72	69	68	69	79	77
53	63	80	65	78	64	72	77	82	77
35	79	71	73	77	76	83	73	78	91
70	88	88	85	77	63	91	94	72	83
88	78	84	78	75	75	86	79	75	87

66	73	62	27	52	47	65	59	77	47
51	47	49	54	58	56	50	54	45	66
39	51	39	27	39	37	43	41	27	29
27	26	29	31	28	38	37	26	31	45
38	33	33	25	24	29	37	35	32	31
28	40	31	37	34	43	38	33	28	35

ARIMA (0, 2, 2) Data, Figure 36 ($n_1 = 15$, $n_2 = 15$):

48.69	47.83	47.89	46.13	46.33	46.81	44.56	44.16
45.16	44.05	43.20	41.21	40.47	39.73	38.09	

43.53	42.57	40.05	39.20	37.47	37.08	35.40	33.94
31.81	30.44	30.49	29.17	26.29	24.91	22.44	

German Divorce Data, Figure 39 ($n_1 = 18$, $n_2 = 15$):

8.7	11.5	12.3	12.8	13.1	12.8	13.3	13.7
13.2	12.6	13.4	13.1	14.5	15.9	15.9	16.5
16.5	17.0						

| 14.0 | 13.8 | 15.6 | 16.9 | 18.2 | 18.7 | 19.8 | 20.5 |
| 21.3 | 22.8 | 22.9 | 24.0 | 25.5 | 26.3 | 26.1 | |

APPENDIX C[*]

LINEAR MODEL AND LEAST-SQUARES THEORY

This appendix is concerned with the development of estimates of parameters and statistical inference in the linear model. There are several methods of statistical estimation available to the researcher such as maximum likelihood (ML), the best linear unbiased estimator (b.l.u.e.), etc. (Searle, 1971, p. 87). However, the most common of the methods, that of least squares (LS), is the one whose development is presented herein. It should be noted that the LS method coincides with the ML method in the important case of normally distributed observations.[**] The LS method, however, is free from distributional assumptions in the derivation of estimators and their properties and requires the normality assumption only in the development of the machinery of statistical inference.

This exposition is modest in scope and is intended as a minimal treatment of the subject. Those desiring comprehensive

---

[*]This appendix was prepared by William L. Padia.

[**]See Kendall and Stuart, Vol. 2 (1971), Chapter 19, for a parallel development of these two methods of estimation.

221

coverage may consult sources such as Rao (1965), Searle (1971) or Mood and Graybill (1963), among many.

Linear Model

The general linear model is represented in matrix form as

$$y = X\beta + a \qquad (C.1)$$

where,

$$y = \begin{bmatrix} y_1 \\ y_2 \\ \cdot \\ \cdot \\ \cdot \\ y_N \end{bmatrix}, \qquad X = \begin{bmatrix} x_{11} & x_{12} & \cdots & x_{1m} \\ x_{21} & & & \cdot \\ \cdot & & \cdot & \cdot \\ \cdot & & & \cdot \\ \cdot & & & \\ x_{N1} & & \cdots & x_{Nm} \end{bmatrix}$$

$$\beta = \begin{bmatrix} \beta_1 \\ \beta_2 \\ \cdot \\ \cdot \\ \cdot \\ \beta_m \end{bmatrix}, \qquad \text{and} \qquad a = \begin{bmatrix} a_1 \\ a_2 \\ \cdot \\ \cdot \\ \cdot \\ a_N \end{bmatrix}$$

The vector y is commonly referred to as the vector of criterion or dependent variable scores; the matrix X is a set of independent variable scores and the vector a is a set of random variables descriptive of measurement error, lack of fit, or, in short, "residual." Thus one particular observation, y_i, may be represented as $y_i = x_{i1}\beta_1 + x_{i2}\beta_2 + \cdots + x_{im}\beta_m + a_i$. The vector y and matrix X contain elements that are observable, but a and β are unknown.

The model representation (C.1) is linear in β, the vector of parameters for which estimators are desired. In time-series analysis applications, the vector $\underline{y}$ is the transformed vector of observations $\underline{z}$, the matrix $\underline{X}$ is analogous to the design matrix of experimental design and the vector $\underline{a}$ is a vector of random variables such that the $\underline{N}$ variables in $\underline{a}$ are normally and independently distributed with mean zero and variance σ^2 (compactly, $a_i \sim NID\,(0, \sigma^2)$). As noted above, to develop an estimator of $\bar{\beta}$ the normality assumption may be dropped and the less restrictive assumption imposed that the a_i are independently distributed with mean zero and common variance σ^2.

The essence of the LS strategy is to minimize the errors of fitting $\underline{X}\hat{\beta}$ to $\underline{y}$, where the criterion to minimize is the sum of squared estimated errors. That is, $\hat{\underline{y}} = \underline{X}\hat{\beta}$ is the estimate of $\underline{y}$ that arises from using β as an estimator of β. Thus error is introduced into the system, namely, $\hat{\underline{a}} = \underline{y} - \hat{\underline{y}}$, the difference between what is observed and what is predicted by the model. It is this error, $\hat{\underline{a}}$, that figures predominantly in the least squares criterion of minimizing $\hat{\underline{a}}^T\hat{\underline{a}}$. In other words,

$$SS = \hat{a}^T\hat{a} = (y - X\hat{\beta})^T (y - X\hat{\beta}) \qquad (C.2)$$

is the scalar sum of squares to be minimized by a choice of values for the elements of $\hat{\beta}$.

A necessary condition that (C.2) is minimized is that $\partial SS/\partial\hat{\beta} = 0$. Applying this criterion, we obtain

$$\frac{\partial SS}{\partial\hat{\beta}} = \frac{\partial}{\partial\hat{\beta}}\left[(y - X\hat{\beta})^T(y - X\hat{\beta})\right]$$

$$= \frac{\partial}{\partial\hat{\beta}}\left(y^Ty - y^TX\beta - \beta^TX^Ty + \beta^TX^TX\beta\right)$$

$$= -2y^TX + 2\beta^TX^TX = 0. \qquad (C.3)$$

To establish sufficiency, it must be shown that the second derivative of $\underline{SS}$ yields a positive definite matrix (Graybill, 1961, p. 17). The second derivative of $\underline{SS}$ is $2\underline{X}^T\underline{X}$, a Gramian matrix that is positive semi-definite, since the elements of $\underline{X}$ are real. The equations (C.3) yield $\underline{X}^T\underline{X}\hat{\beta} = \underline{X}^T\underline{y}$, which are commonly referred to as the normal equations. The LS estimator $\hat{\beta}$ is then found from the normal equations and is given by

$$\hat{\beta} = (X^TX)^{-1}X^Ty, \tag{C.4}$$

assuming that X^TX is non-singular. For convenience, denote X^TX by S.

Some of the properties of the LS estimators may now be developed.

Unbiasedness. An estimator is unbiased if the expected value of the estimator is equal to the parameter. Thus, one must inquire whether $E(\hat{\beta}) = \beta$. From (C.4) we have

$$E(\hat{\beta}) = E(S^{-1}X^Ty) = S^{-1}X^TE(y), \tag{C.5}$$

since $\hat{\beta}$ is a linear combination of y its expected value is therefore the same linear combination of the expected values of y. Now, since $E(y) = X\beta$ we have

$$E(\hat{\beta}) = S^{-1}S\beta = \beta. \tag{C.6}$$

Variances and Covariances. The dispersion or variance-covariance matrix of the elements of the vector $\hat{\beta}$ is found by applying the definitional formula for the covariance. Since $E(\hat{\beta}) = \beta$, we have

$$E[(\hat{\beta}-\beta)(\hat{\beta}-\beta)^T] = E[(S^{-1}X^Ty-\beta)(S^{-1}X^Ty-\beta)^T]$$

$$= E[(S^{-1}X^T(X\beta+a)-\beta)(S^{-1}X^T(X\beta+a)-\beta)^T]$$

$$= E(S^{-1}X^Taa^TXS^{-1}) = S^{-1}X^TE(aa^T)XS^{-1},$$

since X is a constant over the expectation operator. Examination of $E(aa^T)$ yields

$$E(aa^T) = \begin{bmatrix} E(a_1^2) & & & \cdot & \cdot & \cdot & \cdot & \cdot & \cdot \\ & \cdot & & & & E(a_j a_i) & & \cdot & \\ & & \cdot & & & & & & \\ \cdot & & & E(a_i^2) & & & & \cdot & \\ & & & & \cdot & & & & \\ \cdot & & E(a_i a_j) & & & \cdot & & & \\ \cdot & & & \cdot & \cdot & \cdot & E(a_N^2) & & \end{bmatrix} = \begin{bmatrix} \sigma^2 & & & & & \\ & \cdot & & & & 0 \\ & & \cdot & & & \\ & & & \cdot & & \\ & 0 & & & \cdot & \\ & & & & & \sigma^2 \end{bmatrix} = \sigma^2 I.$$

$$(C.7)$$

Thus the variance-covariance matrix of $\hat{\beta}$ is given by $\underline{S}^{-1}\sigma^2$. By means of this formula it is possible to read off variances and covariances of the $\hat{\beta}_i$ once the inverse of $\underline{S}$ has been computed.

Minimizing the sum of squares $\hat{\underline{a}}^T\hat{\underline{a}}$ does not directly provide an estimate of σ^2. However, the estimate of σ^2 which is based on the LS estimate of β and which is unbiased is given by

$$\sigma^2 = \frac{(y-X\hat{\beta})^T(y-X\hat{\beta})}{N-m} = \frac{\hat{\underline{a}}^T\hat{\underline{a}}}{N-m}, \qquad (C.8)$$

where $\underline{m}$ is the number of parameters estimated (Mood and Graybill, 1973, p. 349).

An important feature of LS estimators is that they possess minimum variance among all linear unbiased estimators. In other words $\text{VAR}(\hat{\beta}) \leqq \text{VAR}(\hat{\beta}^*)$ where $\hat{\beta}^*$ is any unbiased estimator of β. This result is known as the Gauss-Markov Theorem and a proof of this theorem may be found in any of the aforementioned references.

Interval Estimation and Hypothesis Testing. The results so far have been based on the assumption that $\underline{E}(a) = 0$ and that $\text{VAR}[a] = \sigma^2\underline{I}$. However, to test hypotheses, or equivalently, to construct confidence intervals about the estimates, $\hat{\beta}_i$, it is necessary to make distributional assumptions. Applying the normality assumption to the vector of errors $\underline{a}$ allows as to construct confidence intervals about the LS estimates. To do this we need the fact that $\hat{\beta}_i \sim \underline{N}(\beta_i, \sigma^2\underline{c}^{ii})$, where $\underline{c}^{ii}$ is the $\underline{i}$th diagonal element of $\underline{S}^{-1}$. The normality follows since the β_i are linear functions of the $\underline{a}_i$, and the mean and dispersion matrix were displayed above. Thus, $((\hat{\beta}_i - \beta_i)/\sigma\sqrt{c^{ii}}) \sim N(0, 1)$ and furthermore, $(((N-m)\hat{\sigma}^2)/\sigma^2) \sim \chi^2_{\underline{N-m}}$ (Rao, 1965, p. 195). It then follows that

$$\frac{\hat{\beta}_i - \beta_i}{\sigma\sqrt{c^{ii}}} \; \frac{\sigma}{\hat{\sigma}} \; = \; \frac{\hat{\beta}_i - \beta_i}{\hat{\sigma}\sqrt{c^{ii}}} \sim t_{N-m}. \tag{C.9}$$

Thus the $100(1-\alpha)$-percent confidence interval about $\hat{\beta}_i$ is

$$\hat{\beta}_i \pm {}_{1-\alpha/2}t_{\underline{N-m}}\hat{\sigma}\hat{\beta}_i. \tag{C.10}$$

If the interest centers on hypothesis testing, then $(\hat{\beta}_i - \beta_i)/\hat{\sigma}\sqrt{c^{ii}}$ is compared with the ${}_{1-\alpha/2}t_{\underline{N-m}}$ percentile point for a decision to accept or reject.

It is also possible to examine several estimates jointly, obtaining a confidence région and a simultaneous hypothesis test of the vector $\hat{\beta}$, rather than one element, $\hat{\beta}_i$. The construction of the interval and the hypothesis test depend on the fact that $((\beta-\hat{\beta})^T S(\beta-\hat{\beta}))/m\hat{\sigma}^2 \sim F_{m,N-m}$ (Box and Jenkins, 1970, p. 266). Thus

$$(\beta-\hat{\beta})^T S(\beta-\hat{\beta}) \leq m\,\hat{\sigma}^2 {}_{1-\alpha}F_{m,N-m} \tag{C.11}$$

defines a $100(1-\alpha)$-percent confidence region for β. The test criterion for the simultaneous hypothesis test $\beta_1 = \beta_2 = \ldots = \beta_m = \beta$ is given by

$$F = \frac{(\beta-\hat{\beta})^T S(\beta-\hat{\beta})}{m\hat{\sigma}^2} > {}_{1-\alpha}F_{m,N-m}, \tag{C.12}$$

for rejecting the hypothesis at the α significance level.

REFERENCES

Aigner, D. J. A compendium on estimation of the autoregressive-moving average model from time series data. International Economic Review, 1971, 12, 348-371.

Airasian, P. W.; Kellaghan, T.; Madaus, G.; & Ryan, J. P. Payment by results: the analysis of a 19th century performance contracting program. Paper presented at the 1972 Annual Meeting of the National Council on Measurement in Education, Chicago, Ill., 4 April 1972.

Ames, E., & Reiter, S. Distributions of correlation coefficients in economic time series. Journal of the American Statistical Association, 1961, 56, 637-656.

Bartlett, M. S. On the theoretical specification of sampling properties of autocorrelated time-series. Journal of the Royal Statistical Society (Series B), 1946, 8, 27-36.

Box, G. E. P. Bayesian approaches to some bothersome problems in data analysis. Chapter 2 in Stanley, J. C. (editor), Improving Experimental Design and Statistical Analysis. Chicago: Rand McNally, 1967.

Box, G. E. P., & Jenkins, G. M. Time-series analysis: forecasting and control. San Francisco: Holden Day, 1970.

Box, G. E. P., & Tiao, G. C. A change in level of a nonstationary time-series. Biometrika, 1965, 52, 181-192.

Bracht, G. H., & Glass, G. V. The external validity of experiments. American Educational Research Journal, 1969, 5, 437-474.

227

Broden, M.; Hall, R. V.; & Mitts, B. The effect of self-recording on the classroom behavior of two eighth-grade students. Journal of Applied Behavior Analysis, 1971, 4, 191-199.

Brown, J. S. The motivation of behavior. New York: McGraw-Hill, 1961.

Campbell, D. T. From description to experimentation: interpreting trends as quasi-experiments. In Harris, C. W. (editor), Problems in Measuring Change. Madison, Wis.: University of Wisconsin Press 1963.

Campbell, D. T. Administrative experimentation, institutional records, and nonreactive measures. Chapter 6 in Stanley, J. C. (editor), Improving Experimental Design and Statistical Analysis. Chicago: Rand McNally, 1967.

Campbell, D. T. Reforms as experiments. American Psychologist, 1969, 24, 409-429.

Campbell, D. T., & Ross, H. L. The Connecticut crackdown on speeding: time-series data in quasi-experimental analysis. Law and Society Review, 1968, 3, 33-53.

Campbell, D. T., & Stanley, J. C. Experimental and Quasi-Experimental Designs for Research. Chicago: Rand McNally & Co., 1966. (Also appears as Chp. 5, "Experimental and quasi-experimental designs for research on teaching," in Gage, N. L. (editor), Handbook of Research on Teaching. Chicago: Rand McNally, 1963.)

Caporaso, J. A., & Pelowski, A. L. Economic and political integration in Europe: a time-series quasi-experimental analysis. American Political Science Review, 1971, 65, 418-433.

Chassan, J. B. Statistical inference and the single case in clinical design. Psychiatry, 1960, 23, 173-184.

Chassan, J. B. Stochastic models of the single case as the basis of clinical research design. Behavioral Science, 1961, 6, 42-50.

Chassan, J. B.   Intensive design in clinical research.   Psycho-
somatics, 1965, 6, 289-294.

Chassan, J. B.   Research Designs in Clinical Psychology and
Psychiatry.   New York: Appleton-Century-Crofts, 1967.

Chassan, J. B., & Bellak, L.   An introduction to intensive
design.   In Gottschalk, L., & Auerbach, A. (editors),
Methods of Research in Psychotherapy.   New York:
Appleton-Century-Crofts, 1965.

D'Abro, A.   The Rise of the New Physics.   Vol. II.   New York:
Dover, 1951.

Edwards, A. L., & Cronbach, L. J.   Experimental design for
research in psychotherapy.   Journal of Clinical Psychology,
1952, 8, 51-59.

Feller, W.   An Introduction to Probability Theory and Its Applications.   Vol. I, 2nd edition.   New York: John Wiley &
Sons, 1957.

Fisher, R. A.   Studies in crop variation.   Journal of Agricultural Science, Part II, 1921, 11, 8-35.

Gastwirth, J. L., & Rubin, H.   Effect of dependence on the
level of some one-sample tests.   Journal of the American
Statistical Association, 1971, 66, 816-820.

Gentile, J. R.; Roden, A. H.; & Klein, R. D.   An analysis of
variance model for the intrasubject replication design.
Journal of Applied Behavior Analysis, 1972, 5, 193-198.

Glass, G. V.   Analysis of data on the Connecticut speeding
crackdown as a time-series quasi-experiment.   Law and
Society Review, 1968, 3, 55-76.

Glass, G. V., & Maguire, T. O.   Analysis of time-series
quasi-experiments.   Final report, U.S.O.E. Project
No. 6-8329, 1968.

Glass, G. V.; Peckham, P. D.; & Sanders, J. R. Consequences of failure to meet assumptions underlying the fixed-effects analyses of variance and covariance. Review of Educational Research, 1972, 42, 237-288.

Glass, G. V.; Tiao, G. C.; & Maguire, T. O. Analysis of data on the 1900 revision of German divorce laws as a time-series quasi-experiment. Law and Society Review, 1971, 4, 539-562.

Goodman, N. R. Scientific paper No. 10, Engineering Statistics Laboratory, New York University, 1957.

Gottman, J. M. Time-series analysis in the behavioral sciences and a methodology for action research. Unpublished doctoral dissertation, University of Wisconsin, 1971.

Gottman, J. M. N-of-one and N-of-two research in psychotherapy, Psychological Bulletin, 1973, 80, 93-105.

Gottman, J. M., & Clasen, R. M. Evaluation in education: a practitioner's guide. Itasca, Ill.: Peacock Press, 1972.

Gottman, J. M., & McFall, R. M. Self-monitoring effects in a program for potential high-school dropouts: a time-series analysis. Journal of Consulting and Clinical Psychology, 1972, 39, 273-281.

Gottman, J. M.; McFall, R. M.; & Barnett, J. T. Design and analysis of research using time series. Psychological Bulletin, 1969, 72, 299-306.

Granger, C. W. J., & Hatanaka, M. Spectral Analysis of Economic Time Series. Princeton: Princeton University Press, 1964.

Graybill, F. A. An introduction to linear statistical models, Vol. I. New York: McGraw-Hill, 1961.

Greenblatt, M. Discussion by Saslow of papers by Matarazzo and Lacey. In Research in Psychotherapy. Vol. I. Washington, D.C.: American Psychological Association, 1958.

Hahn, C. P.   Methods for evaluating counter-measures inter-
vention programs.   Pages 83-108 in Evaluative Research:
Strategies and Methods.   Pittsburgh, Penn.: American
Institutes for Research, 1970.

Hall, R. V.; Fox, R.; Willard, D.; Goldsmith, L.; Emerson,
M.; Owen, M.; Davis, F.; & Porcia, E.   The teacher as
observer and experimenter in the modification of disputing
and talking-out behaviors.   Journal of Applied Behavior
Analysis, 1971, 4, 141-149.

Hannan, E. J.   Time series analysis.   London: Methein
Monographs, 1960.

Hibbs, Jr., D. A.   Problems of statistical estimation and
causal inference in time-series regression models.   In
Sociological Methodology 1974, Costner, Herbert L.
(editor).   San Francisco: Jossey-Bass Publishers,
252-308.

Hilgard, E. R.   The effect of delayed practice on memory and
motor performances studied by the method of co-twin
control.   Genetic Psychology Monographs, 1933, 6, 67.

Holtzman, W.   Statistical models for the study of change in
the single case.   In Problems in Measuring Change,
Harris, C. W. (editor).   Madison, Wis.: University of
Wisconsin Press, 1963.

Huntington, E.   Mainsprings of civilization.   New York: John
Wiley & Sons, 1945.

Jenkins, G. M., & Watts, D. G.   Spectral analysis and its
applications.   San Francisco: Holden-Day, 1968.

Johnston, J.   Econometric methods.   New York: McGraw-Hill
Book Co., 1966.

Jones, R. H.; Crowell, D. H.; and Kapuniai, L. E.   Change
detection model for serially correlated data.   Psychological Bulletin, 1969, 71, 352-358.

232

Kazdin, A. Methodological and assessment considerations in evaluating reinforcement programs in applied settings. Journal of Applied Behavioral Analysis, 1973, 6, 517-532.

Kelly, F. J.; McNeil, K; & Newman, I. Suggested inferential statistical models for research in behavior modification. Journal of Experimental Education, 1973, 41, 54-63.

Kendall, M. G., & Stuart, A. The advanced theory of statistics. Vol. 2. London: Griffin, 1966.

Kepka, E. J. Model representation and the threat of instability in the interrupted time series quasi-experiment. Ph.D. dissertation, Northwestern University, June 1972.

Kmenta, J. Elements of econometrics. New York: The Macmillan Co., 1971.

Lovaas, D. I.; Berberich, J. P.; Perloff, B. F.; & Schaeffer, B. Acquisition of imitative speech by schizophrenic children. Science, 1966, 151, 705-707.

Lovitt, T. C., & Curtiss, K. A. Academic response rate as a function of teacher and self-imposed contingencies. Journal of Applied Behavior Analysis, 1969, 2, 49-53.

Maguire, T. O., & Glass, G. V. A program for the analysis of certain time-series quasi-experiments. Educational and Psychological Measurement, 1967, 27, 743-750.

Meichenbaum, D.; Bowers, K.; & Ross, R. Modification of classroom behavior of institutionalized female adolescent offenders. Behaviour Research and Therapy, 1968, 6, 343-353.

Mood, A., & Graybill, F. Introduction to the theory of statistics. 2nd edition. New York: McGraw-Hill, 1963.

Morris, J. R., & Ammentorp, W. B. Time-series analysis of role performance. Unpublished paper, Department of Educational Administration, University of Minnesota, 1972.

Nelson, C. R. Applied time-series analysis for managerial forecasting. San Francisco: Holden-Day, 1973.

Padia, W. L. Effect of autocorrelation on probability statements about the mean. Masters thesis, Laboratory of Educational Research, University of Colorado, 1973.

Press, S. J. Police manpower versus crime. Pages 112-119 in Tanur, J. M. (editor), Statistics: a guide to the unknown. San Francisco: Holden-Day, 1972.

Quenouille, M. H. Approximate tests of correlation in time series. Journal of the Royal Statistical Society (Series B), 1949, 11, 68-74.

Rao, C. R. Linear statistical inference and its applications. New York: John Wiley, 1965.

Revusky, S. H. Some statistical treatments compatible with individual organism methodology. Journal of the Experimental Analysis of Behavior, 1967, 10, 319-330.

Risley, T. , & Baer, D. Operant conditioning: "develop" is a transitive, active verb. In Caldwell, B. , and Ricciuti, H. (editors), Review of Child Development Research. Vol. III. Social Influence and Social Action. 1969.

Ross, H. L.; Campbell, D. T.; & Glass, G. V. Determining the social effects of a legal reform: the British "breathalyzer" crackdown of 1967. American Behavioral Scientist, 1970, 13, 493-509.

Scheffé, H. The analysis of variance. New York: John Wiley & Sons, 1959.

Schuster, A. On the investigation of hidden periodicities with application to a supposed 26-day period of meteorological phenomena. Terrestrial Magnetism, 1898, 3, 13-41.

Searle, S. R. Linear models. New York: John Wiley, 1971.

Shewart, W. A. The economic control of the quality of manufactured product. New York: Macmillan Co., 1931.

Shine, L. C., II, & Bower, S. M. A one-way analysis of
variance for single-subject designs. Educational and
Psychological Measurement, 1971, 31, 105-113.

Smoker, P. A time-series analysis of Sino-Indian relations.
Journal of Conflict Resolution, 1969, 13, 172-191.

Sween, J., & Campbell, D. T. A study of the effect of proxi-
mally autocorrelated error on tests of significance for the
interrupted time series quasi-experimental design.
Unpublished paper, Department of Psychology,
Northwestern University, August 1965, 41 pp.

Tukey, J. W. An introduction to the calculations of numerical
spectrum analysis. Pages 25-46 in Harris, B. (editor),
Spectral Analysis of Time Series. New York: John Wiley,
1967.

Tyler, V. O., & Brown, G. D. Token reinforcement of academic performance with institutionalized delinquent boys.
Journal of Educational Psychology, 1968, 59, 164-168.

Whittaker, E. T., & Robinson, G. The calculus of observations. London: Blackie and Son, 1924.

Willson, V. L. Estimation of intervention effects in seasonal
time-series. Research Paper No. 51. Boulder, Colorado:
Laboratory of Educational Research, University of
Colorado, 1972.

Willson, V. L. Concomitant variation in the interrupted time-
series experiment. Ph.D. dissertation, University of
Colorado, 1973.

Wolf, E.; Lüke, G.; & Hax, H. Scheidung und scheidungsrecht:
grundfragen der ehescheidung in Deutschland. Tubigen:
J. C. B. Mohr, 1959.

SUBJECT INDEX

AUTHOR INDEX

239